PARKWAY VILLAGE

DELIBERATE
INTENT

Also by Rod Smolla

Free Speech in an Open Society

Jerry Falwell v. Larry Flynt: The First Amendment on Trial

Suing the Press: Libel, the Media, and Power

DELIBERATE INTENT

A Lawyer Tells the

True Story

of Murder by the Book

ROD SMOLLA

Crown Publishers

New York

Published by Crown Publishers, 201 East 50th Street, New York, New York 10022. Member of the Crown Publishing Group.

Random House, Inc. New York, Toronto, London, Sydney, Auckland

www.randomhouse.com

CROWN is a trademark and the Crown colophon is a registered trademark of Random House, Inc.

Printed in the United States of America

Design by Leonard Henderson

Library of Congress Cataloging-in-Publication Data

Smolla, Rodney A.

    Deliberate intent : a lawyer tells the true story of murder by the book / Rod Smolla.

      p.   cm.

    1. Rice, Vivian Elaine—Trials, litigation, etc.   2. Paladin Press—Trials, litigations, etc.   3. Feral, Rex. Hit man. 4. Trials (Homicide)—Maryland.   5. Wrongful death—Maryland. 6. Press law—United States. 7. Accomplices—Maryland. 8. Freedom of the press—United States.   9. Horn, Lawrence—Trials, litigation, etc.   10. Horn, Trevor 1984—1993—Death and burial.   I. Title.

KF228.R488S63   1999

342.73'0853—dc21   98-55296

                                                    CIP

ISBN 0-609-60413-9

10 9 8 7 6 5 4 3 2 1

First Edition

To Michele

Contents

CONTENTS

Preface

In 1983, Paladin Press, of Boulder, Colorado, and its president, Peder Lund, published a murder-for-hire instruction manual entitled *Hit Man: A Technical Manual for Independent Contractors.* On one level, the book is pure recipe—a detailed, step-by-step technical explanation of how to go into the business of becoming a professional hit man, plan murders, and carry them out. On another level, the book is incitement and exhortation, written in tones that incessantly cajole and encourage and embolden, propelling the would-be assassin to take the plunge and become a *real* man, a nihilistic, efficient, cold-blooded murdering machine.

On the night of March 3, 1993, James Perry, a thug from Detroit, traveled to Montgomery County, Maryland, in the suburbs of Washington, D.C., and brutally murdered Trevor Horn, a crippled eight-year-old boy; his mother, Mildred Horn; and his nurse, Janice Saunders.

Perry was hired to perform these murders by Lawrence Horn, little Trevor's father and Mildred's ex-husband. Horn ordered his own son and former spouse killed so that he could obtain insurance money. James Perry was to be cut in on part of the take. Perry planned the executions using the detailed instructions contained in Paladin's *Hit Man* murder manual. Perry and Horn were each caught and convicted on three counts of first-degree murder. In their murder trials, the prosecutors focused heavily on the role of *Hit Man* as the blueprint for the slayings.

I became involved in this tragedy when Howard Siegel, a colorful and iconoclastic lawyer from Rockville, Maryland, called me on behalf of the families of the murder victims. The families believed that Paladin Press had aided and abetted James Perry in committing the murders by providing Perry with an instruction manual. They wanted to sue Paladin Press for civil damages. They wanted me to become a member of the legal team that would bring this lawsuit.

This request presented me with an acute moral dilemma. Throughout my professional life I had been a champion of the First Amendment. As an author, a law professor, and a scholar, I believed that freedom of speech and freedom of the press were numinous and transcendent values. The very idea of suing a book publisher seemed to grate at my soul, running against everything I thought I believed in.

And so I was, instinctually and reflexively, resistant. To be sure, I felt emotionally drawn to the families, impelled to their cause by the pulls of sympathy and empathy. Their grief was devastating. Their outrage overpowering. But this was asking too much. All my life I had defended the rights of publishers. This felt like nothing less than betrayal.

Yet there was something haunting in the plea of the families, something vexing and disturbing. I thought I believed that Paladin Press had a constitutional right to publish a manual on how to commit contract murder. But why did I think that? And was I right? I wrestled with the dilemma, and in so wrestling, experienced a personal metamorphosis.

Hit Man's preface opens with this passage:

> A woman recently asked how I could, in good conscience, write an instruction book on murder.
>
> "How can you live with yourself if someone uses what you write to go out and take a human life?" she whined.
>
> I am afraid she was quite offended by my answer.
>
> It is my opinion that the professional hit man fills a need in

society and is, at times, the only alternative for "personal" justice. Moreover, if my advice and the proven methods in this book are followed, certainly no one will ever know.

Here was an author, writing a preface to a murder manual, openly reflecting on the moral propriety of writing the manual. Strangely, I found myself in much a parallel position. As I grappled with whether or not to take the case on behalf of the families involved, friends and colleagues put essentially the same sort of question to me: "How can you live with yourself, Rod Smolla, if you participate in a lawsuit against a publisher, albeit of an instruction book on murder? What if someone uses the legal precedent you are attempting to establish to go out and engage in censorship?"

Unless I could come up with a satisfactory answer to this query, I had no business getting involved in the lawsuit. Could I come up with a convincing answer? Not an answer formed in quicksilver lawyer-talk and moral euphemism, but one grounded in principle, an answer consistent with my own values and self-identity?

This book is about many things. It is the shocking story of a dysfunctional marriage, an estranged father, and conspiracy ending in cold-blooded butchery. It is the riveting tale of two sensational murder trials. It is the narrative of a civil action for damages against a book publisher, a lawsuit that established landmark First Amendment precedent. But for me, on a very personal level, it is foremost the story of an intellectual and moral transformation, the story of how and why I ultimately came to answer the questions posed by the preface to *Hit Man* and, ironically, to the preface of this very book.

This story is not important because it is mine but because of the conflicts it presents. Those conflicts are not just for me to face, but for all of us.

We are a society deeply and profoundly committed to the ideal of freedom of speech. Yet does that freedom embrace even the right to publish an instruction manual on how to engage in murder for hire? I invite the reader to retrace the steps of my own journey, and in so doing, to answer these questions for yourself.

1

A Boy Named Trevor

Howard Siegel's phone call came out of the bright October blue. I had just returned to my office, a cluster of students still in tow, after teaching my morning class in constitutional law. Sexual privacy was the topic of the day, and the classroom discussion had been passionate and animated.

"All straight space is gay space!" The comment was from Paul, one of my brightest students, an ordained minister and an activist on gay and lesbian rights. "I believe that the Constitution should protect same-sex marriage."

At Paul's remark a hand bolted into the air like a military salute. I called on Jennifer, knowing things were about to get rough. "The very idea of same-sex marriage is a moral abomination," she sneered with disgust, "and I just cannot understand how *anyone* could consider making legal the scourge of homosexuality." Jennifer's comment torched a debate so vehement it verged on the edge of riot. Unsatisfied by my feeble suggestion that we let matters cool until our next session, some ten or twelve students had followed me upstairs after class to carry on the fight in the sitting room outside my office door. Jennifer and Paul were in each other's face and in each other's space, getting louder and louder. The trill of the phone gave me an excuse to duck away from the battle.

"Is this Professor Rod Smolla?" It was a loud, assertive voice, spiced with a touch of growl. For a moment I thought Rush Limbaugh had called me.

"This is Rod Smolla," I said warily, thinking maybe I should have lied.

"My name is Howard Siegel. You've never heard of me, though you've probably read about a case I tried a few years ago that made history. It's in all the law school casebooks now. *Kelley v. R.G. Industries.* I represented the victim in a convenient store shooting in a suit against the manufacturer of the Saturday Night Special the gunman used. Anyhow, that's neither here nor there. I'm calling you about a very unusual case I've got up here in Rockville, Maryland. I've been checking with folks all over the country, and everyone keeps mentioning your name as *the* expert. So that's why I'm calling. We have a chance to make history."

Through the crack in my office door I could see more students gathering to join the quarrelsome din. I had the choice of trying to quell the mob or listen to a madman. I went with the madman.

"Well, before we go making any history," I chuckled, "why don't we take it by the numbers? How about telling me what this is all about?"

Howard Siegel then proceeded to unlock and unload. We didn't have what you could really call a conversation. It was more a declamation, a piece of oratory, like a closing argument to a jury, with soaring waves of emotion, dramatic pauses, and impassioned appeals. I'd never heard anything like it—at least not on the telephone. This guy really thought he was about to make history. And for some cockamamie reason he thought I was going to be part of the program.

"Howard," I said when he had finished, "we've got a little complication here."

"And what's that?"

"Something called the First Amendment. Did you ever hear of a case called *Brandenburg v. Ohio?*"

"No. What's *Brandenburg v. Ohio?*"

"It's a Supreme Court decision from 1969." I pulled a copy of the *Supreme Court Reports* from my bookshelf and turned to the case. "Here's the citation," I said, cradling the phone between cheek and shoulder. "You read the case. Meanwhile, I'll do some thinking about what you've told me. Then we'll talk."

"We need you in this case," Howard insisted. "It'll be the 'dream team'."

•   •   •

Erin, my seven year-old daughter, was swinging hand-over-hand across the monkey bars. Corey, her two-year-old sister, was playing in the sandbox with a bevy of other rugrats. It was a gorgeous Indian summer afternoon in Williamsburg, Virginia. Fluorescent red, orange, and yellow hardwood leaves fluttered in a crisp breeze against a turquoise sky. We were at Kidsburg, Williamsburg's new mega-playground, a place big enough to have its own zip code. There must have been two hundred kids swarming the kiddie metropolis, romping on slides, ropes, tires, swings, ladders, towers, teeter-totters, sand boxes, forts, and playhouses, and about twenty-five or thirty parents, grandparents, older siblings, and nannies, some of the adults pushing kids on swings or holding little ones as they swooped down slides, but most lounging in lazy supervision on benches, reading books, soaking up the last fading rays of fall sunshine, or chatting idly with friends. I spotted a couple of grandfathers, and one other dad, but the adults were overwhelmingly women. Among all these various soccer moms and soccer mom surrogates, I was the only one in a business suit. Our child-care provider, Diane Lee, had the afternoon off for a doctor's appointment, and I'd gone directly from the Marshall-Wythe School of Law at the College of William and Mary to the playground to take over from Diane. Erin and Corey were well-ensconced in play, so I took to an unoccupied bench to watch them. They were angelic children, cavorting in a day made by angels. The air was scented with fresh pine mulch and the pungent fragrance of hundreds of fall mums, blooming purple, yellow, and burnt orange throughout the park. Corey left the sandbox, making headlong for a teeter-totter. I sprang from the bench and trotted over to her. Teeter-totters are not meant for two-year-olds. Putting Corey on one end I took the opposite seat and, keeping my feet on the ground, gave her a ride. As I bounced her gently up and down, she giggled with a laugh that could launch a thousand ships. Her merriment turned to envy, however, as she spied an itinerant toddler grabbing the pail and shovel she had abandoned in the sandbox. Leaving me high and dry, she bolted back for the sand. Violence was averted as I and the other toddler's mother worked out a sharing arrangement.

My mind wandered to Howard Siegel's phone call, and I felt my temples knot and my stomach tighten. Howard's call that morning had come at a vulnerable moment. For two years I had been writing a novel, which I titled *The Nominee*, about the dean of a law school who is nominated to become Chief Justice of the U.S. Supreme Court. As he navigates the shoals of the brutal confirmation process, however, we find that all in his life is not what it seems. You couldn't really call this an "autobiographical first novel," I suppose, because I am never going to be appointed to the Supreme Court. On the other hand, not all in my life was what it seemed. The facade looked real pretty, but beneath the surface I was heavily mortgaged. Professionally, the world was my oyster. Maybe not oysters Rockefeller, maybe more your common everyday oysters on the half-shell, but oysters nonetheless. I held a good job at a good law school, and everything in my life was settled and secure. But something was missing. A line from a Sheryl Crow song kept running through my mind: "If it makes you happy, then why the hell are you so sad?" I was at once paragon and paradox, fulfilled yet discontented, rock-steady but restless and ready for revolution. I didn't need this Howard Siegel.

• • •

One of the courses I taught at William and Mary was "Law and Religion," and one of the prominent issues in the course was the question of whether concepts of God had any place in a secular society that embraced the ideal of separation of Church and State. I often talked to the students about where they thought "law" came from.

"We hold these truths to be self-evident . . ." wrote Thomas Jefferson in the Declaration of Independence—*self-evident* was his phrase. ". . . that all men are created equal, that they are endowed by their Creator with certain unalienable rights . . ."—*endowed by their Creator* was his phrase. It was to secure these rights that governments were instituted among men. And this was why it was necessary for the good people of the British colonies to brashly assert that "separate and equal station to which the Laws of Nature and of Nature's God entitle them"—*Laws of Nature and of Nature's God* were his phrases.

Thomas Jefferson had once walked the streets of colonial Williamsburg, had once studied law at William and Mary. For a millennia, philosophers and lawyers like Jefferson believed that *law* was in a basic and fundamental sense *natural*. Law, the natural-law lawyers believed, was derived from currents of universal being. Law came from *God*.

•　•　•

I called Howard Siegel and told him I did not want to be involved in the case. "You don't need me," I said. "The guy you really want is at Columbia. His name is Kent Greenawalt. He's a great guy, and the foremost expert on this stuff. He wrote the book on the subject."

"I've already got Greenawalt's name, and I bought his book. It's a great book and I intend to call him and pick his brain, but he's not what I'm looking for. We need *you.*"

I put him off again, pleading for more time. But I could feel myself being reeled in, almost seduced, by Howard's passion, and by the magnetism of the case. And there were many magnetic attractions to

the case. It was legally and morally complex, filled with riveting intellectual challenges and puzzling philosophical conundrums. But the
most potent magnet was not of the mind but of the heart. Compassion may be the shortest distance between two points. Howard's story
had planted somewhere inside me the seeds of a bond, a bond intuitive and instinctual, a bond that began with the story of a little boy
named Trevor.

• • •

Trevor Horn and his twin sister, Tamielle, were born eleven weeks
premature, and like many premature infants, their health was fragile.
Trevor's condition was particularly precarious, and he was in and out
of hospitals for much of his first year of life. He was being treated at
Children's Hospital National Medical Center in Washington, D.C.,
in September 1985 when his respirator tube was accidentally dis-
lodged, cutting off his oxygen supply and causing severe brain damage. The mishap left him paralyzed, retarded, unable to speak, barely
able to see, and in need of twenty-four-hour-a-day medical attention.
Trevor was eventually released from the hospital and brought to the
family home. His mother, Millie, thought she was bringing her son
home to die.

But Trevor surprised everyone. He did not die when brought
home, but improved. He gradually learned to breathe on his own,
though he still required an enriched oxygen supply through a tube
fastened to his neck. Despite his pain and many disabilities, he
proved to be a source of inspiration and joy to all who came in contact with him. Whenever his mother was in the room he seemed to
become especially transformed. He would smile and become animated and happy, making sounds and noises in an attempt to communicate his feelings. For all the damage his body and mind had
suffered, he remained profoundly human and alive. Trevor could do
almost none of the things most children could do, but he *could* love.

In 1986, Howard Siegel and a colleague, a lawyer named John

Marshall, filed a medical malpractice lawsuit against Children's Hospital for the alleged negligence that caused Trevor's brain damage. Their case against Children's Hospital ended with a multimillion-dollar settlement, reached at the eleventh hour. The trial had actually begun, and Howard had made his opening statement to the jury. Howard's statement was so logically persuasive and emotionally gripping that the insurance company asked for a recess and then settled the case on the spot.

The money from the settlement guaranteed Trevor the medical attention he would need for the rest of his life. Although he continued to require round-the-clock nursing care, Trevor Horn made greater progress than anyone had ever expected, even in the face of his cerebral palsy and crippling brain damage. Trevor had a tracheotomy, and breathed principally through a trach tube, receiving oxygen and humidification from tubing that ran from machines to a collar that fitted loosely around his neck. While he could not walk, he had learned to crawl on his stomach and lift lightweight objects. He enjoyed playing simple games and even started going to a school, with the aid of a portable oxygen system. His emotional range was simple and pure. When he was happy—and he was usually happy— he was a bundle of smiling joy. When he was upset he would cry. He didn't like to have his picture taken, because the flash from the camera bothered him, so people began to be careful not to use flashes when he was photographed. At school he interacted with other children and learned to say a few words. "El" was Trevor's word for his sister Tamielle, "E.E." his phrase for older sister Tiffani, and "Ma" for his mother. The words and noises he had learned to make indicated that air was passing beyond his trach tube, another positive sign.

• • •

Trevor's story made me wax sentimental about my own children, Erin and Corey. When Erin was born my entire world changed. She became the center of my universe, a center joyfully enlarged by Corey five years later. At seven, Erin was at once astonishingly mature and sophisticated, and yet still very much Daddy's little girl. She had long, black hair, deep brown eyes, and a giant smile. Happy, funny, bright, and gregarious, she was an affectionate, compassionate child with a big heart, wonderful intellectual curiosity, a passion for learning, and a love for athletics. Corey, at two, was an ebullient, bouncy, precocious little bundle of energy and joy, a fearless and merry imp, game for anything, demanding of time and attention equal to her sister, and stunningly beautiful, with blond hair, sparkling blue eyes, and a round cherub's face.

The thought of poor little Trevor, and the accident that had left him paralyzed, left me maudlin. How had his family coped? I guess people find the strength. A superstitious Catholic, I made the sign of the cross and said a short prayer for Erin and Corey's safety. (My prayers too often tended to be like that—sporadic, transparent, self-serving.) Yet Trevor's story was also uplifting. It gave one hope for the resiliency of the human spirit, for the remarkable healing power of love. So I said another prayer, of thanks for that power of healing, on behalf of all humanity. It made me feel magnanimous. I doubt God was much impressed.

• • •

Millie's sister, Vivian Elaine Rice, lived in the same Silver Spring, Maryland, neighborhood as Millie and her family, only three houses away. Friends and family called Vivian by her middle name, Elaine. Millie was a flight attendant for American Airlines, and her schedule was fairly routine. She would usually fly out early on Wednesday mornings and return on Friday afternoons. On Tuesday nights before Millie left town, Tamielle would come to Elaine's to stay the night.

On Tuesday evening, March 2, 1993, Millie stopped by Elaine's home to drop off Tamielle and to pick up a dinner plate that Elaine had fixed for her. The next day, Wednesday, Elaine followed her usual routine. As she always did, Elaine drove by Millie's house around 7:15 A.M., just to check on things. On this morning, Elaine knew immediately that something was wrong. The garage door was open, and she could hear the alarm from Trevor's respirator bleating. As she tried to enter the front door, Elaine spotted the body of her sister lying on the floor. She could go no farther, blocked by the weight of the body against the door and petrified by the terror in her heart at what she had just seen. Elaine ran from the house and jumped back into her car to drive the short distance down the street to her own home. She screamed for Tamielle to call the police.

The first officers arrived minutes after the call. In the house they found the bodies of Mildred Horn, Trevor Horn, and Janice Saunders, Trevor's nurse. They had been brutally murdered.

2

The Motive and the Masquerade

Before you make a final decision *not* to get involved," Howard insisted, "why don't you let John Marshall and I drive down to Williamsburg for a meeting with you? Take a little more time. Let's get to know each other, let's talk it through, and then make your call."

"I don't think it would be worth your while, Howard."

"We'll take that chance. It's always fun to visit Williamsburg anyway. The worse that can happen is you say no, and John and I will stay and get in a round of golf. Just give us a hearing, that's all we ask."

I capitulated. Howard promised to confer with John on his court schedule and get back to me with some possible dates for our meeting. As soon as he hung up I was berating myself for my weakness. *I do not want to get involved in this case. But damn, this Howard Siegel is a relentless son of a bitch.*

•   •   •

Detective Chris Wittenberg arrived on the scene and assumed immediate control of the investigation. Wittenberg had been with the Montgomery County police for fourteen years, five as a detective with the Homicide/Sex unit. Three people were dead. Millie Horn was found at the front door. She had been shot three times in the head. One of the shots had gone through an eye and then through her brain. Janice Saunders, the nurse, was found dead in an upstairs bedroom. She had been shot twice in the head. Again, one of the shots had gone through an eye and into the brain. The third victim was eight-year-old Trevor Horn. A respirator was next to the boy's bed. It had been detached, and its alarm was blaring when the police arrived. Wittenberg guessed that Trevor had died when his respirator tube was removed.

Wittenberg sized up the evidence that was immediately visible. The screen of a basement window had been pulled away and there were pry marks on the window frame. The French doors leading out to a deck had puncture marks in their weather stripping. Wittenberg shut the French doors, putting the dead bolts into place. He walked around the outside of the house and inserted a pen into a space near the bottom of the doors, where the throw-bolt was located. Using his pen, he tried to lift the bolt. It lifted. There was enough play to push in the right door and insert another pen to release the top dead-bolt on the door. Though the door handle was locked and the dead bolt "engaged," all he now had to do was firmly push both sets of doors and he was inside the house. It had taken no more than thirty seconds.

A piece of grass was found on Trevor's cheek. A rug and cocktail table in the living room had been moved and cushions on a sofa in the family room were on the floor. A bookcase in one bedroom had been toppled, and Millie's bedroom appeared to be slightly tossed. The contents of Millie's purse, a Fendi tote bag, had been dumped on the floor. Credit and check-cashing cards were gone from Millie's wallet, and Millie's Gucci watch was missing. But none of the other valuables in the house had been taken, including a five-carat diamond tennis bracelet lying on the counter in the bathroom. The purse of Janice Saunders, the nurse who had been watching Trevor, had not been disturbed, and none of the jewelry on her body had been stolen.

Wittenberg suspected this was murder masquerading as burglary.

What, for example, had been the point of upending the sofa cushions? "What would a burglar do that for?" Wittenberg asked one of the other detectives on the scene. "Was he looking for popcorn seeds, maybe pennies between the cushions?"

A little more physical evidence would gradually accumulate over the next several days, but for the most part there were almost no useful forensic clues. The morning after the murders, a jogger on nearby Norbeck Road found some of Millie's credit cards. Two weeks after the murders, a canine officer and his dog found a small piece of a trigger from some kind of firearm near where the credit cards had been discovered. The police lab was able to identify the trigger piece as coming from an AR-7, a 22-caliber rifle. The serial numbers had been completely drilled through and could not be read. Police also found a rat-tail file with traces of gunpowder on it, as if it had been used to scour the inside of a gun barrel. Stray pieces of bullets and the wound patterns of the victims were consistent with the use of a silencer.

But beyond that, the scene was clean. No prints, no fibers, no incriminating evidence of any kind. This was not a case that looked as if it would be cracked through physical evidence. The crime scene was a transparent masquerade. Wittenberg decided to focus not on method, but motive.

● ● ●

Michael Saunders, the husband of Janice, was at home with his son, Colin, when Montgomery County detective Ed Tarney arrived. Michael and Colin had heard a radio report stating that three persons had been killed at the home of Mildred Horn. Michael was praying that the detective walking up to his door was coming to tell him that Janice was all right. Detective Tarney, a hardened veteran, began to weep as he confirmed Michael's worst fears. Janice was dead. Tarney could hear Colin screaming in a back bedroom of the house, crying that he wanted his mother home now!

"Today we look at two of the most important modern Supreme Court decisions dealing with the connection between freedom of expression and illegal activity. They arise against the backdrop of a time of great cultural ferment, in the midst of the ongoing struggles of the civil rights movement, and growing disillusionment with the Vietnam War. Let's begin with *Brandenburg v. Ohio*, decided in 1969. This is one of the genuine lodestars of the modern First Amendment. Who can tell me what was going on in this case?"

A student named Maria volunteered. "*Brandenburg* involved a Ku Klux Klan rally conducted on a farm in Hamilton County, Ohio, outside Cincinnati. A local Cincinnati television station reporter had been invited to witness the rally, and he and a cameraman filmed the event, portions of which were later broadcast on the Cincinnati station and a national network. The film footage was filled with racist bile. The Supreme Court tells us that the Klan members pronounced that 'the nigger should be returned to Africa, the Jew to Israel,' and that 'if our President, our Congress, our Supreme Court, continues to suppress the white, Caucasian race, it's possible that there might have to be some revengence taken.' "

"Tell me, Maria, then what happened?"

"The state of Ohio prosecuted Mr. Brandenburg, the leader of the Klan group, under an Ohio 'criminal syndicalism' law, which made it illegal to advocate 'the duty, necessity, or propriety of crime, sabotage, violence, or unlawful methods of terrorism as a means of accomplishing industrial or political reform,' or to assemble 'with any group, or assemblage of persons formed to teach or advocate the doctrines of criminal syndicalism.' Brandenburg was convicted, fined $1,000, and sentenced to one to ten years' imprisonment."

"Now, you said this was a *criminal syndicalism* law. What the hell is that? Did the state of Ohio pass this law with groups like the Ku Klux Klan in mind?"

Maria looked at me with befuddled, clueless eyes. Another student in the back of the room had his hand up. "Tom?" I said. "Can you help us out?"

"This was originally an antilabor law," said Tom, our class historian. "It was a capitalist response to labor and socialist movements from earlier in the century. The Wobblies and groups like that. That's why there's the reference to 'industrial or political reform.' "

"Good," I said, and then returned to Maria. "But Maria, Ohio had pressed this old law to new use. And it certainly seemed to fit, didn't it? I mean the Klan quite clearly *did* advocate and teach the propriety of crime, 'sabotage, violence, or unlawful methods' to accomplish its own perverse image of 'political reform,' didn't it. I mean, we are talking about real evil here, aren't we? The damn Ku Klux Klan."

"The United States Supreme Court did not see it that way," said Maria, firmly. "It held that the Ohio law was unconstitutional."

"And why was that?"

"Well, to start, no one was present at the Klan rally except the Klan members themselves, the television reporter, and his cameraman. Nothing in the record indicated that this orgy of race hate posed any immediate physical threat to anyone. In these circumstances, the Court said, the Klan was guilty only of the 'abstract teaching' of the 'moral propriety' of racist violence. 'The constitutional guarantees of free speech and free press,' the Court stated, 'do not permit a State to forbid or proscribe advocacy of the use of force or of law violation except where such advocacy is likely to incite or produce such action.' "

I looked at Tom, up in the back row. "Let's call on our history expert to next take us to Bloomington, Indiana. Tom, what was going on in the sequel to *Brandenburg*, the *Hess v. Indiana* case?"

"This involved a guy named Gregory Hess," said Tom. "Hess was convicted of violating Indiana's disorderly conduct statute in an anti–Vietnam War demonstration on the campus of Indiana University. Between 100 and 150 demonstrators had moved onto a public street, blocking traffic. After refusing to obey the sheriff's command to clear the street, the demonstrators were moved to the curbs by the sheriff and his deputies. As the sheriff passed by, Hess said, 'We'll take the fucking street later.' The sheriff immediately arrested Hess for disorderly conduct, and he was convicted." Tom had spoken Hess's words with an almost gleeful accent, raising eyebrows and smiles from his classmates.

"We can all easily imagine this scene, can't we? It's like a technical foul in basketball. Right? There are certain things you just don't say within five feet of an authority figure in this country. If Bobby Knight had said, as the referee passed him, 'That's all right, ref, we'll foul the fucking guy later,'" you can pretty much figure the ref is going to spin around and lay a T on him, if not toss him right out of the game. And on the street, if you yell 'fucking'-just-about-anything at a cop as he walks by, there's a good chance he's going to spin around and lay the cuffs on you. So Hess does this—probably some long-haired hippie-freak anyhow—and the cop charges him for it. But the Supreme Court says no. You can't do that. It violates the First Amendment! Now, why is that, Tom?"

"The Court first says that Hess could not be convicted merely for having used the word *fuck*, since that word standing alone does not satisfy the legal definition of obscenity. Nor could Hess's statement be seen as a direct verbal challenge to fight the sheriff or his deputies—witnesses testified that he was facing the crowd, not the street, when he made the statement and that his words did not appear to be addressed to any particular person or group."

"Good. Now what about *Brandenburg?* How did the Supreme Court in *Hess* apply its prior ruling in that case?"

"The Court held that Hess was not guilty of any incitement to imminent lawless action. The words *We'll take the fucking street later,* the Court maintained, could be taken as a counsel for 'present moderation' or as advocacy of illegal action 'at some indefinite future time,' neither of which were enough to constitute a present threat of imminent disorder."

As Tom expounded other hands rose, eager students primed to speak. Sometimes the law professor business was just too easy, I thought. A regular loophole in life.

3

The Master of Motown

Detective Chris Wittenberg began his investigation by learning everything he could about the Horn family. Millie had come from a large family with fourteen children, eight brothers and five sisters. Millie and three of her sisters—Elaine Rice, Marilyn Farmer, and Gloria Maree—had all escaped their impoverished beginnings in South Carolina to become professional success stories. They all lived near one another in the Washington area, and had remained very close. Elaine was a principal at Galludet High School in Washington, and Marilyn was a teacher there. Gloria worked in the computer business. Elaine and Millie were especially close. Elaine lived only a few houses down from Millie on Northgate Drive in Silver Spring. She would usually stop by Millie's house twice a day. "There are 365 days in a year," said Elaine. "And I was at Millie's house on 360 of them."

Millie had three kids. Trevor, killed with her, was eight. Trevor's twin sister, Tamielle, had been away from the house on the night of the murders, staying with Elaine. Millie's oldest daughter, Tiffani, was away at college at Howard University.

Wittenberg learned about Trevor's medical malpractice incident, and the large pot of money that had been set away in trust for his medical care. He learned that Janice Saunders, the nurse who had been killed, had been one of Trevor's nurses from the beginning, and she was like a sister to Millie and Elaine Horn. On March 2 at about 6:30 P.M., Janice had dropped off her three-year-old son, Colin, with her husband, Michael. It was the last time they would see her alive.

Millie, Wittenberg found, was divorced. Her former husband was Lawrence Horn. Under Maryland law, if Millie and Trevor were both to die, Lawrence would inherit the multimillion-dollar trust fund. From the moment they learned of the murders, Millie's sisters were pointing suspicious fingers at Lawrence. The man certainly had a motive. Wittenberg set out to learn what he could about Lawrence Horn.

• • •

The assigned reading for "Law and Religion" was on Natural Law. The reading was dense, but I always enjoyed presenting it to the students. The Natural Law philosophy that "law" as we know it on earth descends from the will of God was one that I, a Polish Catholic kid from Chicago, well understood and, on some visceral level, perhaps believed. I certainly knew my Thomas Aquinas. At the apex is God, and Eternal Law. Is God above the Eternal Law, or is the Eternal Law above God? This is a conundrum, like asking "Could God make a rock so heavy he couldn't lift it?" If you say God *could* make such a rock because God is omnipotent, you are trapped, because you would then be admitting that there is something God *can't* do—lift the unliftable rock—so your God can't really be God. On the other hand, if you answer that God *could not* make a rock so heavy he couldn't lift it, you are also trapped, because again you are confessing that there is something your God can't do—make an unliftable rock. But what kind of God would not "obey" Eternal Law anyway? If Eternal Law is perfection, then God should obey it, because God wouldn't want to be anything other than perfect. On the other hand, if God is supposed to be omnipotent, how can something else, like Eternal Law, bind him? And what kind of omnipotent God can't do as he pleases? One solution is to think of Eternal Law as an extension of God, or as the *mind* of God itself, and thus treat the question of whether one is above the other as silly, irrelevant logic-chopping.

In the thought of Thomas Aquinas, Natural Law is that imperfect glimpse of Eternal Law that is visible to humans on earth. We may be made in God's image and likeness, but we are so far beneath him, so inferior to him, that we cannot come close to knowing or understanding him completely, or to knowing or understanding Eternal Law. Through the haze of our fallen state we look upward and attempt to discern what we can of God and Eternal Law. Those dim perceptions are Natural Law. Aquinas also has a category called Divine Law. The precepts of Divine Law are direct commands from God that may appear to humans to be contrary to Natural Law, but because they come from God, who must have his reasons, they must nonetheless be obeyed. Thus God's command to Abraham to slay Isaac seems contrary to Natural Law, but since there was no doubting, at least in Abraham's mind, that it was God talking to him, it was Abraham's duty to obey and not ask questions.

Human Law is the lowest category of law in Aquinas's philosophy. Human Law is the law that kings and queens make, the law of human governments. A just government will derive its Human Law from Natural Law. This means Human Law is traceable to God, because Human Law is modeled on Natural Law, which is in turn modeled on Eternal Law and God. Aquinas understood, however, that Human Law may at times be perverse. It may run contrary to Natural Law. The king may be a devil. When that happens, the just person must disobey the Human Law and instead follow the Natural Law and its proximation to the will of God.

In class we explored the thought of Thomas Aquinas neutrally, as scholars and students interested in the intellectual origins of the American legal traditions regarding the relationship of law and religion. I didn't ask any of the students whether they personally believed in Natural Law, nor did I reveal my own beliefs. What *were* my beliefs? I guess I was ambivalent. Much of this was part of my childhood Catholic education; whatever I thought intellectually, I could not deny that on some visceral level it remained part of me, like the fragments of the Mass I could still recite in Latin.

•   •   •

Lawrence "L.T." Horn once owned Detroit. It was his town and his sound. He grew up in a show business family. His mother, Pauline, ran a modeling school in Detroit and worked with local performers to develop their careers. His sister, Elaine, was a jazz dancer who married William Tyler, the legendary ventriloquist, who traveled the world with his dummy "Lester." In the navy, he'd been a disc jockey, where he picked up the name "L.T., the Man with the Plan."

Lawrence was the Man with the Plan, and in his early days in Motor City the plan was to create a new sound. He linked up with Barry Gordy, and together they became the masters of the "Motown Sound," producing records for the Supremes, the Temptations, Smokey Robinson, Stevie Wonder, and many others. Horn was a brilliant recording engineer, and he rode the Motown meteor as the sound took off. He had plenty of cash, drove a Porsche, and was always in the fast lane.

"People insist on confusing marriage and love on the one hand, and love and happiness on the other," wrote Albert Camus. "But they have nothing in common." If Camus only knew. In Lawrence Horn's life, love, marriage, and happiness were much confused.

Horn's first marriage was to Juana Royster, a receptionist at the Detroit building known as Hitsville USA, the headquarters of Motown Records. The wedding ceremony had been secretly arranged by Horn, who had not bothered to tell his fiancée. Royster walked into her basement recreation room one night in 1966 and found herself in a wedding. "He was absolutely fun," Royster remembered. But fun as it was, the marriage lasted only eight months.

In 1973, Horn married Millie Maree, an attractive flight attendant with American Airlines. Virtually from the start, the marriage was a roller-coaster. Millie and Horn had their first child, Tiffani, in 1974. But the marriage soon deteriorated. Motown Records moved from Detroit to Los Angeles. Horn made the move to L.A. with Motown, but Millie did not. She and Horn split up, and Millie moved to the suburbs of Washington, D.C., to live close to her sisters. Several years passed, and Millie and Lawrence remained separated. Divorce seemed imminent. Yet the couple could not completely cut off their mercurial romance, and Millie became pregnant by Lawrence again, this time with twins.

On August 14, 1984, Trevor and his sister Tamielle were born, eleven weeks premature. Tamielle was not released from the hospital for a month. Trevor's problems were worse. He had underdeveloped lungs and chronic respiratory problems, and was constantly in and out of hospitals.

The birth of the twins precipitated the real end of the marriage. In a bitter divorce and custody battle, Horn went deeply into debt. Then Motown Records was acquired by a larger record company, and in the ensuing downsizing at Motown, Horn lost his job. He went more deeply into debt. He was $16,000 behind in his child-custody payments and $65,000 behind in his legal bills.

To Detective Chris Wittenberg, it looked as if Lawrence Horn had reached a troubled impasse in life. It sounded like the Man with the Plan had needed one.

4

Alibis and Videotape

Chris Wittenberg interviewed Tiffani Horn. He found out that at 2:30 in the morning on March 3, Tiffani had called her mother at home from her dormitory room at Howard University, where she was studying broadcast journalism. Tiffani said that she had mistakenly dialed the number, actually intending to call her boyfriend. Then Tiffani told him that the night before the murders she had talked to her father, Lawrence, who had called from Los Angeles. Her father had been obsessed with questions about where everyone in the family would be the following night, including what Tiffani knew about when Millie would be home, and whether Tamielle would be sleeping over that night at Elaine's.

It sounded to Wittenberg like Tiffani had not had an easy time dealing with her mother and father's stormy relationship. For about two years, starting in 1989, Tiffani had lived in Los Angeles with her father and his family. She had sometimes been at odds with her mother, and the two had often fought. But her relationship with her father was also difficult. She told Wittenberg that her dad paid almost no attention to Trevor.

Wittenberg was bothered by Tiffani's call to her mother's home at 2:30 in the morning of March 3, a call so close in proximity to the time of the murders. Could Tiffani have been involved in some way?

Her explanation, that she had simply dialed her mother's number by mistake, touching the speed-dial button on her phone, was plausible, and Wittenberg found Tiffani's demeanor convincing. But he wanted to be sure. He asked Tiffani to submit to polygraph examinations. She agreed. Three examinations were administered. She passed all of them with flying colors. There were no indications of deception or untruthfulness. The tests were enough to confirm Wittenberg's instinct—that the call from Tiffani was nothing more than a strange and poignant coincidence.

•   •   •

Wittenberg knew that everyone in the Horn family thought Lawrence Horn was somehow connected to the murders. Horn certainly had the motive—greed. But would a man actually kill his own child for money?

Wittenberg and his assistant, Detective James Leasure, flew to Los Angeles on March 12, nine days after the murders. At Wittenberg's request, three detectives from the Homicide unit and two uniformed officers from the Los Angeles Police Department joined Wittenberg and Leasure to conduct a search of the apartment Horn occupied with his girlfriend, Shiri Bogan. The apartment—at 1776 North Sycamore—was a modest one-bedroom, one-bath, garden-style flat that had originally been Bogan's. When Horn moved in he split the rent and expenses with her. At 7:15 in the evening on March 13, ten days after the murders, the detectives entered the apartment. Neither Bogan nor Horn was there. The police found a videotape Horn had made that showed him driving along the route from the Days Inn in Rockville to Millie's neighborhood in Silver Spring. They also turned up a hand-drawn map of Millie's block, showing her house and the location of the houses near it. A yellow piece of scrap paper had handwritten notes on it, including the initials "MMH," followed by the address "13502 Northgate, 20906, Silver Spring, Maryland." A telephone number was written on the pad, with a note under it saying "Tiff dorm." There was a hotel notepad from the Days Inn with the name "Bishop" on it, and several fragments of numbers.

At 8:15, Horn and Bogan arrived. Horn seemed nonplussed. He had an alibi. Horn gave the police a videotape that he had made on the night of the murders, showing him in his own apartment. The tape was made from a camera mounted on a tripod. Wittenberg watched the tape with keen interest. At first the lens zoomed in on the television screen in the apartment. On the screen, the date and time were prominently displayed: "03-02-93 - 11:03 P.M." The camera then panned back to a wider-angle shot, showing Horn and his girlfriend, Shiri.

Wasn't it a terrific coincidence for Lawrence Horn that he just happened to be taking a home video on the night of March 3, and he just happened to have that video focus on his television screen, which just happened to be displaying the date and time—11:03 P.M. Pacific time—the approximate time of the murders?

A terrific coincidence, thought Wittenberg. A bit *too* terrific.

•   •   •

Another videotape seized at Horn's apartment showed the inside of Millie's residence on Northgate Drive, and had scenes of Trevor playing. Wittenberg learned that Horn's daughter Tiffani had made the tape, at Horn's request, with the explanation that Horn wanted to be able to show film clips of Trevor to Horn's mother.

At Wittenberg's direction, the police methodically examined all hotel registrations in the vicinity of the murders. One registration at the Days Inn got Wittenberg's attention. A man named James Perry had checked in at midnight and was gone by 6:00 A.M. He had paid cash but used his driver's license as identification. Wittenberg and his officers began pouring over phone records. They found that Horn had received a call from a pay phone at a nearby Denny's two hours after the murders. They also found a call placed from a pay phone at the U.S. Post Office on Wilcox Avenue in Los Angeles to the Days

Inn, made at 11:50 A.M. on March 3. The call had been charged to the calling card of one Kamella MacKinney. Further investigation revealed that this was a false name, adopted by one of Horn's cousins, Marsha Webb, to obtain telephone service after Pacific Bell cut her off for nonpayment. Webb stated that she obtained the fake card at the urging of Horn. She did not know anyone named James Perry. But police found sixty-six calls on Webb's card from Los Angeles to Detroit, including calls to a joint called Farcel's Bar in Detroit, where Perry liked to hang.

Wittenberg began to learn more about James Perry. He found out that Perry fashioned himself "a spiritual adviser and case buster." His business card described him as "Dr. J. Perry." It did not disclose that among the credits on his résumé were felony convictions for assault and armed robbery, or that his ministry was that of the con artist. The police went more deeply into the phone records and found a trail of phone traffic between pay phones in Los Angeles near Horn's residence and pay phones in hangouts that Perry frequently haunted in Detroit. Most damning, they found a phone call from the Days Inn, at 5:12 in the morning, to Horn's residence. It was obvious from the phone records that Perry had some kind of relationship with Lawrence Horn.

Wittenberg sought the help of the FBI and the Detroit police. Perry was placed under surveillance and his phone was tapped. On September 24, an FBI agent from the Detroit office, Robert Casey, paid a visit to Perry. Using a "Peter Falk as Columbo" act, Casey fumbled through a nonchalant interview, claiming he was simply carrying out a routine inquiry he had been given from another FBI office. For some reason the Maryland FBI wanted to know if Perry had been in the Rockville, Maryland, Days Inn on the night of March 2. Perry said that he had been there, but had stayed only a few hours. He had been driving and had simply checked in to get a few hours' rest.

The day after the interview, the surveillance team spotted Perry making more calls from a pay phone. Wittenberg did more digging through the phone records. Phone calls from Perry's credit card to Los Angeles were found from pay phones at highway stops on the route from Rockville, Maryland, to Detroit. Wittenberg himself drove the route, stopping at each pay phone to photograph it. The trip was about five hundred miles and took nine hours.

It was decided that the phone connections already established between Perry and Horn were enough evidence to obtain a search warrant. With the help of the Detroit police, a warrant was issued, and in November 1993, James Perry's residence on Glenfield Avenue in Detroit was searched. Nothing directly incriminating was found. But Perry did seem to have unusual reading habits. The search turned up a cache of catalogs, books, and magazines on crime and weapons. It was a long shot, but Wittenberg began calling some of the magazines and publishing companies to see if any of them had a record of Perry buying anything. One of the places he called was an outfit called Paladin Press, located in Boulder, Colorado. To his amazement, Paladin told him that Perry had purchased two books from them in 1992. One was called *How to Make Disposable Silencers.* The other was entitled *Hit Man: A Technical Manual for Independent Contractors.* Perry had purchased *Hit Man* and *Silencer,* a Paladin sales representative stated, with a personal check. Wittenberg sensed from the title of the books alone that he was on to something. He ordered the books from Paladin Press.

5

"But You Don't Stand for Anything"

Wittenberg received his copy of *Hit Man: A Technical Manual for Independent Contractors* and took meticulous notes as he read its pages. What first grabbed him was the book's discussion of the 22-caliber AR-7 as the ideal weapon for most contract kills. A piece of an AR-7 rifle had been found by police near the place where Millie Horn's credit cards had been found. *Hit Man* also instructed the killer to drill out the serial numbers on the weapon. The serial numbers on the fragments of the rifle the police had discovered had been completely drilled through and could not be read. *Hit Man* told the killer to use a rat-tail file to scour the inside of the gun to defeat ballistics tracing. Police had found a rat-tail file with traces of gunpowder on it, and believed it had been used to scour the inside barrel of a gun. *Hit Man* also contained very detailed instructions on how to build a silencer for the AR-7. The stray pieces of bullets and the wound patterns of the victims had already led Wittenberg to conclude that a silencer had been used by the murderer. *Hit Man* told the assassin to fire from a distance of three to six feet. The police had established that Janice Saunders and Millie Horn had both been killed from a gun fired at that distance. *Hit Man* told the killer to fire at least one of the shots through an eye. Both Janice and Millie had been shot through an eye.

Wittenberg was satisfied that the modus operandi used to commit the three murders came directly from *Hit Man*. He was certain that whoever killed Trevor, Millie, and Janice had read the book.

• • •

A small herd of white-tail deer grazed on the edge of the highway, indifferent to my headlights, impervious to the storm. Erin and Corey were half-asleep in the backseat. I was nervous, on edge, squinting through a gray fog and gusting sheets of sleet and snow. We were on the Colonial Parkway, a federal highway that winds through national parkland in tidewater Virginia along the marshy shores of the York River. The parkway runs from Jamestown, the site of the first European settlement in the New World, to Yorktown, where George Washington's ragtag army defeated British troops to end the Revolutionary War.

Suddenly, my rearview mirror was lit with blinding lights. My daughters were startled awake by the rude warbles of a police siren. I pulled to the shoulder of the road. *Not just one cop car pulled up, but three.* Three black vans, one behind us, one alongside, and one angled across our front bumper, cutting off any forward escape. The flashing lights were terrifying the children. From the rear van an officer emerged. A woman. She walked to my window and tapped against it with a flashlight. Sleet pounded on her felt hat, which was covered in clear plastic. She flashed a badge, too quickly for me to read, and said, "Sir, I need for you to step out of the car."

The vans didn't seem to have any markings, and I had never seen a uniform like hers—special federal park service cops or something. I glanced back at my daughters, simpering in the backseat. "Kids, it's okay. Daddy has to talk to the police lady."

"*Why* Daddy? What's going *on*?"

At that moment a tall man in a hideous yellow-green pinstripe suit and matching fedora stepped out of the front van and stood in the beam of my headlights. He nodded to the woman.

Panic swelled inside me. *"You're not real cops!"* I shouted.

She pulled back her topcoat, revealing a leather shoulder harness strapped tightly against her white blouse. I reached for the switch that would roll up my window, but she was faster on the draw. Whipping out a chrome-plated pistol fixed with a fat silencer on the end of the barrel, she trained the gun at my eyes, and fired.

Haaaggggh!

I sat bolt upright in the bed, sweating and panting. *Jesus! God!* I took several deep breaths to try to calm myself. *Well, that disproves one myth: When you are killed in a dream it doesn't actually mean you die.*

Spooked and disoriented by my nightmare, I padded down the hallway to check on the kids. They were in their bedrooms, sleeping like angels. It was four in the morning. I walked to the kitchen. I could pull out a beer and hope to relax myself enough to get back to sleep. Or I could give up on the night, make coffee, and start the day early. *Hell, I'm too shaken. I'll never get back to sleep.* I made the coffee. It was going to be a busy day. I was picking up my best friend, Roger Reitzel, in Virginia Beach. He was spending the next two days with me. I'd tell him about the case, and let him advise me. Maybe I'd even tell him about my dream. He liked to play Sigmund Freud.

• • •

"As a realtor motivational speaker, I have to travel a lot. I really don't like to travel because I don't sleep well on the road. I'm married, so I'm used to having a good fight right before I go to bed. Sometimes I call up the desk clerk and tick her off just so I can get some rest."

Standing against a table in the back of the convention center of the Cavalier Hotel in Virginia Beach, Virginia, I was hypnotized by the spectacle. Some two thousand real estate agents all wearing the same tan Century 21 Real Estate blazers were cheering wildly as Roger Reitzel, a stand-up comic and comedy writer from Los Angeles, regaled them with two hours of unrelenting real estate comedy.

"Of course, as real estate agents, you travel plenty, too. You go on 'tours' or 'caravans,' which I would define as the act of real estate agents traveling from home to home to criticize people's decorating taste while they decide where to have lunch." *Peels of laughter.*

"And speaking of lunch, what time is it?" *Jovial titters.* "I've tried every diet there is. I've tried high-fiber diets where you eat gravel and pocket change." *More titters.* "I've tried aversion therapy where you put your cigarettes out in your food. After a couple months, cigarette butts don't taste all that bad." *Hoots, howls, applause.* "I've tried calorie diets, but I keep borrowing from the next day's calories." *Huge laughs.* "I was doing what they call deficit eating." *Laughs.* "I embarked on a massive exercise program and started jogging. Seven miles every other day. On the other days I was on life support." *Laughs again.*

"People, it's amazing to me that we are members of the largest trade association in the world and half of us can't seem to pronounce what we are. It's not 'real-*a*-tor,' it's 'real-tor.' It's not 'doc-*a*-tor,' it's 'doc-tor.' It's not 'hook*a*-ker,' it's '*law-yer.*' "

Laughs and more laughs. They love him.

This was the kickoff of a bacchanal weekend convention of Century 21 agents. Ostensibly, Roger was conducting a "training session," but it was really a corporate pep rally. The "show" had opened with the house lights dark and a sound system louder than at a rock concert booming the same high-powered technobeat rhythms used to introduce the Chicago Bulls at the United Center. It was *exactly* like the opening of a Bulls game, actually, with laser lights flashing across the ceiling and Century 21 sales "superstars" running up the aisles to the stage, slapping each other high-fives, their faces blazoned across enormous television screens. The emcee whipped the crowd into a frenzied sea of tan-jacketed crazies, standing on their chairs cheering wildly as Roger Reitzel, Superstar, hit the stage. For two hours he sang real estate songs and told real estate jokes, with lights and sounds and pitches to buy his complete set of videotapes after the show.

He was the Wayne Newton of corporate comedy. And he was my oldest and closest friend.

It took half an hour to appease the throng of autograph-seekers and women looking for love in all the wrong places before we were able to make our escape to my jeep in the hotel parking lot.

"So basically," I said, once we were inside with the doors locked, "when you do one of these gigs, you could pretty much get laid by bouffant-hair-types round-the-clock from the moment you get off stage."

"Yes I could, if I were into that kind of thing." I knew he wasn't.

Roger and I had known each other since childhood. Together we'd played football, dated high school sweethearts, smart-assed teachers, and wrecked cars, with a fealty unflinching through college, careers, marriages, and kids.

"And so how many of these conventions do you do a year?" I asked.

"Oh, fifty."

"*Fifty!* Chrissakes. You know, watching you up there, I realized how much our lives are still in parallel. We're both successful failures."

"*Ungh,*" Roger grunted a halfhearted laugh.

"You didn't move to Los Angeles for a career in real estate comedy."

Now it came, his huge cackling belly laugh, from way down in his huge cackling belly. "You were unbelievably *hilarious* up there," I continued. "I was in tears. So why do other funny fat guys like John Belushi, John Goodman, and Chris Farley make it with feature films while you're still doing the Century 21 convention in Virginia Beach?"

"And why are Alan Dershowitz, Johnny Cochran, and F. Lee Bailey defending O. J. Simpson in prime time while you're on C-Span at three in the morning?" he rejoined.

"Because they're headliners," I said, "and I'm a lounge act." We bantered on during the hour drive from Virginia Beach to Williamsburg, past the picturesque Norfolk skyline and harbor, and the navy base in Hampton Roads, with the silhouettes of aircraft carriers and battleships backlit against a brilliant orange sunset. "I can see why you live here," Roger said. "It's beautiful." We caught up on jobs and kids and dreams. Roger had been asked to do a "spec script" for a "Seinfeld" episode, and had been hired to write two "Rugrats" shows—potentially big breaks. I told him about the call from Howard Siegel, and how I was grappling with whether to take the case. "I'm worried that getting involved in this would be going against all I stand for."

"Yeah? And the problem is? You don't think I'd sell out in an L.A.-second if I could land a 'Seinfeld'? Turn my back on all *I* stand for? Hell yes, I would. That's called commitment."

"But Roger, you don't stand for anything."

•   •   •

We stopped for dinner. On the table between us lay my copy of *Hit Man: A Technical Manual for Independent Contractors.* It had a glossy purple cover with a blood-red silhouette of a dead body sprawled upside down across the front, and a man in a yellow-green pinstripe suit brandishing a revolver fitted with a fat silencer superimposed over the dead body. The author was listed as "Rex Feral," an obvious pseudonym. It was published by Paladin Press, from Boulder, Colorado. A warning appeared in the front of the book, on a page facing the table of contents:

WARNING

IT IS AGAINST THE LAW to manufacture a silencer without an appropriate license from the federal government. There are state and local laws prohibiting the possession of weapons and their accessories in many areas. Severe penalties are prescribed for violations of these laws. Neither the author nor the publisher assumes responsibility for the use or misuse of information contained in this book. **For informational purposes only!**

Roger flipped through the book quickly, and then turned to the beginning. He began to read from the opening lines of the preface:

> A woman recently asked how I could, in good conscience, write an instruction book on murder.
>
> "How can you live with yourself if someone uses what you write to go out and take a human life?" she whined.
>
> I am afraid she was quite offended by my answer.
>
> It is my opinion that the professional hit man fills a need in society and is, at times, the only alternative for "personal" justice. Moreover, if my advice and the proven methods in this book are followed, certainly no one will ever know.

Roger looked at me. "This is unbelievable," he said.

"What we have in this little diddy," I said, "is a detailed, step-by-step instruction manual in the dark arts of assassination." I took it back from him and flipped the pages as I spoke. "Just look," I continued. "You got your instructional photographs, your engineering specifications, your chemical formulas, your checklists, descriptions of tools and weapons, surveillance methods, sample maps and floor plans, and specific instructions on killing techniques. The early chapters deal with mental and physical preparation." I turned to a passage I had marked. "Here our friend Rex is setting his narrative tone.

> You might be like my friends—interested but unsure, standing on the sidelines afraid to play the game because you don't know the rules. But within the pages of his book you will learn one of the most successful methods of operation used by an independent contractor. You will follow the procedures of a man who works alone, without backing of organized crime or on a personal vendetta. Step by step you will be taken from research to equipment selection to job preparation to successful job completion. You will learn where to find employment, how much to charge, and what you can, and cannot, do with the money you earn.

"When I first received the book from this guy Howard Siegel, the lawyer who is trying to get me to do this, I was tempted to skim-read it, but I found it too engrossing. Or maybe I should just say grossing. I decided to follow Rex's admonition. 'But deny your urge to skip about, looking for the "good" parts,' says Rex. 'Start where any amateur who is serious about turning professional will start—at the beginning.'

"Roger, you are looking at a lean, mean, killing machine, even as we speak. I've read the book, baby. Rex has assured me that after completing all of the book's instructions 'you will have honed your mind, body and reflexes into a precision piece of professional machinery.' I am the man's *student*. And Rex says the student will have 'assembled the necessary tools and learned to use them efficiently.' The student's 'knowledge of dealing death,' upon graduation from this course of instruction, will have made the student 'confident and competent enough to accept employment.' "

The waiter brought us our mineral waters and a basket of baguette bread. "Why don't you sit back and listen, and I'll read you the highlights of what I have learned," I said to him. *"Hit Man* methodically explains everything you need to know to go into the business of murder-for-hire, including how to find clients, negotiate contracts, and determine what to charge. The suggested retail price for killing a federal judge is $250,000. A county sheriff is a relative bargain, between $75,000 and $100,000. The book contains detailed instructions on how to plan a hit, including what to learn about the so-called mark's routines and habits, how to assess where best to stage the execution, the preferred methods of surveillance, what to wear for the job, how to travel into the jurisdiction, what weapons to use, how to retool and reconfigure the weapons, how to conduct the kill without leaving incriminating evidence behind, how to escape, and how to launder the money received in the payoff. A major part of the book was dedicated to canvassing a range of killing techniques.

"For example, it says, 'The kill is the easiest part of the job. People kill one another every day. It takes no great effort to pull a trigger or plunge a knife. It is being able to do so in a manner that will not link yourself or your employer to the crime that makes you a professional.'

"The book gives the chemical and engineering specifications for techniques requiring bombs or arson. Kills with knives, guns, explosives, poisons, and ice picks were all described in graphic detail:

> The knife should have a double-edged blade. The double edge, combined with the serrated section and six-inch length, will insure a deep, ragged tear, and the wound will be difficult, if not impossible, to close without prompt medical attention. . . . Make your thrusts to a vital organ and twist the knife before you withdraw it. If you hit bone, you will have to file the blade to remove the marks left on the metal when it struck the victim's bone. . . . Using your six-inch, serrated blade knife, stab deeply into the side of the victim's neck and push the knife forward in a forceful movement. This method will half decapitate the victim, cutting both his main arteries and wind pipe, ensuring immediate death. . . . An ice pick can . . . be driven into the victim's brain, through the ear, after he has been subdued. The wound hardly bleeds at all, and death is sometimes attributed to natural causes.

The waiter brought our order of smoked salmon and focaccia. "Now, Rex also describes 'special order' jobs," I said, pushing forward, undaunted by our food, "for which such extras as torture or the procurement of information are required. The assassin, of course, should charge extra for services from this à la carte menu:

> Although several shots fired in succession offer quick and relatively humane death to the victim, there are instances when other methods of extermination are called for. The employer may want you to gather certain information from the mark before you do away with him. At other times, the assignment

may call for torture or disfigurement as a "lesson" for the survivors.

There is no end to the various ways of torturing a mark until he would tell you what you want to know, and die just to get it over. Sometimes all it takes is putting a knife to his throat. Not from behind with the blade across the throat the way they do in the movies, but from the front with the tip of the blade creasing the soft hollow of the throat, where the victim can see the gleaming steel and realizes what damage it would do if fully penetrated.

"Rex also explains methods of disposing of bodies. I found this very informative. I had never realized, I guess, that even something as basic as burying your victim requires informed scientific technique. 'If you bury the body, again deep stab wounds should be made to allow the gases to escape. A bloating corpse will push the earth up as it swells. Pour in lime to prevent the horrible odor of decomposition, and lye to make that decomposition more rapid.' Cutting off the victim's head is especially recommended: 'You can simply cut off the head after burying the body. Take the head to some deserted location, place a stick of dynamite in the mouth, and blow the telltale dentition to smithereens! After this, authorities can't use the victim's dental records to identify his remains. As the body decomposes, fingerprints will disappear and no real evidence will be left from which to make positive identification. You can even clip off the fingertips and bury them separately.' "

Neither of us had touched our dinner. Something about the book had gotten us out of the mood. "You wanna beer?" I asked. "Reading from Rex Feral makes me feel the need for something stronger than San Pellegrino."

"Glass of wine for me," he said. "Keep reading. I can take it if you can."

I signaled for the waiter, and we ordered drinks. "Of course I can take it," I chided. "I'm a killing machine." I picked up the book. "We were on body-disposal," I said. "Maybe you're thinking, Rog, well, why not just throw the body in a lake somewhere?"

"Yes. You read my mind."

"Well I'll bet you didn't know that sinking the corpse in water requires particular precautions:

> If you choose to sink the corpse, you must first make several deep stabs into the body's lungs (from just under the rib cage) and belly. This is necessary because gases released during decomposition will bloat these organs, causing the body to rise to the surface of the water. . . . The corpse should be weighted with the standard concrete blocks, but it must be wrapped from head to toe with heavy chain as well, to keep the body from separating and floating in chunks to the surface. After the fishes and natural elements have done their work, the chain will drag the bones into the muddy sediment.

"You're right, I didn't know that. You learn new things every day."

The drinks came. We began to work on our food, and were quiet for several minutes. "What about psychology?" Roger asked shortly. "He tells you *how* to kill. But I should think that having the mind and the will would be as critical as the technical know-how."

I nodded. "Absolutely right. In fact, that's exactly what Rex says, again and again, page after page. This book is filled with counseling, exhortation, and encouragement. Rex is constantly seeing to it that the hit-man-in-training has the psychological resolve necessary to undertake his new profession."

"So how does it feel—to kill somebody?"

"It's a look into the void, Roger. You feel absolutely nothing:

> And you are shocked by the nothingness. You had expected this moment to be a spectacular point in your life. You had wondered if you would feel compassion for the victim, immediate guilt, or even experience direct intervention by the

hand of God. But you weren't even feeling sickened by the sight of the body.

After you have arrived home the events that took place take on a dreamlike quality. You don't dwell on them. You don't worry. You don't have nightmares. You don't fear ghosts. When thoughts of the hit go through your mind, it's almost as though you are recalling some show you saw on television.

"But the emptiness that follows the kill ultimately gives way to a feeling of profound superiority:

By the time you collect the balance of your contract fee, the doubts and fears of discovery have faded. Those feelings have been replaced by cockiness, a feeling of superiority, a new independence and self-assurance. Everything seems to have changed. The people around you have suddenly become so aggravatingly ordinary. You start to view them as an irritating herd of pathetic sheep, doing as they are told, doing what is expected, following someone, anyone, blindly. You can't believe how dumb your friends have become, and your respect diminishes for people you once held in awe.

You too have become different. You recognize that you made some mistakes, but you know what they were, and they will never plague you again. Next time (and you know there will be a next time), there will be no hesitation, no fear. Your experience in facing death head-on has taught you about life. You have the power and ability to stand alone. You no longer need a reason to kill.

"The key, Roger, is to learn to keep this aura of superiority in check. Discretion, Rog. Discretion is everything. The true professional must learn to bide his tongue.

The things you have learned about life are important. You may wish to pass on your observations to someone you care about.

3 7

When the bullshit starts to flow, you may feel compelled to set the record straight and tell those morons how it really is. When someone starts to brag, in confidence, about something he's done, the intimacy of the moment, the shared confessions, may inspire you to do a little bragging of your own. Or you may want to overawe some new woman in your life with your masculinity and you feel the urge to shock her just a little by hinting at your true profession.

"Rog, what we are talking about here is nothing less than ego-control: 'Start now in learning to control your ego. That means, above all, keeping your mouth shut! You are a man. Without a doubt, you have proved it. You have come face to face with death and emerged the victor through your cunning and expertise. You have dealt death as a professional. You don't need any second or third opinions to verify your manhood.'

"But of course, all good things must pass, and even the professional hit man will some day retire. When he does, however, a literary career may be waiting. This really piqued my interest, what with my own literary aspirations and all: 'Then, some day, when you've done and seen it all; when there doesn't seem to be any challenge left or any new frontier left to conquer, you might just feel cocky enough to write a book about it.' "

Roger stared at me. "So explain to me again why the hell you're having moral qualms about suing these bastards?"

"I didn't say I had moral qualms. I said the whole thing made me depressed. The first time I read the book, I was totally disgusted. It wasn't that the violent images were so revolting—they were bad enough but I'd seen far worse. It wasn't that the *idea* of murder-for-hire, or the methods described, were so original. I had not known most of the details disclosed in the book, but many have a sort of intriguing common sense and cleverness to them, and they're not intrinsically the most shocking things I'd ever read. I think it was the confluence of two emotions. I was depressed at the absolute incarnate *evil* of the thing, the brazen, cold-blooded, calculating, meticulous instruction, and repeated encouragement in the black arts of assassination. Roger, I didn't even want to *touch* the damn book. I couldn't leave it on the night table—I had to take it back to my office in the house and lock it in my briefcase. It didn't even seem like it was a book at all, really. It was more like someone had sent me a loaded pistol, or a vial of poison. The physical *thing* had a stench of evil to it."

"What was the other emotion?"

"Fear."

"Fear of what? That the publisher would take out a hit on you?"

"Not really. It wasn't physical fear. It was psychological. It was the fear that taking this case would somehow change my life."

6

The Tort-Mobile

Wittenberg wanted more evidence. He dug into the life of James Perry and found that one of Perry's best friends, a buddy he'd met in prison, was a guy named Thomas Turner. Thomas Turner just happened to be Lawrence Horn's cousin. Turner had rented a car using his American Express card in March 1993. Wittenberg believed it was the car Perry had used when he drove to Maryland. He began to pressure Turner, making Turner believe that he would soon be indicted as part of the murder conspiracy. Turner turned, and agreed to testify against Perry and Horn in exchange for immunity. Turner knew nothing about any murder plot, he insisted, but could verify that he had put his cousin Lawrence Horn and his buddy James Perry into contact with one another. Wittenberg also widened the search for phone records. Within a few weeks over 140 phone calls between Perry and Horn were found.

And then came a semblance, at least, of a cash link. Wittenberg found that James Perry and his girlfriend had received some $6,000 in money orders from Los Angeles. The orders were sent from a building at 6255 Sunset Boulevard, which was the new Los Angeles home of Motown Records. Wittenberg knew the location was close to Horn's home, and the connection to Motown Records was tantalizing. There was only one problem: The money orders were sent from somebody named Mary Wells. Who the hell was she? Wittenberg wondered.

The name rang a bell in Detroit. Mary Wells had once been a Motown recording artist. She had moved to Los Angeles. Wittenberg checked on her, and found out that Mary Wells had died, destitute. Her obituary had run in the *Los Angeles Times*—and was dated the same day the money orders were sent from Sunset Boulevard to James Perry in Detroit. Wittenberg guessed that Horn had seen the notice of Wells's death and seized on her name when sending the down payment to Perry. One thing was sure: Destitute dead women don't send money orders.

It was a circumstantial case, and in some respects thin. The clincher, however, was *Hit Man.* The book was the blueprint for the murders, the blueprint that Wittenberg knew James Perry had used. Wittenberg had both James Perry and Lawrence Horn arrested and charged with three counts of murder. Perry was picked up in Detroit, Horn in Los Angeles. By coincidence, Horn was arrested at the same time as O. J. Simpson and placed in the same holding tank as O.J.

•   •   •

Howard and John Marshall were scheduled to drive down from their law offices in Rockville, Maryland, to Williamsburg, to finally meet with me in person. On the morning of their planned trip I awoke to an inch of fresh snow on the ground and a sky heavy with wet, swirling flakes. I love snow, and the scene outside my window was beautiful, but I was worried about Howard and John driving. I checked the Weather Channel. There was even more snow around Richmond, and the highway conditions were treacherous. Howard had given me the number for his car phone. Figuring they'd already left Maryland, I tried it.

"Tort-mobile," Howard answered.

"Yeah, roger, tort-mobile," I chuckled. "You got heavy weather ahead. Sure you want to do this today?" Howard assured me that a little snow was not about to deter them from their appointed rounds. They'd be in Williamsburg in a couple of hours, right after my morning class was over.

•   •   •

"Natural Law philosophy took a fateful turn in the seventeenth century, with the social contract thinkers Thomas Hobbes and John Locke, philosophers who would come to have a major influence on those who wrote the American Constitution and Bill of Rights," I pronounced from the lectern. "Thomas Jefferson and James Madison may well have believed that human beings were endowed by their Creator with certain inalienable rights. But they also believed that to secure these rights, governments were instituted. Among men. The Bill of Rights—including the First Amendment's guarantees of freedom of speech, freedom of the press, and freedom of religion—were drafted to provide that security."

I read to the class a passage from Hobbes's famous work *The Leviathan*.

> Nature hath made men so equal in the faculties of body and mind, as though there be found one man sometimes manifestly stronger in body, or of quicker mind than another; yet when all is reckoned together, the difference between man and man is not so considerable, as that one man can thereupon claim to himself any benefit, to which another may not pretend as well as he. For as to the strength of body, the weakest has strength enough to kill the strongest, either by secret machination, or by confederacy with others.

Setting the book down on the podium, I asked, "Who can tell me what Hobbes is talking about?"

A hand bolted up from the middle of the room, a student named

Cindy. I called on her. "That passage, those two sentences you just read, are the anchor for all of Hobbes's thought," she said. "For me, when I read it, it was like, well, I think the ideas in that passage, you know, from those ideas everything else in his philosophy seems to tumble forth inexorably."

I pushed her, "Explain what those ideas are."

"They're wicked, really. Cynical and wicked." Cindy was smiling wryly, as if she relished the wickedness. "But they're true. What Hobbes is saying is that nobody's really safe. Nobody is secure. Just about any human being can kill just about any other human being. It's a jungle out there, you know? You've got to watch your back every minute."

"And you think that Hobbes is right?" I asked. "You think that anyone on earth can kill anyone else?"

Another hand shot up, from Sidney, a former all-American defensive tackle. "No, it's not true," said Sidney. "I would say I'm pretty safe from anyone in this room."

"Not true!" shouted Cindy, choosing not to wait for my permission to speak. "You're missing Hobbes's insight. You gotta take your shoulder pads off sometime, don't you? Everybody's got to eat, drink, sleep. In a conspiracy with the right people, I could easily arrange to have you killed with a little well-timed poison, and no one would be the wiser."

Squeals, whistles, claps, and desk-pounding filled the room with freaky holiday as diminutive Cindy the Cynic confronted Mr. Varsity. Would he dare spear-tackle her in a room with eighty witnesses and a law school professor at the podium?

Sidney smiled. "I will concede the point," he said, seeking orderly retreat. "I'm totally convinced that *Cindy* could kill me if she wanted to." *Clever,* I thought. Sidney's jibe drew a gentle wave of approving murmur. Sidney was just getting warm. "But it seems to me that Hobbes is trying to pull a fast one," he continued. "The basic idea, I guess, is that all human beings are created equal. But Hobbes does not mean equal in their talents, or their accomplishments, or their human dignity, or in anything else particularly uplifting or inspiring. He means equal in their ability to *kill* people. Even though the earth has strong persons and weak persons—even though in this room, for example, we have sitting among us certain powerful athletic types and other more delicate cerebral types—Hobbes argues that any one of us could conceivably murder any other one of us. None of us is really secure, no matter how strong or quick or tenacious we may fancy ourselves. If that's what Cindy is saying, okay, I agree, as far as it goes. Just fine. None of us in this room can ever be perfectly sure that we might not die at the hand of another, with a gun, or poison, or a sudden knife in the back. But that's a helluva notion on which to build a philosophy. It's evil incarnate."

I looked back at Cindy, to see if she wanted time for rebuttal. I was pleased to see that she did. "Hobbes's philosophy is not really evil," she insisted. "It's just reality. It's the natural order of things. He's a Natural Law philosopher, get it? What I like about Hobbes is that he's not a wuss. He has the guts to tell it like it is. No smarmy mysticism. In the state of nature, he says, society has yet to form. There is no good or evil, no right or wrong. It is a world of all against all. A jungle world." She looked down at her reading, and began to quote. "Hobbes writes that in the state of nature: 'The notions of right and wrong, justice and injustice, have no place. Where there is no common power, there is no law; where no law, no injustice.' There is no property in the state of nature—or as Hobbes puts it, *no mine and thine distinct.* But what is more, there is no murder in the state of nature. There is no rape. In the state of nature, Hobbes argues, every man has the right *even to another's body.*"

"Very good," I said. It was very good. "And this leads to Hobbes's most famous sentence, in which he summarizes the state of nature by explaining that in such a condition, 'there is no place for industry; nor use of the commodities that may be imported by sea; no commodious building; no instruments of moving and removing such things as require much force; no knowledge of the face of the earth; no account of time; no arts; no letters; no society, and which is worst of all, continual fear, and danger of violent death; and the life of man, nasty, solitary, poor, brutish, and short.' And this leads people, naturally, as it were, out of the state of nature, and into society, through formation of the social compact, in which every person agrees to surrender the total liberty they enjoy in the state of nature, for submission to law and order, imposed by the sovereign, which gives them a measure of security against the brutish violence of the jungle. And notice what it is that causes people to enter this social contract," I pointed out. "When we studied Thomas Aquinas, we saw that his philosophy is grounded in a belief in God. To believe in Thomas Aquinas's Natural Law, you have to believe in God. Is that true for Hobbes?"

"No," answered Cindy. "That's another reason I think Hobbes is so brilliant: He takes God out of the picture."

• • •

Howard and John arrived early, and were waiting for me in a meeting room at the Institute of Bill of Rights Law as I returned from class.

"Nice digs," said John, smiling as we shook hands. He was thin, lanky, and easy-mannered. He wore khakis and a well-broken-in sweater. "How long have you been the director of this place?"

"Eight years," I said. "Can I get you coffee? Soft drinks?"

"We're fine," said Howard. "So what does this institute do?" He was muscular and dark, with swarthy good-looks, dressed in blue jeans and a shirt with an open collar. He had the well-tanned look of a person who's money makes money while he plays golf.

"Oh, we run conferences, put out books and journals, stuff like that," I said. "Have a seat." The institute's meeting room had just been remodeled. While we were not exactly flush, I had wanted the institute's suite to look dignified and elegant for the many distinguished guests and potential donors we entertained. I figured you had to spend money to make it. The deep cherry-wood bookshelves held copies of the complete set of *United States Supreme Court Reports*, framing elegant portraits of scenes from the Constitutional Convention and enactment of the Bill of Rights. A start-of-the-art computer workstation for on-line research was recessed into the wall. We sat in plush high-backed chairs around a coffee table that held a glassed-in poster from a national conference the institute had conducted on the fortieth anniversary of the school desegregation case, *Brown v. Board of Education*. The poster contained a famous painting by Norman Rockwell, showing a pretty young African-American schoolgirl in pigtails and a pastel dress being escorted up the schoolhouse steps by federal marshals, with tomatoes splattering at her feet.

We spent the morning getting to know each other. John and I discovered that we'd overlapped at Duke—he was there as an undergraduate at the same time I was in law school. We swapped stories about Duke basketball. My hero in those days was a pure-shooting point guard named Tate Armstrong, who went on to play for the Chicago Bulls. By coincidence, Armstrong had moved to Rockville after his playing days, and Howard and John both knew him. Said he was a great guy.

Howard and John both worked in separate small firms in Rockville but often collaborated on cases. John's wife, Cindy Callahan, was also a lawyer with her own practice, specializing in domestic relations. She was one of the best, with famous clients like Patrick Ewing. Howard said that he split his time between Rockville and a beach house he owned on Harbour Island in the Bahamas. Though we'd only known each other for a little over a month, he offered the beach house free of charge anytime, a courtesy he extended to all of his good friends and associates. I was apparently already in that category.

"It's an amazing place," John chimed in. "The most breathtaking beach I've ever seen. And a charming island. Totally unspoiled."

John was thoughtful and self-deprecating. Howard was bombastic and self-promoting. I was beginning to sense how they worked. John exuded an aura of forceful but unassuming competence, a calm, thoughtful, meticulous lawyer. Howard came off as a wild man in his quieter moments. As they told me stories about their cases, I could see how the two men made for an effective team, with a good guy/bad guy routine that made juries weep and insurance companies shudder. I couldn't help but like them both—John for his easy grace, Howard for his unvarnished chutzpah. I sensed a closeness between them, a circle of abiding allegiance. And I could sense myself already being drawn into that circle.

Howard's greatest claim to legal fame was a victory in a lawsuit entitled *Kelley v. R.G. Industries.* Howard's client, Olen Kelley, was shot in the chest during an armed robbery at the grocery store where he worked. The robber used a Saturday Night Special, the kind of cheap handgun of little use for anything but violent crime. The particular weapon in the case was a Rohm Revolver RG-38S, manufactured by Rohm Gesellschaft, a West German corporation, sold in the United States through R.G. Industries, a Miami-based subsidiary. The suggested retail price of the gun was thirty-five dollars.

Howard brought a lawsuit for civil damages on behalf of Kelley against R.G., arguing that the manufacturer should be liable to the victims of crimes injured or killed by its shoddy handguns. The suit made Howard Public Enemy Number One with the National Rifle Association (NRA) and the world's weapons industry, ranking right up there with Sarah Brady and all the others who dared to defile the right to bear arms and defy the homespun wisdom that "Guns don't kill, people do."

"I actually had a road show with the NRA media spokesman. The case became a major fund-raising item for them. We went on the 'Today Show' to debate the suit, and I kicked his ass. I was the master of sound-bite warfare. You never get more than two minutes. Whatever you are asked, ignore it, and make your three canned sound-bite points. Screw the deep issues. Jump all over your opponent with righteous indignation and make him fight your fight—"

"Tell him about the nuclear weapons," John broke in.

"On the 'Today Show' I said, 'If nuclear weapons were available at low cost, you people would fight for the right of every working man to have them by his bedside in case the Communists came over the border to gang-rape his pickup truck."

I laughed, though with forced conviction. Howard was funny, no doubting that. But was he playing with a full deck? "Oh, and armor-piercing bullets," Howard was continuing, "I told them, 'Armor-piercing bullets—something every NRA member needs in case a burglar is hiding behind a refrigerator.' "

"So it sounds like you really had fun with the case," I said, a bit too lamely.

"Not just fun," said John, shaking his head. "It was the right thing." John was loyal. I liked that.

"The profiteers who make these Saturday Night Specials know that their guns are going to be used primarily for crime," Howard said, jabbing his finger in the air. I felt like I was sitting in the jury box. "That's all these pieces of shit are good for. They're inaccurate, unreliable, poorly crafted. Cops can't use 'em, sportsmen can't use 'em, people don't buy 'em to keep in their house or their businesses for self-defense. These things sell because they're cheap and easy to conceal." I just nodded. Howard was on a roll.

In the trial, Howard introduced testimony from an R.G. sales rep who had said to a gun-store owner, "If your store is anywhere near a ghetto area, these ought to sell real well. This is most assuredly a ghetto gun." Another salesmen once said of an R.G. handgun, "This sells real well, but, between you and me, it's such a piece of crap. I'd be afraid to fire the thing." The Maryland Court of Appeals, in a landmark ruling, held that the manufacturer of a Saturday Night Special could be held liable to crime victims injured by their shabby guns. Howard had made history.

"So now let's talk about *this* case," I finally said, bringing our conversation around to the business at hand.

"Well, it's pretty simple," Howard began. "We want to sue Paladin Press and its publisher, Peder Lund, for aiding and abetting the murders of Trevor, Millie, and Janice through the publication of the murder manual *Hit Man*. We want you as our resident First Amendment expert."

• • •

I shuffled and stalled through the morning, managing to avoid any commitments. We repaired for lunch, walking three blocks through the still-falling snow to a tavern in Colonial Williamsburg. The snow was heavy and sticky, blanketing the holly leaves and light posts and rustic red brick of the old colonial square where Thomas Jefferson had studied law and Patrick Henry had declaimed revolution. We walked in silence. Maybe it was the cold that kept us quiet, or the snow pelting our faces, or the peace of the phantasmal winter land-scape. Or maybe it was just instinct on the part of Howard and John. Maybe they knew I needed some time to collect and reflect.

By the time we reached the tavern on the edge of Duke of Gloucester Street it was two in the afternoon, and the lunch crowds had waned. We found a secluded booth in a corner of the bar and ordered beer and sandwiches. We talked about the financing of the case. I was having hard times financially, and the idea of making some money on a case was attractive. But I couldn't take a case I didn't believe in, even if the money was potentially good. And the money wasn't really very likely, given my intuitions about the suit. I felt paralyzed by indecision. I made a pitch for more time. I was leaning toward joining them, I said, but there were still things I needed to think through. One of them was the question of physical danger. "So what about *our* safety?" I asked, somewhat shamefully. "Our families? I don't want to seem melodramatic, but these are frightening people we'd be taking on. I mean, who knows what they might do?"

John nodded. "It's a legitimate concern. We've given it a lot of thought ourselves, and talked about it with our wives." He took a pull from his beer. "You gotta understand something, Rod. My wife, Cindy, can only take so much of Howard. Which isn't much. When I told her about this case, we discussed the danger. But the real ques-tion wasn't about our opponent." John nodded toward Howard. "It was about Howard. Cindy asked me, 'How bad is it going to be?' She meant, how bad with Howard. 'I just told her, real bad.' But she didn't try to talk me out of it. All I'm saying is, if you can learn to handle Howard, Peder Lund will be the least of your worries."

Howard laughed heartily at this, nodding in vigorous agreement.

"So tell me more about Peder Lund," I said.

"You pronounce it Pay-dar," John said. "That's Swedish for Peter. He's a Vietnam vet. He likes to say he was a Green Beret but actually he was just an army Ranger. Got into the business in the 1970s with another 'Nam vet. His buddy later split from him to start *Soldier of Fortune* magazine. Lund has got stuff for all terrorists and assassins great and small. Particularly popular with your right-wing suprema-cists and militia boys. His outfit actually sold to Timothy McVeigh the instructions that were used to make the bomb that blew up the federal building in Oklahoma City."

"Where does he live?" I asked.

"London and Boulder, Colorado," Howard replied.

I took a swig of beer. "Does he hire assassins to rub out unfriendly lawyers?" I asked.

"We had a former FBI agent check out that question for us," said John. "He doesn't think Lund would go that far."

This was not exactly the unequivocal assurance I was hoping for. Howard shifted ground. "You know, if you take this case, a lot of peo-ple are gonna say that you're a traitor. They'll say you're turning your back on the Bill of Rights, the Constitution, and everything that made this country great."

"Uh-uh," I agreed. "They sure as hell will."

"We need a decision, Hamlet," said Howard. "It's time to launch the lawsuit and go public. Sometime this week. You're either on board or you're not."

7

The Year of Living Dangerously

The philosopher John Locke leavened the harsher tones of Thomas Hobbes's social contract theory," I lectured to the class. I called on George. "Can you tell us how Locke differs from Hobbes?" I asked him.

"Locke also theorized that men began in a state of nature," George began. "But Locke's image of that state of nature was far more benign—perhaps not the Garden of Eden, but certainly not a jungle where life was nasty, brutish, and short. Locke believed that in the state of nature people enjoyed the natural rights of life, liberty, and property, and that to secure and preserve those rights people entered into a social contract."

"That's good," I said. "Unlike Hobbes, who envisioned a draconian social contract, in which individuals surrendered their liberty to an all-powerful and dictatorial government—the *Leviathan*—Locke thought the social contract was far more limited and provisional. People granted to government the power to keep law and order in order to preserve liberties such as freedom of speech or due process of law. If the government began to trample on those liberties, the people had the right to rebel, canceling the social contract, forming a new government, a just government, one dedicated to honoring the rights it was instituted to protect. It was much more the thought of

John Locke than Thomas Hobbes that influenced the drafters of the American Constitution and Bill of Rights. When the framers wrote in the First Amendment that 'Congress shall make no law . . . abridging the freedom of speech, or of the press,' they thus thought of themselves as proclaiming the *natural rights* of human beings."

George raised his hand with a question. "One of the problems I have with all this social contract theory," he said, "is that none of us is ever asked to sign it. I mean, nobody gave *me* the option."

Several students laughed. "Yup," I agreed. "It's not like we reach some magic age at which society says to us, 'Okay, there's this social contract, see, and if you sign it, you'll become a member of society, with all its rights and duties, and if you don't—well then, you better move to Canada.' The notion, I guess, is that once people are adults, they do, in some sense, have the option to 'opt out,' at least of the social contract that governs the country they are in, by picking up stakes and leaving."

"But that's not a realistic option," George observed.

"I agree. The social contract is thus a kind of grand myth, a philosophical and legal fiction, that can be used to both explain the legitimacy of government and the natural rights that individuals may demand the government respect. Which is the topic I'd now like to explore. Robert Bork, the scholar, judge, and failed Supreme Court nominee, argued very elegantly that freedom of speech did not include the right to advocate the violent overthrow of the government. The purpose of freedom of speech, in Bork's view, was to facilitate the processes of democracy and the enterprise of self-government. Freedom of speech, in effect, is the method through which we continuously work out the management of our social contract. But Bork says it is not part of the contract to overthrow the contract. The Constitution is not a suicide pact. What do you folks think of Judge Bork's claim?"

Katherine raised her hand. "Who is Robert Bork to say that the purpose of freedom of speech was merely to assist in self-governance?"

"I take it you don't accept that?" I prodded. "Others have suggested that freedom of speech deserves a special place in our hierarchy of constitutional values because of the linkage of speech to thought, to man's central capacity to reason and wonder? Is that more persuasive? Are freedom of thought, conscience, and expression numinous values, linked to the defining characteristics of man?"

Ryan came into the discussion. "I think Bork's argument makes good sense," he said. "What he's asking us to think about is whether freedom of speech is something inside or outside the social contract. I agree with Judge Bork when he argues that we would have no freedom of speech if it were not for the social contract. This means freedom of speech cannot include the right to advocate the repudiation of the social contract itself."

"So does this mean," I asked, "that freedom of speech would not include the right to urge people to be vigilantes, to go outside the formal governmental justice system and commit individual acts of 'justice,' for revenge or retribution?"

The question ignited a vigorous debate among the students. Little did they know that the polemic they were engaged in was also now raging inside my own mind. I was willing to let my conscience be my guide—that was the easy part. The hard part was figuring out where it was trying to guide me.

• • •

A few days after my meeting with Howard and John, I was in Washington, D.C., giving a speech about the First Amendment rights of advertisers. Anheuser-Busch had retained me to assist the company in fighting advertising restrictions on beer. The City of Baltimore had banned most alcohol and tobacco advertising on billboards on the theory that such advertising influences children to smoke and drink. And there were proposals being floated to regulate beer advertising on television, such as the idea of "channeling" all beer advertising to late-night hours, when most children would not likely be viewing. I was working with John Walsh, a terrific lawyer from New York who had long been an outside counsel for Anheuser-Busch, and P. Cameron DeVore from Seattle, one of the very best First Amendment lawyers in the country. Playing to an audience packed with congressional aides, lobbyists, and other inside-the-beltway policy wonks, I was on the stump, arguing that freedom of speech should include freedom of speech for advertisers, and that included Budweiser's frogs and lizards. Beer was a lawful product, I claimed, and perfectly healthy when taken in moderation. Kids were influenced in their decisions to drink not by frogs or lizards or billboards but by their immediate family and social interactions, primarily peers and parents.

Howard Siegel was standing in the back of the auditorium, listening to my speech. "So you're not just a champion of little guys, are you?" Howard was pleased with himself as we walked to the hotel bar together. "Do you represent tobacco companies, too?"

"No. Strictly beer. I thought you liked beer, Howard."

"I'm just jerking you. I came to hear your speech because I thought maybe it would give me some insight into your character, something I could use to try to get you to leave the dark side of the force and join the rebellion."

"Funny, I've been thinking the same thing. I'd actually like to learn a bit more about you." We sat down and ordered a couple of Anheuser-Busch products.

"Ask me anything," Howard said.

"Well, where are you from? Around here?"

"Yeah. I grew up in D.C. My parents struggled to be part of the great American middle class. Neither had a college education. I was an underachiever with a short attention span, no self-discipline, lazy, and irresponsible. My adolescence was devoted entirely to getting laid."

"So you were a normal kid."

"No, I had an edge. I was the dark Jew-boy who wanted to steal the blond surfer babes from the Aryan quarterback with the mane of sandy blond hair flying back across his forehead in the perfect position to cover the only zit he ever had. I like to think the dude is now driving a truck for the *Washington Post*, delivering my headlines."

"You seem to like your headlines."

"I admit it. Something I grew into. As a kid, I had a pathological fear of public speaking."

"That's hard to believe."

"I began to change in college, at the University of Maryland. It was there I realized that most of my fellow students were dumb as fence posts. This was a confidence-booster. I was sort of against the Vietnam War, but I detested the phony pseudointellectual groovy hippy types."

"People like me."

"Well, I became a critical thinker and developed my most sacred philosophical principle: All worldviews suck. I also learned that I could bullshit my way through virtually every essay exam by rewriting the question. I graduated with a 3.8 average and Phi Beta Kappa."

"And so armed with these insights, you went to law school."

"I went to Georgetown, at night. I couldn't dance or do math, and I figured babes liked lawyers. I definitely was not one of those wannabe lawyer-boomers who went to law school with grandiose dreams of saving the world or arguing *Brown v. Board of Education*."

"But you seem so grandiose now."

Howard laughed. "I'm not saying I didn't have convictions. I just didn't have the focus to do anything about them. But I was a terrific railer. My fear of public speaking had evaporated."

"To the world's great benefit."

"Imagine a huge globe spinning in front of you with millions of little handholds."

I tried to imagine this, but found it difficult. "Go on," I said.

"You want to grab ahold and go on this terrific ride, but you can't decide where to grab. Too many choices and too big a decision. So you just watch it spin and complain about how fast it's going. You know how many people get overwhelmed by the shear number of worthy charities and decide they won't give to any of them because what's the point? I'm one of those people."

"Still? You're still one of those? Pretty cynical."

"Well, yeah, I agree. Probably too much so."

Was Howard just being a seductive chameleon, willing to tell me whatever he thought I needed to hear?

"Did you ever see the movie *The Year of Living Dangerously?*" he asked.

"Sure. Linda Hunt. One of my favorite movies."

"Mine, too. Linda Hunt's character said that there wasn't much she could do about the state of the world around her, so she just decided to start in front of her, one child at a time. That's what I believe in. The only real heroes are those kinds of people. The nurses who clean you up after you puke on yourself. The people who work in the trenches of suffering. Not the scientists, the doctors, the moral and spiritual leaders. Not the lawyers. It's the people who hold the hands of the dying. The rest of us are noisemakers and glory-addicts."

"Including you?"

"There was a time when that's all I was. Now there's something more. That's why I want you in this case. To help me in the quest for the something more."

"So what did you do after law school?" I didn't want to talk about questing.

"I started off clerking for a Montgomery County trial judge with a soft spot for smart-asses. Connie Chung got called for jury duty in our court once, and as a gag I got the judge to sign an order commanding her to appear in his chambers for lunch with his law clerk. The sheriff served it on her and she went with the flow. We actually did lunch. After clerking I opened up my own crappy little office on top of a bank. My rent was $75 a week. I took public defender cases, divorces, rear-end accidents, and DWI's. Little-people law. The crap nobody wanted. I hated it."

This didn't sound very Linda Hunt–like to me, but I let the contradiction pass. "Were you able to make a living?"

"Adequate. I was single. As long as I made enough to cover the rent, the payments on my little Italian sports car, and trips to Club Med, life was good enough."

"But not entirely satisfying."

"Not entirely. My first adventure into complex litigation was a dog of a malpractice case. A kid had overdosed on Dalmane and was put into the psychiatric ward of a local hospital. When he woke up he tied some bedsheets together and jumped out a third-story window. The sheets broke and he fell into a petunia bed, sustaining a broken body."

"You sued the hospital."

"I actually toyed with suing the sheet manufacturer, but it turned out the sheets didn't rip—the lunkhead kid didn't know how to tie knots. So I was stuck with suing the hospital, on the theory that they should have given the kid the proverbial 'room without a view.' Everybody thought it was the dumbest suit in the history of tort law, that I had no chance. On the eve of trial I uttered the trial lawyer's prayer: 'Oh Lord, I don't care if I win or lose. Just please don't make me look like an asshole.' "

"Were your prayers answered?"

"I won. Upset of the year. Pretty soon I was getting swamped with cases. Won some big money in a few of them. Developed a local reputation as the Wild Man of Borneo. I had a shtick. I was the leftover lawyer from the sixties who was pissed at something. Nobody ever quite knew what it was I was pissed at, but I always *looked* sincere. At some point in every trial I would explode. Go off like a Polaris missile. I'd yell and rant and wave my hands like a madman. I knew how to play it just right, up to the point where the judge was almost ready to order the bailiffs to unholster their weapons. Then I'd back down. Apologize to the judge. It always unnerved the other side, and the trial judges never held it against me. It seemed to amuse them, actually, keep them awake, give them something to live for. And I kept winning."

"So is that all you are? Tantrum-shtick?"

Howard grinned. "No, I'm also clever. I'm not smart, but I am clever. Smart gets beat by clever every time."

"Connect this to *The Year of Living Dangerously* for me. I mean, since you want me to live dangerously. You're a lot of fun, Howard.

I'm not saying it wouldn't be a thrilling ride. But would it be a worth-while ride? Or am I just going to watch Howard Siegel freak out in a friggin' freak show?"

"Friggin' A. Okay, here's the connection. My midlife crisis."

I gestured to the waiter for a couple more beers. "Now we're get-ting somewhere."

"One day I realized I was tired of suing doctors and engineers, making them hate lawyers and hate the legal system. I was tired of my life. I wanted to do something entirely new. Like Ernest Hem-ingway would have done, buy a boat and sail around the world or something. Above all, I wanted to begin to believe in something. In anything. It was right then that Jackie came along. She was married. Had a nine-year-old son. Had just gotten separated."

"She was married when we first met, soon to be divorced. Got her out of a jam I guess, but I used a little too much force." Imitating Bob Dylan's twang, I sang the lines from "Tangled Up in Blue."

Howard half-laughed and half-grunted. "Okay, Bobbie. Well, I was *in love*. Because the divorce and separation were still being worked out, for the first four months our relationship was entirely on the telephone. She was intelligent, beautiful, and blond. The cheer-leader with a brain I'd always wanted. We got married two years later in the Montgomery County Courthouse wearing jeans and exchang-ing cigar bands."

"Did Jackie change your worldview? Your ideas about practic-ing law?"

"She didn't so much change it as help me to change it. Help me to find myself. After about a year of marriage I'm laying on the couch one day telling her how miserable I was with my practice. It was all bullshit, I said. All I knew how to do was make people miserable. 'Okay,' Jackie says. 'If your only talent is making people miserable, why don't you get up off the couch and make somebody miserable who deserves it?' It was the insight that changed my life. That's what I started to do."

"And that's what this case is all about?"

"Yup. Have you ever read the book *A Civil Action* by Jonathan Harr?"

"Yeah." Howard was referring to the best-selling book about the lawyer Jan Schlichtmann and his crusading lawsuit in a toxic tort suit involving environmental pollution that allegedly caused an outbreak of leukemia.

"It was reading that book that got me fired up for this case."

"Do you think of yourself as Jan Schlichtmann."

"Honestly? I don't really admire Schlichtmann. The whole time I was reading the book I kept wanting to grab the guy and kick him in the balls, because he constantly let his ego get in the way of being a sensible lawyer. But I admire the *idea* of Schlichtmann—at least the idea of Schlichtmann without the oversized ego."

I raised my eyebrows. Howard knew what I was thinking. "I know your wondering if I'm really no different from Schlichtmann. I've got a gargantuan ego. But the difference is, I admit it. And I've learned how to keep old glory under control."

"Okay, Howard. So you obviously know what you're doing. What I want to know is why you need *me* in this?"

"I've told you a hundred times why we need you. What I'm wondering is why you're so goddamn dense." He paused, and then shifted tacks. "I noticed on your résumé that you've bounced around a little yourself. I even saw Arkansas on there."

"Ever been there?"

"No."

"The University of Arkansas is in Fayetteville, a little college town nestled in the rolling Ozark Mountains of northwest Arkansas. I loved it there, actually." It was the truth. In Fayetteville, red-jacketed and red-shoed Razorback boosters would sit in street cafes next to artisans, artists, writers, and musicians, mixing in a bouillabaisse of rednecks and poets. I could watch football, watch Bill Clinton, and get in touch with my poetic self.

"But you're from Chicago, right? How'd you end up in Razorback country?"

"A friend of mine from Yale had gone to Arkansas with his Yale Law School friends, Bill Clinton and Hillary Rodham, to help with one of Bill's political campaigns. He stayed on the Arkansas law faculty after Bill and Hillary moved on to greater glory. He's the one who recruited me."

"I know you've been involved in a lot of high-profile cases. But let me ask you this. Have you ever taken a case on the *plaintiff's* side?"

"I've sort of flirted a few times, you might say. But never really acted on it." I chuckled. "So Howard, you think I've got 'plaintiff's block'?"

"Didn't you file some kind of libel suit for Chuck Robb, when he had that nasty sex scandal with the beauty queen? I remember you in the papers on that one."

Howard was referring to a time when I had helped represent Charles Robb, Virginia's Democratic senator, who had been caught in a whirlwind of scandal over allegations of an affair with a former Miss Virginia. "We threatened to sue for libel but never did."

"Because Robb actually *did* have the affair with her, didn't he? I remember seeing a television show about it. He met her at the Pierre Hotel in New York. She said they committed adultery. But Robb said that there was no sex, right? Only a massage. It was the hand-job defense. Was that your legal handiwork, Rod Smolla, world-renowned constitutional scholar? The hand-job defense? Did Bill Clinton call you, too?"

"Attorney-client privilege."

"When we were checking up on you the Jerry Falwell case came up. The one over the cartoon, or whatever."

"Yeah, that's right." Howard was talking about a notorious case in which Reverend Jerry Falwell sued *Hustler* magazine and its publisher Larry Flynt over a parody that *Hustler* had published, in the form of a fake advertisement for Campari Liquor. Campari is not instantly pleasing to most palates; affinity for the drink is an acquired taste. So the problem, if you're trying to sell Campari to people, is to get them to try it enough times that they will actually acquire this acquired taste. Campari hit on this clever ad campaign, with various glitterati talking about their so-called first time. People like Jill St. John, Elizabeth Ashley, Tony Roberts would be interviewed for these ads and would tell about their first times. It was a double entendre—you couldn't tell if it was their first time with Campari, or their first time with sex. The subliminal message was that Campari, like sex, gets better with practice.

Hustler decided to run a parody featuring a mock interview with Jerry Falwell talking about his "first time," which turned out to be in an outhouse, with his mother. It was prescient that Howard had mentioned the case, for I'd been giving it a lot of thought as I consternated over whether to get involved with Howard and the suit against *Hit Man*'s publisher. In the Falwell case I'd been a member of the First Amendment in-crowd. But privately, I'd always felt some empathy for Jerry Falwell. I was especially intrigued by the moment in the trial when Falwell was asked about his reaction the first time he was confronted with the *Hustler* parody of him having sex with his mother in an outhouse. "I have never been as angry as I was at that moment," Falwell testified. And then his anger, he said, gave way to a more rational and deep hurt. I had memorized this testimony: "I somehow felt that in all of my life I had never believed that human beings could do something like this," Falwell had said. "I really felt like weeping. I am not a deeply emotional person. I don't show it. I think I felt like weeping." Falwell went on to say that, in his entire life, he had never experienced a personal feeling of such intensity as the moment he first saw the *Hustler* attack.

Yet how could this have been the most intense moment in Falwell's life? More intense than the birth of his child? The death of his mother? His conversion experience? After I read *Hit Man* for the first time, I understood what Falwell was saying. It wasn't that I now, in recanting retrospect, thought he deserved to win his case against Larry Flynt. It was rather that, for the first time, I understood. I understood what Falwell felt. He was just shocked at the crudity of *Hustler*'s humor. He was shocked by the sheer calculating mendacity of it all—*"I somehow felt that in all of my life I had never believed that human beings could do something like this."*

That was how the book *Hit Man* made me feel the first night I read it. I could barely hold it in my hands. When I finished, I couldn't leave it in the bedroom, like its mere physical presence would send off menacing vapors and bring me horrifying nightmares, stinking the rot of cold-blooded murder.

"I wrote a brief in the United States Supreme Court on behalf of a group of newspapers and publishers in support of *Hustler*," I explained to Howard, "arguing that, under the First Amendment, Larry Flynt had a right to publish his parody. It's the same crowd that will jump all over our asses in *this* case, Howard, if we file a suit."

"You see, that's your problem. You're in this chummy club of rich First Amendment lawyers, and I'm asking you to bolt and sue a fellow member of the club. And you can't bring yourself to do it."

"Go to hell. That has nothing to do with it."

"Sure it does. Same guys who pay you to represent Budweiser. They're all club, too, aren't they?"

"I'm not a rich First Amendment lawyer. Wish I was, but I'm not. I'm a poor pro bono-help-the-ACLU-and-occasionally-scrounge-up-a-real-fee guy. The folks in the First Amendment crowd aren't the ones dangling money in front of me."

"Neither am I. Odds are we'll never see a dime from Paladin Press."

"It's not the money. It's not the club. If I thought you and the families were on the right side, I'd be a coward *not* to help you."

"Then what's the problem?"

"Whether you *are* on the right side."

"Well, how the—"

I cut him off. "And on *that* score, I have something to tell you, so shut up a minute."

"You just won the right to argue this case in court," Howard said. "Now what are you vacillating about?"

I took a swig of beer, and then I took the plunge. "I'm not," I said, reaching over to shake Howard's hand. "You got yourself a partner."

• • •

Joseph Conrad once wrote, "They talk of a man betraying his country, his friends, his sweetheart. There must be a moral bond first. All a man can betray is his conscience."

I finally knew where my conscience was trying to take me. I felt a moral bond—to Trevor, Millie, Janice; to Howard; to John. I had not yet worked out all the math. I had not yet figured out exactly how we should structure our legal arguments, or how we should deal with such First Amendment precedents as *Brandenburg v. Ohio*. But I knew in my heart that the First Amendment simply could not plausibly be interpreted to protect a book like *Hit Man*. I had studied pretty much every First Amendment decision ever decided by the Supreme Court. None of them exactly covered our case. None of them clearly established us as winners, or as losers. Yet I was convinced that the First Amendment should not protect the *Hit Man* book. We would not be attempting to punish Paladin Press for publishing unpopular or offensive ideas. We would simply be attempting to hold it responsible for aiding and abetting murder by training, counseling, encouraging, and inciting hit men, *with deliberate intent.*

8

"Trevor Lives Through Me"

Attorneys for James Perry and Lawrence Horn made several
early moves in defense of their clients. They did not want
the two men tried together, and they were successful in
getting the Montgomery County Circuit Court to sever the two
cases. A sharp battle was then fought over the admissibility of certain
wiretap evidence that had helped link Perry to Horn. In a preliminary hearing, Perry's attorney, Roger W. Galvin, asked Montgomery
County circuit judge Paul Weinstein to throw out a wiretap placed
on a phone in a Detroit cocktail lounge. Galvin argued to the judge
that police investigators had intercepted conversations between
Horn and his mother that they deemed pertinent to the investigation, but in applying for permission to wiretap Perry in Detroit, the
investigators had said in an affidavit that "no pertinent calls were
monitored or intercepted on Horn's phone." The police, Galvin
claimed, had lied. Assistant State's Attorney Teresa Whalen countered by arguing that the wiretapped conversations between Horn
and his mother were not disclosed because they did not link Horn to
Perry or yield pertinent information about the alleged conspiracy.
Judge Weinstein refused to suppress the wiretap evidence.

The trial of James Perry came first. The trial was assigned to
Montgomery County circuit judge .D. Warren Donohue. Robert
("Bob") Dean and Teresa Whalen of the Montgomery County State's

Attorney's Office were the chief members of the prosecution team. Roger Galvin and Amy Brennan of Rockville defended Perry. An unusually large jury pool of 250 prospective jurors were assembled for the case. Galvin asked Judge Donohue to sequester the jury, but the judge refused, although he did acknowledge the need for special care with the jury, given the sensational publicity that had surrounded the case and the prosecution's decision to seek the death penalty.

Montgomery County is a relatively liberal enclave in Maryland, and capital punishment cases were rare. There had not been a case in which the prosecution sought the death penalty since 1987, when an unemployed house painter named Mitchell Moore was convicted of killing a Silver Spring woman in front of the children she was babysitting. The jury in that case refused the death penalty for Moore, sentencing him to life in prison.

Judge Donohue questioned the prospective jurors, as a group and then individually in his chambers, about their attitudes toward the death penalty. To speed up the process, he prepared in advance a handout listing the questions the lawyers would raise in their jury voir dire. But even so, it took over a week to select the jury panel of seven women and five men.

As the prosecution opened its case, it was clear that the book *Hit Man* would be central to the prosecution's presentation. Bob Dean, who lead the prosecution team, thought *Hit Man* was the critical piece of evidence. His colleague Teresa Whalen opened the prosecution's presentation by candidly admitting to the jury that the case against Perry was based solely on circumstantial evidence. The linchpin, she explained, was the book *Hit Man*. "James Perry did better than leaving his fingerprint at the scene," Whalen said, "because James Perry followed a blueprint for murder." She showed the jury a chart listing twenty-two steps taken directly from *Hit Man* that were used to commit the murders. Whalen described how Perry had used the book to carry out a "diabolical plot" and a "gruesome conspiracy."

Perry's defense lawyer Roger Galvin countered that the state's opening statements were simply "the beginning of a process where the state tries to kill James Edward Perry."

Howard Siegel and John Marshall carefully monitored Dean and Whalen's prosecution of Perry. Howard and Dean were friends. It was Bob Dean, in fact, who had sent Olen Kelley to Howard, which resulted in the *Kelley v. R.G. Industries* Saturday Night Special case that had first made Howard famous as a maverick plaintiff's lawyer and antigun advocate. Howard and John wanted to see Perry convicted. They also wanted to see what kind of case could be made against *Hit Man*.

The case proved to be impressive. "In the course of criminal conduct," wrote William Wordsworth, "every fresh step that we make appears a justification of the one that preceded it, it seems to bring again the moment of liberty and choice." And so Lawrence Horn and James Perry, emancipated to further evil by every fresh step in their wicked scheme, assiduously advanced their evil mission. *Hit Man* was the blueprint.

Hit Man, the prosecution explained, largely relieved James Perry of the need to do much independent thinking in planning the murders. Every step required for the murders was right there in front of him in the book, all laid out. The book described numerous alternatives and techniques for contract murder. There was also a tenor to the book that made the job seem at once achievable and even laudable. "Dr. J. Perry, Spiritual Adviser, Case-Buster, Independent Contractor" could do this. *Hit Man* told him so. James Perry culled the detailed instructions in the book and from them put together his method for murder. He would purchase an AR-7 rifle, as the book instructed, and use his own machine tools to modify the weapon according to the book's specifications. He would follow the book's instructions on how to manufacture his own silencer to place on the rifle. He would follow the book's formulas for casing the mark's home in advance, for using a rental car with stolen tags for the drive to Maryland, for dressing for the hit, for shooting the victims in the eyes at a range of three to six feet, for disposing of the weapons, and for getting out of town. He could do this. He'd always had the guts, the toughness. He certainly had the need. All he had required was the confidence, the training, and the plan. And with *Hit Man*, he had that.

The prosecutors explained to the jury that the story actually began way back with poor Trevor Horn's hospital accident and a chilling incident that took place during the malpractice suit brought by Howard Siegel and John Marshall against the hospital and doctors who treated Trevor. Lawrence Horn was in Maryland for the malpractice trial because he wanted a piece of the action. Millie wanted no part of Horn, and had no intention of sharing any malpractice award with him. Howard Siegel said this to Horn during a break in the proceedings. Horn wrote in red ink on a yellow legal pad that he expected to leave court that day with $1 million, and showed it to Howard. There was no way that would happen, Howard insisted. Horn then looked at Howard with cold eyes and said: "You don't understand. Trevor lives through me."

•　•　•

"In *Miller v. California* the Supreme Court holds that hard-core obscenity is not protected under the First Amendment," I stated to the class. "Obscenity is treated by the Court as beneath the dignity of the Constitution. It is speech left in the deep chill, devoid of First Amendment protection. How can this rule be explained? Obscenity clearly *is* a form of expression, isn't it? Why isn't this the kind of viewpoint discrimination that we normally condemn under the First Amendment?"

I called on Jennifer. "Because obscenity has no serious redeeming social value," she asserted confidently. "It does not have anything to do with democracy or self-governance. It contributes nothing to the marketplace of ideas. Hard-core obscenity has nothing to do with politics, or art, or religion, or education; nothing to do with any of the intellectual or emotional capacities of men and women that truly nourish the mind or spirit. It doesn't communicate ideas at all, really, but simply arousal. It is a means of facilitating masturbation. It encourages lascivious fantasies. It encourages people to cheat on their husbands and wives, breaking up families. It treats human beings as sexual objects, appropriate for exploitation and domination. It portrays rape and dismemberment and other perverse forms of sexuality as legitimate and pleasurable. It degrades human dignity, and corrodes society's quality of life. For all these reasons, it is not deserving of protection."

"All right Jennifer," I countered, "you've certainly made a very eloquent statement about why we should not protect obscene speech. Yet I seem to remember you favoring the Supreme Court's decision in *Brandenburg v. Ohio.* Everything you said about obscenity could also be said about violent speech, could it not? So there seems to be some inconsistency here. Some hypocrisy."

At this comment, Katherine's hand shot up. I called on her. "I agree," she said. "There is duplicity. I think it is probably traceable to hang-ups in American culture. We've always had hang-ups about sex. It's our puritanism. It's *The Scarlet Letter.* Violence is different. We are a violent people, a nation of cowboys. So speech about guns and revenge and revolution we treat as part of our First Amendment tradition, while erotic and arousing speech is taboo."

"So what would be your solution, Katherine?" I cross-examined. "Would you protect obscene speech?"

"No, I'd end the duplicity. But the other way around. For all the reasons that Jennifer would ban obscenity, I'd ban calls to violence. Jennifer doesn't see any redeeming value in explicit sex. I don't see any redeeming value in preaching murder."

9

The Man with the Plan

Meticulously, the prosecutors set before the jury the dreadful sequence of events. Lawrence Horn went back to Los Angeles, where he was scraping bottom. He had lost his Motown job and was deeply in debt, borrowing heavily from family and friends, and over $16,000 behind in his payments for child support. And so he made a pilgrimage to Detroit, seeking rest and rehab among his family and old friends in the haunts of his glory days. Horn tracked down his cousin, Thomas Turner, whom he had not seen in twenty years. Over a couple of beers, he complained to Thomas about his wife, Millie, and how bitter and expensive the custody battle had become. The two men met several more times, at the home of Jean Baker, another cousin, and at one of those meetings Thomas said to Horn that he knew a man who might be able to help Horn with his troubles, an old prison pal named James Perry. Turner considered Perry one of his best friends. He frequently drummed up business for Perry, handing Perry's business cards to passengers in the taxi he sometimes drove, and keeping Perry's "House of Wisdom" handout flyers in his house. "Give Mr. Perry a call," Turner told Horn, "because he helps people."

A meeting between Horn and Perry was arranged. They quickly discovered common ground. Both were hard up for cash. And both were willing to do whatever might be necessary to change that. The Man with the Plan now had one. Perry would travel to Maryland and murder Millie and Trevor. Horn would set Perry up with all the advance reconnaissance materials needed to make a clean hit, and would also arrange for Tamielle and Tiffani to be away from the house when the hit went down. Horn would advance Perry several thousand up front, and when the insurance money came through, there would be plenty more to divide. Perry liked Horn's plan, and he began to prepare himself for the job. For that task, he turned to *Hit Man*.

Using over six hundred exhibits, the prosecutors carefully laid out before the jury the impressive array of telephone, credit card, and hotel records linking Horn and Perry. Horn could not be compelled to testify because of his right to invoke his Fifth Amendment privilege against self-incrimination. His only "appearance" in the trial was in the form of a photograph displayed by the prosecution, a color mug shot of "L.T." that showed him with a cocked eyebrow and sinister gleam, suggesting the personality that Teresa Whalen told jurors was "diabolical."

One of the strangest pieces of evidence to emerge in the case was a lawyer's business card found in Lawrence Horn's Los Angeles apartment. The card was for a Maryland lawyer named "D. Warren Donohue," the very lawyer who would later be appointed to the Montgomery County bench and was, in fact, the presiding judge at James Perry's trial. When Perry's lawyer Roger Galvin pointed out this curiosity to Judge Donohue, the judge dismissed it as nothing but an odd coincidence, saying that he had scanned his business records and searched his own memory for any recollection of any prior contact with Horn, but could find or recall nothing.

In a rented car procured by Thomas Turner on March 1, 1993, James Perry drove to Maryland. On March 3, just after midnight, he checked into the Days Inn on Shady Grove Road in Rockville. Sometime around 3:00 A.M., James Perry entered Millie's house in Silver Spring. Janice Saunders was shot first, through the eye, at a range of three feet. Perry knew from *Hit Man* that shots through the eyes were preferred, and that three feet was the ideal range. Because his gun was fitted with a silencer the shots were muffled. Perry then disconnected Trevor's respirator—a mistake! A high-piercing alarm filled the house. Perry knew from Horn's instructions that Trevor could breathe on his own now, and that merely disconnecting the respirator would not ensure death. So he quickly smothered Trevor. Up in her bedroom, Millie heard the alarm. She came down the stairs. She must have seen Perry and tried to escape, for she was heading for the front door when James Perry intercepted her and shot her through the eye. Perry wanted to make the hit look like a burglary, as *Hit Man* instructed. But the alarm was making a terrible noise. Hurriedly, he made a token pass at ransacking the house, knocking over some furniture and throwing sofa cushions on the floor. He stole some of Millie Horn's credit cards and found the keys to the family van. He drove the van away to where he had parked his rental car. He tossed the stolen credit cards and pieces of his gun along the roadside as he drove. At 5:12 A.M., Perry used a pay phone at the Denny's Restaurant on Quince Boulevard in Gaithersburg to make a call to Los Angeles. The number was Lawrence Horn's.

Prosecutors played for jurors the twenty-second snippet of tape-recorded conversation captured on Horn's Los Angeles answering machine that they claimed was made from that Denny's phone. In the cryptic message, which was difficult to hear on the poor-quality tape, a voice that appeared to be Perry's said, "Can you talk? Okay. All right. So I mean I'm sittin' there. . . . I could take a picture. I could take a picture of him. You know, right there. . . . But I couldn't. The noise, you understand what I'm saying? I wasn't able to do the others. Didn't, I didn't want to go, uh, frontwise—" And then the tape abruptly stopped. What did the message mean? Was Perry explaining why he had not photographed his kills? Was the "noise" the medical monitor on Trevor's bed, screaming its desperate alarm into the night?

• • •

In his closing argument, prosecutor Bob Dean told the jury that "what emerges is a plan that is so evil it is almost beyond our comprehension." The jury agreed. On October 12, 1995, after five hours of deliberation, the jury found Perry guilty on all counts. Perry stared directly ahead as the verdicts were read, his eyelids fluttering and mouth moving silently.

On the afternoon of Monday, October 16, the jury was convened again to consider the sentence. After only four more hours of deliberation, the jurors unanimously agreed on death sentences for all three counts. Perry stood. Placing his hand on the defense table, he spoke to the jury for the first time, speaking contemptuously. "The *finders of fact*," he snarled, "have found me guilty and have imposed the death penalty. But I stand before you this evening and say I had nothing to do with these crimes. I am innocent, and I will continue to fight the good fight."

One of the jurors, Jeff Neely, an employee of the General Services Administration, told the *Washington Post* that the jury had found the circumstantial evidence against Perry "overwhelming" and basically "undisputed." Although they had not deliberated long, Neely said that the jurors' deliberations over the appropriate sentence had been challenging, but that in the end the nature of Perry's crime had outweighed the arguments that Perry posed no continuing threat to society, or that the jury should be moved by the general plea for mercy for a fellow human being. Perry was placed on death row, facing execution by lethal injection.

10

"He'll Die Knowing"

Today's assignment is *New York Times Co. v. Sullivan*, the landmark 1964 Supreme Court decision that revolutionized much of our modern thinking about the media, personal reputation and privacy, and freedom of speech. Who can tell us what was going on in the *New York Times* case?"

Alberto volunteered. "The case involved Dr. Martin Luther King and the civil rights movement in the Deep South," he began. "King had been arrested in Alabama on what turned out to be trumped-up charges. A group calling itself the Committee to Defend Martin Luther King and the Struggle for Freedom in the South took out a full-page ad in the *New York Times* describing the pattern of massive resistance and violence that blacks and civil rights activists had been subjected to in their struggle for freedom. The ad contained some relatively trivial factual inaccuracies. A petty official from Alabama, a Montgomery City commissioner named L. B. Sullivan, sued for libel the *Times* and four African-American preachers who had signed the ad. A jury awarded Sullivan $500,000. The Alabama Supreme Court affirmed the verdict, and the case then went to the United States Supreme Court. The Supreme Court, in an opinion written by Justice Brennan, reversed the jury award, holding that a public official like Sullivan could not recover in a libel suit involving matters relevant to his performance in office unless he could prove that the false statements of fact made against him were published with knowledge of their falsity, or reckless disregard for their truth or falsity."

"And what was the basis for the Court's ruling?" I asked.

"Justice Brennan wrote that the First Amendment embodied a national commitment to 'the principle that debate on public issues should be uninhibited, robust, and wide open,' and may often include 'vehement, caustic' attacks on public officials. The knowing or reckless falsehood standard, he argued, was needed to give this public debate 'breathing space.' "

"That's outstanding," I said, and then, reaching underneath the podium, I took out a copy of the famous full-page ad that gave rise to the suit, and held it up for the class to see, in an exercise of law school show-and-tell. "Here is a copy of the ad, exactly as it appeared," I said. "Up here is the text that Alberto has described. Below the text you see the illustrious names of some of the people on the committee that took out this ad: Harry Belafonte, Maureen Stapleton, Nat King Cole, Diahann Carroll, Sammy Davis, Jr., Nat Hentoff, Mahalia Jackson, Rabbi Edward Klein, Langston Hughes, Sidney Poitier, Jackie Robinson, Shelley Winters, Eleanor Roosevelt, Marlon Brando." I then focused my attention back on Alberto. "Commissioner Sullivan sued the *Times* for libel, Alberto. My first question is very basic. Why does our legal system permit libel suits at all? Why do we let people go to court to sue just because somebody says something about them that hurts their feelings?"

"It's not just hurt feelings we're talking about," Alberto replied. "We are talking about honor. Reputation. Good name. It may be the most valuable thing a human being possesses. Shakespeare called it the jewel of the soul."

"Alberto has conjured for us the lines from *Othello*. Who remembers them?"

Daniel, an actor before he went to law school, practically leaped from his chair. I knew him as a diffident student with at best a sketchy grasp of legal principles. But he was a gregarious and affable character, and I had always liked him. This was his chance for glory. "Daniel? Would you indulge us?"

Daniel stood up to recite, sending eddies of murmur and giggle through the class. They were quickly quieted by his mellifluous voice:

> Good name in man and woman, dear my Lord,
> Is the immediate jewel of their souls:
> Who steals my purse steals trash; 'tis something, nothing,
> 'Twas mine, 'tis his, and has been slave to thousands;
> But he that filches from me my good name
> Robs me of that which not enriches him,
> And makes me poor indeed.

Daniel was regaled by whistles, cheers, and sustained applause. Daniel might not know much law, I thought, but he could please a crowd, and someday he would undoubtedly woo juries. He'd probably end up the richest kid in the class. "Daniel," I said, "you are an estimable thespian. Now, let's see how well you *really* remember your Shakespeare. What you just gave us was perhaps Iago's most famous speech in *Othello*. But, it turns out, that is not Iago's last word on the topic of reputation. Do you happen to remember his other lines on the subject?"

Daniel was up to the task. "It comes a few scenes later. Othello is despondent, because he is worried about his loss of reputation. Iago can't believe what Othello is telling him. So the same Iago who just called reputation the 'immediate jewel of their souls' now turns around and gives what are probably his real views." Daniel looked around the class, to be sure he had our collective attention. He did.

> As I am an honest man,
> I thought you had received some bodily wound;
> there is more sense in that than in reputation.
> Reputation is an idle and most false imposition;

oft got without merit and lost without deserving.
You have lost no reputation at all,
unless you repute yourself such a loser.

Again, whistles and applause. "Daniel has now laid out for us one of the great legal questions—or perhaps I should say, one of the great questions of life. Which speech of Iago gives us the best advice? What really matters, ultimately? What people think of us, or what we think of ourselves?"

• • •

We knew the basic outlines of the history of Paladin Press and its publisher, Peder Lund. In the early 1960s, Robert Brown, an ex–Green Beret, created a maverick publishing company called Panther Publications, specializing in the reprinting of military manuals and action books. In 1970, Peder Lund, another Vietnam vet, joined the business as Brown's partner. They renamed the company Paladin Press to avoid association with the Black Panthers. Brown became increasingly interested in starting a "hairy-chested" magazine, and Lund in pushing the envelope of instruction publications on how to commit violence and crime. They split. Lund bought out Brown's share of Paladin, and Brown created *Soldier of Fortune* magazine. Lund turned Paladin into a multimillion-dollar business, with more than 350 titles, including a line of do-it-yourself manuals such as: *Be Your Own Undertaker: How to Dispose of a Dead Body*; *Fun, Games and Big Bangs: The Home and Recreational Use of High Explosives*; *Kill Without Joy: The Complete How-to-Kill Book*; *The Poor Man's Sniper Rifle*; *21 Techniques of Silent Killing*; *The Ancient Art of Strangulation*; and *How to Make Disposable Silencers*. Paladin books teach readers how to manufacture bombs and use them to destroy bridges and buildings. The books often contain detailed chemical formulas, engineering instructions and diagrams, photographs, checklists, and similar technical information. *Hit Man* was first published in 1983. We did not know the true identity of its author, listed on the cover as "Rex Feral."

As we planned the launching of our suit, we were conscious both of our position in the court of law and in the court of public opinion. "When we file this lawsuit," Howard argued, "we've got to go out into the media and explain what we're doing, or they're going to crucify us. The case will be over before we get started."

"I don't agree," said John. "I say we quietly file the suit, with no hubbub, no publicity. Just an old-fashioned, professional, discrete bit of traditional, dignified lawyering. If the press picks up on the case, we either say 'no comment,' or we make very general and brief comments."

Howard and John turned to me. I was the tie-breaker. The problem was that I saw no real way to contain the "Howards" that periodically rose up inside Howard, balloons of ego, exuberance, and showboat-showoff that had to be released before they bloated and choked him. These Howards were magical wellsprings of energy and imagination, they were Wynton Marsalis blowing jazz, they were Michael Jordan floating above the rim, they were fits of cantankerous genius and tweaking creativity. I didn't want to muzzle the Howards inside Howard. Neither did John. We just wanted a little control, was all. Just a little.

"What about a compromise?" I suggested. "We don't do a media blitz, because that would look tacky and unethical. But we don't put our heads in the sand either. I say we script out our sound bites and stick to them. Howard is the telegenic one, he can be our media darling."

We argued for an hour. Ultimately, John relented, agreeing with my compromise. But John and I both knew we had just papered matters over. The Howards in Howard would never be able to stick to the script.

•　•　•

The same prosecution team that had successfully prosecuted James Perry undertook a reprise with the trial of Lawrence Horn. The case was heard in Frederick, Maryland, after Horn exercised his right as a defendant facing a possible death sentence to have the trial venue changed. Although the case was physically tried in another part of the state, Montgomery County circuit judge Ann S. Harrington presided at the trial. The trial was postponed several months when Horn's original lawyer, Robert E. Morin, was appointed by President Clinton to a superior court judgeship in Washington, D.C. Jeffrey O'Toole was appointed by the Montgomery County Public Defender's Office to assist Paul DeWolfe of Rockville in handling Horn's defense.

In many respects the Horn trial was a replay of James Perry's case, but the Horn trial was far more emotionally intense. Prosecutor Bob Dean held up a picture of the triggerman, James Perry, for the jurors to see. "This guy," he said, pointing to Perry, "and that guy sitting right there," he said, pointing to Horn sitting in the defendant's chair, "maintained close and steady and deadly contact to make him a millionaire." Dean described Horn's finances as in "absolute shambles." He had already blown the entire $125,000 he had received from the settlement of Trevor's malpractice case, and was borrowing thousands from family members and friends, including his nephew Cory Tyler, who had money from an acting career, including appearance as the character "Terrance" on the NBC situation comedy "A Different World."

The first witness called by the prosecution was Dana Rogers, an employee of Paladin Press. Rogers testified that Perry had purchased the books *Hit Man* and *Silencers* from Paladin. On cross-examination, DeWolfe had Rogers read passages of *Hit Man* aloud to the jury, including passages suggesting that prospective hit men should look for clients in messy divorce cases, attempting to establish that Horn was vulnerable prey for Perry.

In a gripping moment of testimony, Elaine Rice described her discovery of the tragedy, as she first opened the front door to Millie's home. When asked on the witness stand why she did not enter the home, Elaine cried out, "Because I saw Millie's body!" She broke down and wept, generating a wave of sobbing through the courthouse gallery where family members were seated. Her sister Gloria began to cry uncontrollably, and then collapsed between two narrow rows of seats. Deputies rushed to Gloria's aid, radioing for paramedics as she began to convulse. Judge Harrington immediately ordered the jurors out of the courtroom and called for a recess.

Later, the jurors heard testimony from Tiffani. Horn had rarely seen Trevor, she explained, and had never really accepted him. "He told me once that Trevor could never be a real son to him because of his condition," she testified. Tiffani explained how Horn had asked her to videotape the interior of her mother's home, a tape that prosecutors suggested Horn had used to help Perry plan the murders.

As in Perry's trial, prosecutors carefully laid out the matrix of phone records showing the pattern of calls between Horn and Perry in the months leading up to the murders. The hundreds of credit card, hotel, and telephone records that formed the prosecution's case linking Horn to Perry were compiled in the prosecution's "Summary of Records," a compendium suggestively bound within a green cover, the color of money. Chris Wittenberg was the prosecution's final witness, setting out all the circumstantial links between Perry and Horn. Once again, the capstones were the phone call on the night of the murder from the Days Inn at Rockville, where Perry was registered, to Horn's Hollywood apartment, and the second call that the prosecution claimed captured Perry and Horn together for some twenty seconds of conversation on tape.

Horn wanted to spare from death his daughter Tamielle, the prosecution claimed. So Horn made sure that Perry conducted the hits on a night when Tamielle would not be home. He called the house the night before to confirm that Tamielle would be staying at Elaine's when Perry's planned hit was scheduled to go down.

Horn's cousin Thomas Turner testified against Horn under a grant of immunity, just as he had against Perry. Turner repeated how he had brought Horn and Perry together, and then proclaimed his own innocence in the scheme. He had no idea what Horn and Perry were plotting, Turner said, until after he saw newspaper clippings about the March 1993 slayings. It was then that he became suspicious, testifying that "I got to thinking I was brought into something and I didn't know exactly what." After FBI agents searched Perry's home, there was a flurry of phone activity from Perry to Turner and Horn to Turner. At this point, Turner decided to withdraw his services as a middleman. "I approached Mr. Perry," Turner said, "and told him whatever business he had with my cousin, they should conduct it between themselves." On cross-examination, Paul DeWolfe asked Turner if he knew that Perry had purchased the book *Hit Man*. "No," Turner claimed.

Among the highlights in the case against Horn was a videotape of Horn answering questions in a civil suit that had been commenced against him by the families to block any claim he might make to Millie's and Trevor's estates. The families had filed a claim under Maryland's Slayer's Law, a law that prevents someone who has killed another person from inheriting any of the proceeds of that person's estate. Under the Fifth Amendment, a defendant in a criminal case has a constitutional right to avoid self-incrimination, a right that includes a choice whether or not to take the witness stand. Horn could also have invoked the Fifth Amendment in his civil case, because the possibility of criminal prosecution was looming over him. But Horn, foolishly, thought the police investigation had dead-ended, and he wanted the money. And so, with phenomenal hubris, Horn testified in the civil case, answering questions under oath in videotaped deposition. Glen Cooper, a lawyer from Bethesda, interrogated Horn for two days in July 1994 as part of the civil suit.

The criminal charges were then formally entered against Horn, and the civil suit was suspended. But the videotape deposition was turned over by the families to the prosecutors, and ultimately played at Horn's criminal trial. The videotape showed Horn constantly denying links to Perry, denying that he had received calls from Perry the night of the killings, and evasively and lamely attempting to explain such things as his trips to the Days Inn prior to the murders, his possession of the videotapes, and the hand-drawn map of Millie's neighborhood.

The videotape was devastating to Horn's defense. Horn appeared arrogant and cocky on the tape. But far worse, because virtually everything Horn said on tape, particularly his denials of any relationship with Perry, had been directly contradicted by the well-documented trail of links the prosecution had already set before the jury, Horn came off as a liar, a murderous liar. During a break in the presentation, Horn's attorney Jeffrey O'Toole pleaded with Judge Harrington to stop the showing of the videotape, claiming that the tape was so effective it was depriving Horn of a fair trial." Judge Harrington declined.

Horn's attorneys spent only four hours presenting his defense to the jury. Horn did not take the stand. Paul DeWolfe's strategy was to admit that Perry and Horn had been in contact with one another, but to attempt to place all the blame for the murders on Perry. "This was a case that was born in the mind of a street hustler in Detroit, of a scam artist, of someone who turned out to be a cold-blooded killer," DeWolfe told the jury in his opening statement. "Apparently, this was James Perry's next step up. Apparently, this was where he hit the big time." The defense called only seven witnesses. Cory Tyler testified that he had been happy to lend Horn money, and that he was now living in the town house Horn had used as collateral. Horn's sister, Elaine Tyler, described his reaction on learning of Trevor's death. He was devastated, she claimed, repeatedly saying, "Trevor, Trevor. Why is this happening? Why is this happening?" Horn would laugh and cry at the same time, Tyler testified. She had never seen him like that before, and it scared her. Horn's girlfriend, Shiri Bogan, testified that when Horn learned of Trevor's death, he "looked like a little boy who had had something bad happen to him. I opened my arms to him. He literally collapsed in my arms." When she climbed down from the stand, she blew him a kiss.

In a seventy-minute closing argument, Paul DeWolfe delivered a soft-spoken but eloquent summation, assailing the circumstantial case against his client. Showing the jury a screen illuminated with the words HORN, NO INTENT TO KILL, DeWolfe claimed the murders were an idea Perry had kept to himself until he and Horn spoke by phone two days before the killings. "Lawrence Horn, ladies and gentleman of the jury, never agreed to kill these three people," DeWolfe said. "There has been no evidence presented to you that Lawrence Horn intended to kill anyone." DeWolfe admitted that Horn had told some lies about his relationship with Perry when he learned that Perry had committed the murders, but these, he said, were simply Horn trying to cover himself when he knew he would be a prime suspect. Attempting to plant in the jury's mind an alternative explanation of the events, DeWolfe suggested elliptically that Horn was not the one who had planned the murder of his only son and ex-wife. Horn, DeWolfe admitted ambiguously, had learned about the existence of such a plan, by someone Horn had been "in business with," and Horn had kept silent. But he was not guilty of the murders.

The mysterious intrigue insinuated by DeWolfe was derided by Bob Dean, who mocked the theory that James Perry was simply on a frolic of his own. "To say that James Perry for some reason decided to do this atrocity on his own is absolutely incredible," Dean scoffed to the jury in reply. "This was a business arrangement. In the coldest business imaginable."

As the jury was rising to retire to the jury room for deliberations, Horn's sister Elaine Tyler rose up and shouted from the rear of the gallery, "Lawrence, you got to tell 'em the truth! Tell 'em what Tommy told me. It's a lie! It's a lie!"

Tyler's son Cory grabbed at his mother's arms and began to whimper, "Mom, Mom."

"He's being double-crossed!" Tyler screamed. "He told us he would kill his family if he talked. He would kill all of us!"

Frantically, the bailiffs rushed the jury from the courtroom. As soon as they were out of hearing, DeWolfe asked Judge Harrington for a mistrial, though, if anything, Tyler's outburst should have helped his client, perhaps lending a wisp of verisimilitude to the intimation, made only moments before by DeWolfe in his closing argument, that the real murderer was someone Horn had been in business with. Tyler never explained who she meant by her reference to "Tommy," but it could well have referred to Thomas Turner, who had arranged the liaison between Perry and Horn, and then testified against both under a grant of immunity.

On May 4, 1995, after seven and a half hours of deliberation, the jury found Horn guilty of murder on all three counts. Horn stood expressionless in the blue suit he had worn every day of the trial, shifting his eyes only briefly as the jury forewoman announced the verdict.

Bob Dean said it brought "a certain completion and finality" to the case. But it was clear that the families were far from any sense of emotional closure.

"There's no joy in this decision, because joy was taken from us on March 3, 1993," said Terry Krebs, Janice Saunder's sister. Krebs, who had vanity license plates on her car spelling MISUJAN (for "Miss you, Jan"), said that Horn's conviction was more important than Perry's to the families. Perry, she pointed out, "was just a means to an end. There are many, many people like Perry out in this world. But to conceive of a scheme like this, to plan the death of your own child, to totally disregard the life of an innocent caregiver like my sister— He did the unthinkable."

The Horn family felt the same way. Her voice breaking, Tiffani said, "Not only were my mother and my brother and Janice killed, but my family was destroyed. I hope when this is over, we'll be able to rebuild it. Because that's all we have, family."

Two weeks later, the jury sentenced Horn to life imprisonment on all counts. When the verdict was announced Horn looked at Tiffani, as if searching for some sign of grudging but lingering compassion, some sore residue of mercy. It was not there. Tiffani screamed through tears, "I hate you! I hate you so much! You killed my family!" Horn's face dissolved into tears. He removed his glasses, wiping his eyes and shaking his head. Tiffani continued to scream "I hate you!" as deputies lead Horn, weeping through red eyes, to his holding cell.

The state had made a strong plea to the jury for the death sentence. Bob Dean argued that "to make the punishment fit the crime is what this proceeding is all about." He reminded the jurors that Maryland reserves the penalty of death by lethal injection for only "the worst of the worst."

Michael Saunders testified about the day Janice was found dead, and how he broke the news to his son, Colin. "I had to look at him and tell him that his mother had been killed. I'll never forget the look in his eyes until the day I die." When Michael was dismissed from the witness stand he walked directly toward Horn, glaring at him with hatred as he passed by Horn's chair.

Marilyn Farmer testified for the Horn family, repeatedly struggling for composure as she spoke. The family would never be the same without Millie, she said. Millie was their ever-smiling confidante and charmer. "She always had a smile," said Marilyn. "That was something she had in common with Trevor." Tiffani described Trevor in radiant terms. When he was first brought home in an incubator after his premature birth, she recalled, "I can remember being afraid to really see him and love him because I was afraid he might die." But Trevor survived and grew strong, and filled the family with love even after his hospital accident left him brain-damaged. He was buoyant. He was inspirational. He was pure love. As Tiffani testified, Horn dabbed his face with tissue, and tried to catch his daughter's eye. But she would not look at him.

Yet unlike the James Perry jury, Horn's jury rejected capital punishment. Horn's lawyers pointed to the lack of any prior violence in his record and presented testimony from relatives, friends, and former colleagues. "In a case like this one," defense attorney Jeffrey O'Toole told the jury, "there's no winner, only losers." O'Toole put on a full day of witnesses to try to demonstrate, as he put it, that "this life is worth saving." There was testimony that Stevie Wonder had particularly valued Horn's abilities as a recording engineer. Another record executive recalled a session in which Donny and Marie Osmond had embraced Horn's advice.

Still, the life sentence caused a furor of its own. Opponents of the death penalty pointed to the incongruity between the two verdicts as evidence of the arbitrariness of capital punishment. Both defendants were African-American. But Perry presented the profile of a Detroit thug, while Horn was a successful, upwardly mobile, middle-class achiever who just went bad. Commenting on the verdict, Alan Dershowitz at Harvard thought the disparity was predictable. The logic for the jurors, said Dershowitz, was that "for the contract person, it's a crime of passion. For the hit man, he's in it for the business." But this could not explain the Perry and Horn case, where Horn was in it for greed, not passion, and his cold-blooded calculation seemed more egregious than Perry's. Even the chief of the Montgomery State's Attorney's Office, Andrew L. Sonner, expressed dismay at the disparity between the two verdicts. Sonner was no fan of the death penalty; as a prosecutor he sought it only in extreme cases. "Here's Perry," Sonner pointed out, "one of life's losers, and Horn, on the other hand, is obviously intelligent and well-spoken." This, for Sonner, was one of the problems with the death penalty. "You end up executing the poor, the deprived, a lot of human flotsam."

Members of Millie's family reacted angrily to the verdict. They had now lived through the horrors of the murders many times: in the awful and surreal first minutes and hours of awareness; Elaine as she came to the house to see the garage door open and hear Trevor's alarm blaring and feel Millie's body blocking the door; the other family members being told by telephone or visits from police, stunned and disbelieving and unable to absorb the shock; the agonizing investigation; the identification of bodies; the pouring over of evidence— Millie's purse, Janice's knitting, Trevor's respirator; the endless interviews with detectives, venting outraged suspicion at Lawrence Horn; the frustrated waiting as police methodically pursued their wispy leads; the dribbling out of information from the police department and prosecutor's office, wondering whether Horn would ever be brought to justice, fretting over who the others were that had helped him in his appalling plot; the ordeal of Perry's trial with more anguishing testimony, more reliving of every grisly detail; and then the spectral recapitulation of it all in Horn's trial, where the horror and grief of their loss commingled with loathing and disgust.

In their nightmares the survivors of the victims saw Millie and Janice at the moment of their brutal deaths. In their nightmares they glared at the silent silhouette of James Perry as Millie and Janice must have glared, in ghastly paralysis of anticipated death, staring through eyes that an assassin's bullets would obliterate. Millie knew she was going to be killed, and still more dreadfully knew that her son and friend upstairs had already been murdered, and in those milliseconds of awareness Millie probably knew who was behind it all, and why.

And if in the nightmares of the survivors they could at least comprehend the sick mind of the Lawrence Horn who would kill his ex-wife for money, they could not comprehend the sick mind of the Lawrence Horn who would kill his own son. The murder of a hated spouse cannot be condoned but it can at least be understood, at least processed as part of the perverse evil of human experience. People kill their spouses and ex-spouses in fits of jealousy, rapacity, spite, or revenge. People even kill their spouses or ex-spouses out of greed, to recover the insurance or inherit the land. These murders are repulsive and deserving of society's highest punishments, but they are not incomprehensible. They happen—sporadically, rarely—but they happen. It is a cardinal rule of homicide: Always suspect the spouse.

But not a child. The calculating avarice that would lead Lawrence Horn to purchase the execution of his own son was unique in its depravity. In their nightmares, this was an evil the survivors could never comprehend. For here was a man who could say to his own son, you are no part of me, we do not touch at any point, you are not human in my eyes, you survive at my sufferance, you *live through me*, and you will live no longer. I need the money.

This was a mind that the survivors could not understand, and its continued existence on this earth goaded them like a horrible haunting spirit. "It gives us no peace, no peace at all," said Gloria Maree of the life sentence the jury had given Horn. "The evil that's in this man will live on. It doesn't matter where he lives. . . . We were looking for a decision that would still Lawrence Horn's mind."

After the case, one of the jurors, Richard C. Bowers, said simply that the jury felt there had been enough killing. "My gracious, there's so much death involved already and so much grief, you don't want to keep piling it up." Another juror, Julius Breczinski, explained, "I didn't feel that the death penalty would assuage all of those people. I felt it would add pain to a lot of them." Maybe he was right, but if he was, on the day of the sentence the family members certainly did not agree.

The outcome was especially upsetting to Tiffani, who felt not only the remorse of her loss but the confusing guilt over her own unwitting complicity in that loss. Her father had used her, getting her to videotape the house and disclose the family schedules. He had used her to kill her own mother and brother. He had destroyed their family and destroyed a part of her. "I feel that he should be on death row," said Tiffani. "He knows how I feel, and he'll die knowing."

11

The Shadow of His Preen

And so our case began. The surviving members of the families of Millie, Trevor, and Janice Saunders filed a civil damages suit for wrongful death in federal district court in Maryland against Paladin Press and its publisher, Peder Lund, for aiding and abetting the murders committed by James Perry and Lawrence Horn. Howard Siegel and John Marshall represented the members of the Horn family. Another Maryland attorney, Tom Heeney, represented the family of Janice Saunders. I represented all of the family members, and the team of Siegel, Marshall, and Smolla would manage the lawsuit. Tom Heeney would participate and assist but agreed to play a backup role.

Vivian "Elaine" Rice was listed first in the complaint as a plaintiff, filing the suit as the "guardian and next friend" of Tamielle Horn; Marilyn Farmer and Tiffani Horn sued as the corepresentatives of the Estate of Mildred Horn; and Michael Saunders sued, individually and as "next friend" of his son, Colin Saunders, and as representative of the Estate of Janice Saunders. Because Elaine Rice was listed first in the court papers, the lawsuit would become known by the name *Rice v. Paladin Enterprises, Inc.*

• • •

"Now, in *R.A.V. v. City of St. Paul*, the Supreme Court seems to push the envelope of the free speech principle to its outer limits, if not beyond," I began. "Here we have the story of an African-American family, Russ and Laura Jones and their five children, that had just moved into a white working-class neighborhood in St. Paul, Minnesota. A bunch of white hooligans began harassing them from the beginning, and one night one of their leaders suggested that they cause some 'skinhead trouble.' One of the hoodlums says, 'Do you want to burn some niggers?' So they put together this half-assed makeshift cross, and at 2:30 in the morning, they go into the Joneses' backyard, plant their pathetic cross in the ground, douse it with paint thinner, and then set it afire. Russ Jones woke up from the commotion, looked out the window, and called the police. These wonderful outstanding young citizens are summarily arrested and charged with crimes. The cops could easily have booked them on some run-of-the-mill crimes, like trespass, assault, or disorderly conduct. If the local prosecutor had gone that route, this would have been a routine case, and it would never have reached the United States Supreme Court. The case would have been open-and-shut, because obviously these guys were guilty of things like trespass and disorderly conduct. But instead, the prosecutor decided to charge them under a newly enacted 'hate speech' law just passed by the City of St. Paul. That law made it a crime—" I looked down at my book to quote from the ordinance, "to place 'on public or private property a symbol, object, appellation, characterization, or graffiti, including, but not limited to, a burning cross or Nazi swastika, which one knows or has reasonable grounds to know arouses anger, alarm or resentment in others on the basis of race, color, creed, religion or gender.' So the prosecutor charged these guys under this ordinance. And they were found guilty. And there's not much debate about the fact that they *were* guilty. They did exactly what the ordinance said they could not do. Yet lo and behold, when they appeal their case to the Supreme Court, the Court says 'No, they can't be prosecuted under this ordinance. It violates the First Amendment.' Now how on *earth* can the Supreme Court say that?"

There were many hands in the air. I called first on Katherine, an African-American student. There was a time when I might not have called on Katherine first, a time when I was overly self-conscious about not appearing race-conscious, or gender-conscious, in class. So I would not call on an African-American student to lead off discussion of *Brown v. Board of Education*, because I did not want it to appear that I had purposefully selected a black student to discuss one of the most important race discrimination decisions in history. Nor would I call on a woman to lead off on a landmark case involving women's rights. I'd gotten past such silliness, however, realizing that I was overthinking things, and that in my zealotry to appear neutral I was actually indulging an unconscious racism and sexism. So I called on Katherine, because I could see intensity in her face. I was not disappointed.

"I have *real* trouble with this case," Katherine said.

"Tell us why."

"The Court seemed to think these were just idle words, like 'sticks and stones may break my bones, but words will never hurt me.' That trivializes what the Jones family was put through. This speech was an insult to their human dignity. This is not freedom of speech. This is an attack. A *racist attack*. I'm sure the Joneses were terrified. We've already studied *Chaplinsky v. New Hampshire*, the fighting words case, and *Brandenburg v. Ohio*, where the Court said the speech had to be directed to imminent lawless action. Where here, there *was* imminent lawless action."

"But the Court doesn't say that these guys could not be prosecuted under a general 'fighting words' law, or under a law that made it illegal to incite imminent lawless action, a law that mimicked the *Brandenburg* standard," I pointed out. "It wasn't that the actions of these criminals were constitutionally protected. Rather, it was that the *particular* law they were prosecuted under was constitutionally defective. What, in the Court's view, was that defect?"

I called on Katherine again, even though I knew she would not find the answer palatable. "Well, I don't buy the Court's reasoning, but according to Justice Scalia, the problem with this law was that it engaged in 'viewpoint discrimination'."

"And what is that?" I asked.

"Justice Scalia argued that the City of St. Paul picked just a few topics from the spectrum of fighting words, such as race, religion, and gender, and made only those kinds of attacks illegal." She looked down at her casebook, and continued, "Justice Scalia said that 'St. Paul has no such authority to license one side of a debate to fight freestyle, while requiring the other to follow the Marquis of Queensbury Rules.' "

"But you don't find Justice Scalia's position persuasive?" I pressed her.

"No, I don't. I think it's illogical. Since St. Paul could ban *all* fighting words, why does it violate the First Amendment to select just a few of the *worst ones* for special treatment?"

"Because that smacks of censorship, doesn't it? This ordinance was born of political correctness, isn't that obvious? And that's what offended the Court."

"And that's what offends me. It's just too easy to dismiss the law as politically correct. Sometimes politically correct *is* correct. This decision encourages all the crazies out there. The militia cells and Ku Kluxers who think it is permissible to take the law into their own hands and lynch niggers and torch Jews and bomb Baptist churches and blow up federal courthouses. I read what you wrote in your book, Professor Smolla, praising the *R.A.V.* decision as a great victory for freedom of speech. Well, with respect to you and the Supreme Court, I think it's a great defeat for human decency, and for the rule of law."

I took Katherine's criticism with aplomb. I liked it when students showed the mettle to challenge me. Moreover, she might well be right and I might well be wrong. The Supreme Court's hate speech ruling in *R.A.V.* bothered a lot of people, including me, one of the decision's defenders. Katherine, I knew, was like of lot of students. She saw me as a caricature, a "free speech freak," who would defend freedom of speech in any circumstance, no matter what the consequences. My students could not know, of course, about the lawsuit we were about to file. *That'll sure as hell confuse 'em,* I thought.

• • •

We filed the suit and simultaneously issued a press release announcing the filing and setting forth the basic facts of the case. There was immediate and overwhelming media interest. Because of the O. J. Simpson saga, there was a general public consciousness that whenever a crime is committed, the victim (or the victim's survivors or estate) has the right to sue the perpetrator, wholly aside from the criminal prosecution brought by the state. But it was the murder manual *Hit Man* that seemed to galvanize public curiosity.

The morning the case was announced, a CBS News team arrived at Howard's office for an interview for the "CBS Evening News" with Dan Rather. John sat in the back of the office and watched as Howard sat for an hour in front of the cameras, attacking Paladin Press and the book *Hit Man.* Other news crews arrived for more interviews. Phone messages lined up from journalists around the country.

At the end of the morning, John looked at Howard gravely. "I can't do this," he said. "I want out."

"*What?* What's your problem?" Howard was shocked.

"I can't go through with this. I can't sit back and watch you do this. I can't sit back in your shadow as you preen for the cameras and pontificate for the next two years. You're going to go crazy with this. You're going to be out of control. And I am always going to be in the background, playing Watson to your Sherlock Holmes. I just can't do that. It will destroy our friendship. And it will kill me." John was absolutely serious. Howard's morning performance had completely turned him off. They went to lunch and tried to patch things up. Howard tried to appease John by promising that he would share the media spotlight with both John and me. "We'll divvy up the interviews," he said. "You take a third, Rod takes a third, I take a third. And I'll promise to tone it down." John was temporarily placated, but it was a shaky and tenuous peace.

If the fissure between Howard and John made me wonder about the stability of our newly formed partnership in the case, it also provided me with a better glimpse into John's character. If Howard was all high-decibel bombast and bravado, John tended to be quiet and self-contained, qualities that made him at once easy to get along with but difficult to know. John grew up in Auburn, New York, a small, blue-collar, heavily Catholic city in central New York's rust belt. His father had graduated from Yale in 1938, and then returned home to run the family business, a small men's clothing store in Auburn that had been in the Marshall family for three generations. John wondered whether his father was a failure or a great success. He was a brilliant man, and it didn't take a Yale education to run a clothing store. But his father had also taught him the values of work, family, and extracting enjoyment from the pleasures of books and nature. By that measure, his father was his hero.

Not that many kids in Auburn went to college, and fewer to prestigious ones, but John was a good student, if somewhat undirected and lazy, and he managed to get into Duke. After college he worked for a few years in Washington, and married Cindy Callahan, a law student. Restless, John applied to law school himself, and got into American University in Washington. For most students, law school is an intense experience, filled with memories of thrills and spills, an intellectual boot camp hated for its stresses and loved for its challenges. But for John, law school was but a tepid wash, rinsing over him without stain or imprint, bereft of memory. The only event of his entire time at American that left any lasting impression was not a curricular experience but a job, an internship he served with a sage Superior Court judge who tutored him in the rich fascinations of the game of litigation.

And so he became a litigator, starting off as an insurance defense lawyer, gaining trial experience in local courts. One of the cases he tried was a routine auto accident case involving a guy who was driving like a bat out of hell and collided with another car making a turn on a green light. The passenger in the car being driven like a bat out of hell was the driver's brother, who was badly injured. He wouldn't sue his own brother, so instead he sued the hapless guy who was making the turn—John's client. The plaintiff-brother was represented by Tom Heeney. One of John's first moves was to file a cross-complaint against the plaintiff's brother who was driving the car. The court appointed a lawyer to represent the driver-brother: Howard Siegel.

It was through this lawsuit that Marshall met his future collaborators in the *Hit Man* suit, Siegel and Heeney. The case chugged along uneventfully until a couple of weeks before trial, when Howard called John. It was the first time they had ever conversed. Howard had done no work on the case, and suddenly realized that he was in trouble, facing trial in two weeks with no preparation. The gist of Howard's call was to ask for John to sever his client from the case, so that the question of his client's culpability could be litigated later. "This is Howard Siegel," said Howard the moment John picked up the phone. "If you don't agree to sever my client out of this case you will find my foot so far up your ass that you'll need a crowbar to get it out."

Even as a still relatively inexperienced trial lawyer, John knew what reaction was called for. He sat back and laughed. Who was this guy? John rejected Howard's proposal, and Howard promptly filed a severance motion with the court. John first met Howard in person at the hearing over the motion. Howard won the motion, strutting out of the courtroom with the grin of a child who'd just beaten a rap. John ultimately won the case against Heeney's client.

Shortly after the trial, John hooked up with another Rockville lawyer, Alan Moldawer. As it turned out, Moldawer had been sharing office space with Howard, though the two were not partners. Howard left the office suite as John entered. Howard had just scored his big victory in the *Kelley v. R.G. Industries* Saturday Night Special case, and was peacocking around town. John would simultaneously insult and compliment Howard, a motif that seemed to suit them both. They discovered a mutual love for tennis, began playing together, and a friendship formed.

It was John's wife, Cindy, who first represented Millie Horn, as her divorce attorney against Lawrence Horn. Cindy referred Trevor's medical malpractice case to John. Knowing that it was a potentially big case, John felt he needed someone with more experience to help show him the ropes, and approached Howard to join him in handling the suit. The case cemented their friendship.

Meanwhile, John began to attract significant cases in his own right. He settled one brain injury suit for $2.4 million. Soon he was hooked on high-stakes cases. They engaged his mind and stimulated his competitive juices. But big cases don't come along that often, and before long John found himself in the middle of a long and stale stretch of humdrum litigation, handling routine suits that were dumbing down and dulling his life. He felt unchallenged and undistinguished, and toyed with the idea of quitting law practice.

Then came the murders of Millie, Trevor, and Janice. These were people John had known. They were killed to get money John had helped earn for them. The killings were violent and repulsive, and John, like the members of the families themselves, was consumed with rage. Howard called John, much like he would later call me, with the idea of suing Paladin Press. By this time John was used to Howard's brainstorms and had made a hobby of deflating them. But this scheme of Howard's seriously intrigued John. A book I had written on the First Amendment was on John's shelf, and John found in it a passage that seemed to hold a scintilla of hope that such a suit might have a chance. John was tempted to join with Howard again, in a reprise of their successful joint venture in Trevor's malpractice case.

But John also had major reservations. He did not want to play second or third fiddle to Howard as Howard frolicked and detoured through his magnum opus. John was particularly peeved by Howard's tendency to constantly use the first person singular when talking about a case. Like the boxing manager who says "I had him in trouble in the third round," or the waiter who says "I've got a clam and corn bisque this evening," the word *we* was not in Howard's usable vocabulary. John's law partner Alan Moldawer, no fan of Howard's, did not approve of John getting involved in the suit. More pointedly, John's wife was opposed.

Despite these reservations and oppositions, John decided to jump in. Quoting Pink Floyd, John said, "I decided to take 'a walk-on part in a war instead of a leading role in a cage.' " John sat down with Alan Moldawer and offered to leave the partnership if Moldawer was adamantly opposed to John's involvement. Moldawer backed off, though he was never really happy with the suit.

It was against this backdrop that John had balked at Howard's preening. Yet it was something both John and I had to get used to, for it simply wasn't in Howard's makeup to keep himself under restraint. If we were staying in, we were staying in with Howard as Howard.

• • •

Three innocent people had been killed early in the morning of March 3, 1993, but in the compressed staccato beat of television sound bites and newspaper crime reporting, attention was invariably focused on only two of them—Millie and Trevor—to the weary dismay of the grieving family of the third victim, Janice Saunders. In the media it was "the Horn case," and accounts often failed even to mention Janice by name, relegating her to the character role of the "attending nurse," who was "also killed." Family and friends of Janice found this so disheartening that they talked of canceling their newspaper subscriptions, that last feeble act of reader protest.

It was Michael Saunders who came up with a fitting antidote, the creation of a nursing scholarship in Janice's name. Michael contributed the first $2,500 to a $50,000 fund that would pay the tuition, books, and fees for a year at Montgomery College, where Janice had graduated in 1983. The scholarship fund was successful, with most of the money coming in through local businesses and family friends.

The first recipient of a $2,700 scholarship was Katie Wheatley, of Aspen Hill, Maryland. Hundreds gathered at the Montgomery College auditorium and watched, through tear-filled eyes, a video that played silently on a screen behind the podium—images of Janice, home videos, family scenes, Janice smiling as she dressed her three-year-old son as a pumpkin for Halloween, Janice buckling Colin into a car seat and then waving to the camera, her arm extended toward the dashboard, Janice cupping and uncupping her hand, showing Colin how to say good-bye.

On the night of her murder Janice had been completing her fifth piece of cross-stitching needlework from patterns designed by the artist P. Buckley Moss. The print was called "The Parade," and showed a boy pulling a wagon with a girl and a throng of black kittens. She had just started on the boy's hat when she was shot. Moss attended the scholarship memorial ceremony, and presented Michael and Colin with a gift: a newly designed print entitled "Stitching Nurse," depicting a Civil War nurse doing needlework. The nurse in the print was knitting a pattern reminiscent of "The Parade," but instead of kittens in the wagon, Moss placed a single black cat at the nurse's feet. Moss dedicated the print to Janice, and donated two hundred copies to her scholarship fund; their sales would contribute $15,000.

Reverend Larry Schmidt, a Lutheran minister, delivered the benediction. "When we are precious," he said, "then nothing is ordinary. Janice no longer belongs just to this family. She belongs to the community."

• • •

"In the nineteenth and early twentieth centuries," I said to the class, "Natural Law philosophy was challenged by a school of thought known as legal positivism. The positivists did not believe that law came from God, or Eternal Law, or nature, or the currents of universal being, or any other transcendent realm. The positivists did not believe that law came from a social compact promulgated to preserve natural rights. There was simply no such thing as Natural Law, the positivists argued. This was a myth invented by humans to make themselves feel better about law, but it was smarmy and weak-minded.

"Positivist thinkers such as the English philosopher John Austin thus taught that law is simply a command to a political inferior from a political superior armed with the power to enforce it. This was positive law—the only *real* law, and it had nothing to do with nature, or God, or even morality. Positivists truly did take God out of the picture, to quote the remark Cindy made several weeks back. At most, God was now an irrelevant artist, as James Joyce's character Stephen Dedalus says in *Portrait of the Artist as a Young Man:* 'The artist, like the God of creation, remains within or behind or beyond or above his handiwork, invisible, refined out of existence, indifferent, paring his fingernails.'

"For the positivist, not merely God but good and evil may evaporate into the mystic mist. A law's goodness or badness is simply a subjective judgment, Austin argued, something in the eye of the beholder, and had nothing to do with whether the precept was or was not law. The existence of law was one thing, Austin instructed, and its moral merit or demerit quite another. For positivists, the study of law was no longer intertwined with theology, philosophy, or morals. It was, rather, a much more concrete and objective science, an essentially sociological inquiry into the anatomy of power and force. As Chairman Mao Zedong would later write, 'Political power comes from the barrel of a gun.'"

• • •

Howard called me early in the morning. He was livid. "Have you seen the *Washington Post* story?" he screamed. "It's terrible! I hate it! It makes it sound like we're apologizing for bringing this case!"

"Howard, slow down, I'm not out of bed yet. Let me walk down to the driveway, get the paper, read the story, start my coffee, and I'll call you back."

The *Washington Post* story on our case was written by *Post* reporter David Montgomery. The *Post* quoted John on the motivation of the families in bringing the suit. "It may sound corny," John said, "but if they can prevent this from happening again, then they're going to feel that they have made a positive contribution out of what has been a devastating family event." The *Post* also quoted me. " 'Nothing like this has been attempted before,' said Rod Smolla, an authority on the First Amendment, a professor at the College of William and Mary School of Law and a member of the legal team that filed the suit. 'This will be, from a First Amendment perspective, a path-breaking test case with important implications. . . . In my judgment, the First Amendment does not protect that kind of speech.' "

I called Howard back. "I see why you're so pissed," I said with mock concern. "They didn't quote you."

That week, Howard, John, and I were all over the media. Stories appeared in the *New York Times*, the *Wall Street Journal*, and the London *Times*, and scores of other papers around the world. Howard appeared on the "Today Show" with Bryant Gumbel, on the "CBS Evening News" with Dan Rather, and on "Larry King Live." While on Larry King a caller from southern California said that he had served on a jury in a multiple-murder case several years before in which the murderer had used a Paladin Press book as the blueprint for his killings. We tried to trace the caller's identity, but we were unsuccessful.

The media appearances proliferated. Howard seemed to thrill to each of them, a media junkie on a heroin rush. For the time being John and I were content to live in the shadow of his preen.

On National Public Radio, John Marshall debated Jane Kirtley, the general counsel to the Reporters Committee for Freedom of the Press, a prestigious First Amendment organization. Jane and I had worked with one another in the past, and I considered her a friend. She and John went hard at each other on the air. Afterward she told John that she was very disturbed that I had gotten involved in the case.

That week I did the show "Burden of Proof," with Roger Cossack and Greta Van Susteren, on CNN. My adversary on the CNN show was Paul McMasters, a longtime First Amendment advocate with the Freedom Forum, a public interest foundation created by Al Neuharth and the media giant Gannett Company to advance freedom of speech and freedom of the press. McMasters and I knew each other from past events and causes in which we had been allies. In the makeup room outside the studio he took me aside. "A lot of people in the First Amendment community are very upset that you took this case," he said. He wasn't tweaking me. I knew that the First Amendment was like a religion to McMasters, and that he probably saw me as the constitutional equivalent of Judas Iscariot.

"Paul, I believe I'm on the right side."

"Well, I'll grant you this much: Of all the First Amendment cases I've ever been involved with, this case probably tests my mettle more than any of them. At the Freedom Forum we think this is one of the most important First Amendment cases of the last ten years. I understand why you might think this suit is justified. But what worries me is the damage you're going to cause freedom of speech in the long run if you prevail. Frankly, some people are saying you sold out."

12

H-Bombs and Copycats

Paladin Press responded to our lawsuit by hiring two of the nation's finest First Amendment lawyers to defend it, Lee Levine and Tom Kelley. I knew and respected both men. Paladin Press might be a maverick within the publishing industry, but it had hired mainstream "establishment" media lawyers who were pillars of the First Amendment bar.

One of the first things the Paladin legal defense team did was to strike back in the court of public opinion. Our suit was a brazen act of censorship, they claimed, masterminded by Howard Siegel, an "avowed anti-gun advocate." Howard relished the epithet, and began signing correspondence "Howard Siegel, Avowed Anti-Gun Advocate." The network of First Amendment lawyers and advocates also simmered with hint and innuendo. Somehow, the whispers went, this crazed antigun zealot Siegel had seduced Rod Smolla into joining his half-cocked cause.

Lee Levine, from Washington, D.C., had been a leader in communications law for years. He was the chairman of the American Bar Association's Section on Communications Law, a highly prestigious position. Tom Kelley, from Denver, was probably the most well-known media lawyer in the Rocky Mountain region. Together they were a formidable team.

The case that had first brought Kelley fame and established his credentials was a victory over the Wyoming cowboy-lawyer Gerry Spence. Kelley had defended *Penthouse* magazine in a suit brought against it by Kimerli Jayne Pring, Miss Wyoming of 1978. In its August 1979 issue, *Penthouse* ran an article depicting the sexual exploits of a fictional beauty queen named "Charlene" who entered the Miss America contest as Miss Wyoming. Throughout the article Charlene has lascivious fantasies, and during the final competition begins to perform fellatio on her coach, an act that causes the coach to levitate. Gerry Spence represented the real Miss Wyoming, Ms. Pring, who claimed that the fictional piece was actually aimed at her, and constituted libel. The jury agreed, and returned a verdict of over $25 million in damages. But Kelley was successful in getting the case overturned on appeal. The appeals court held that no reasonable reader could have understood the story as anything but fiction and fantasy. The court described the *Penthouse* piece as "a gross, unpleasant, crude, distorted attempt to ridicule the Miss America contest and its contestants," and noted that it had "no redeeming value whatsoever," but insisted that "although a story may be repugnant in the extreme to the ordinary reader, and we have encountered no difficulty in placing this story in such a category, the typical standards and doctrines under the First Amendment must nonetheless be applied." One judge dissented, stating bluntly that "I consider levitation, dreams, and public performance as fiction. Fellatio is not."

Howard called me for a scouting report when Levine and Kelley surfaced as Paladin's defense team. Levine was assisted by a younger lawyer, Seth Berlin, and Kelley by an associate named Steven Zansberg. Although I didn't know Berlin or Zansberg, I knew Levine and Kelley. I told Howard we were fighting the first-stringers.

"What kind of strategy are these guys likely to take?" Howard asked.

"They are quintessential First Amendment lawyers," I said. "The mantra is going to be First Amendment, First Amendment, First Amendment, from beginning to end. The good news is that these guys won't necessarily be that good at jury trials. Many media lawyers expect to lose in front of juries, and often do. They win their cases with legal argument, either by getting the trial judge to toss the suit, or getting a jury verdict reversed on appeal. I think what we're going to see is the claim that this is nothing more than an attempt by us at censorship, an attempt to silence Paladin Press because its ideas are unsavory. Levine's and Kelley's instincts will be to take to the high First Amendment ground. They're going to portray Peter Lund as a free speech martyr. They're going to try to make him look like another Larry Flynt."

"But sex ain't the same as murder," said Howard.

"Sure, that's what *we'll* say." I told Howard about Kelley's *Penthouse* victory. "He's going to try to pretend that *Hit Man* is a piece of fluff, a fantasy like Miss Wyoming's levitating blow jobs. But we know what to say to that. Floating fellatio may be fiction, but shooting people through the eyes is not."

•   •   •

"It's a pleasure to welcome as our special guest for today's class, Professor Kent Greenawalt from the Columbia University Law School." The students politely applauded. Some twenty-five law students were gathered in my backyard, munching chips and drinking Cokes and beers. The law school had a guest scholar, Kent Greenawalt, staying in residence for several days, and he had agreed to meet with my seminar at my house, and then to stay for a late-afternoon cookout when it was over.

There are some coincidences in life that seem simply too propitious to be the product of random chance, auspicious fortuities that make one believe there must be providence in the universe. Kent's appearance in my class was just such a stroke of cosmic good fortune, for the topic of the day was whether a person could be held criminally liable for furnishing to another person information used to commit a violent act of terrorism. "Imagine," I said to the class, "that a terrorist group wants to smuggle an altimeter bomb onto a commercial airliner, a bomb that will explode and destroy the plane once it reaches a predetermined altitude. And imagine that a mad and malevolent scientist who wishes to make a little extra income on the side decides to write and sell to anyone who wants to buy it a book entitled *Everything You Ever Wanted to Know About Blowing Up Airplanes But Were Afraid to Ask.* The book is a detailed instruction manual on how to build a bomb and sneak it onto the airplane. It is sold through a publisher who specializes in such how-to books. Anyone can order the book through the publisher's catalog, or even by placing an order via the publisher's Web page on the Internet. If a terrorist group bought the book, followed its instructions, and brought down a plane with it, could we indict and convict the mad scientist for aiding and abetting murder? Professor Greenawalt, as you know, has literally 'written the book' on this subject, and for today's reading you read excerpts from that book: *Speech, Crime, and the Uses of Language.* We'll hear his views on this hypothetical in a bit. But first he and I would like to get your opinions. What do you think?"

This was a synergistic moment, when law practice, scholarship, and teaching all converged and worked together. Kent's book was regarded in scholarly circles as a classic. In it he documented over twenty-one examples of crimes that may be effectuated through the use of language. I asked the students if any of Greenawalt's examples might cover my hypothetical case.

The students were not shy about jumping into the debate. Jeffery started the discussion. "I guess I would begin with Professor Greenawalt's list," he said. "It looks to me like what you described falls within the definition of item number nine. 'A person commits a crime if the person participates in a criminal endeavor by communicating—for example, by telling thieving friends the combination of the employer's safe.' "

Felicia immediately challenged Jeffery. "But there's a difference. In the safe combination example, the person who furnishes the combination knows the thief, knows the victim, knows exactly why the thief wants the information, and what the thief intends to do with it. There is a directness, an immediacy to the whole transaction. In Professor Smolla's hypothetical, the book is being sold in the open marketplace. The author and the publisher don't have any idea who is buying it, or the purpose for which they are buying it, or what the purchaser will do with it. To me, Professor Smolla's hypothetical is closer to the copycat cases we read for class last week, in which the courts always hold that there can be no liability."

Felicia was referring to a series of cases we had just read involving the problem of "copycat" or "imitative" behavior. In these cases material presented for artistic, entertainment, or educational purposes depicts activity that is dangerous or violent. A person exposed to the depiction, often a child, engages in "copycat" behavior emulating the dangerous activity, resulting in injury or death. Felicia was exactly right—in every one of those cases the courts held that there could be no liability against the author or publisher of the information. The list of cases was impressive. In a case entitled *Walt Disney Productions v. Shannon*, for example, Disney's "Mickey Mouse Club" television program ran a feature on the "magic you can create with sound effects," demonstrating how to reproduce the sound of a tire coming off an automobile by putting a BB gun pellet inside a large round balloon, filling the balloon with air, and rotating the BB inside the balloon. Craig, an eleven-year-old boy, tried the trick at home, using a piece of lead about twice the size of a BB, and a long skinny balloon in place of a fat round one. The balloon burst and the piece of lead was projected into Craig's eye, partially blinding him. The court ruled in favor of Disney, saying that there was no "clear and present danger" that injuries would have resulted from the "Mickey Mouse Club" show. Similarly, in *DeFilippo v. National Broadcasting Co.*, the court rejected a claim arising from a stunt on the "Tonight Show," in which Johnny Carson was "hung" by a professional stuntman, when a thirteen-year-old boy, emulating the stunt, hung himself. In *Sakon v. Pepsico, Inc.*, the court held there could be no liability arising from an advertisement for the soft drink Mountain Dew, showing kids riding up a ramp and landing their bicycles in the water, in a claim brought by a fourteen-year-old boy who attempted the stunt and broke his neck. In *Olivia N. v. National Broadcasting Co.*, NBC ran a program about the harm suffered by an adolescent girl at a state-run home, including a scene in which it was suggested that the girl had been "artificially raped" with a toilet plunger. A few days later, a group of boys who had watched the show raped a nine-year-old boy with a soda bottle. The court applied the *Brandenburg v. Ohio* test, and held that there could be no liability because the television program did not advocate or encourage violent acts. In *McCollum v. CBS, Inc.*, the court rejected a claim brought by the parents of a teenager who shot and killed himself while listening to a record by the musician Ozzy Osbourne in a suit against Osbourne and his record company. And in *Zamora v. Columbia Broadcasting System*, the court rejected the argument that television violence caused a minor to become addicted and desensitized to violent behavior, resulting in said minor killing an eighty-three-year-old woman.

The most graphic and perhaps most famous of these copycat cases was *Herceg v. Hustler Magazine, Inc.* The case was a wrongful death suit brought by the mother of a fourteen-year-old boy who emulated the practice of autoerotic asphyxia, as depicted in an article in *Hustler* entitled "Orgasm of Death." Autoerotic asphyxia entails masturbation while "hanging" oneself in order to temporarily cut off the blood supply to the brain at the moment of orgasm. The article described how the act is performed and the physical pleasure those who engage in it seek to achieve. An editor's statement warned: "*Hustler* emphasizes the often-fatal dangers of the practice of 'auto-erotic asphyxia,' and recommends that readers seeking unique forms of sexual release DO NOT ATTEMPT this method. The facts are presented here solely for an educational purpose." The plaintiff sued on the theory that the *Hustler* article constituted "incitement."

The court was understandably dubious that the traditional legal cases dealing with incitement were ever meant for such facts. What was it that *Hustler* was accused of, after all, incitement to masturbate?

The court noted that "Incitement cases usually concern a stated effort to punish the arousal of a crowd to commit a criminal action. The root of incitement theory appears to have been grounded in concern over crowd behavior. As John Stuart Mill stated in his dissertation, *On Liberty,* 'An opinion that corn-dealers are starvers of the poor, or that private property is robbery ought to be unmolested when simply circulated through the press, but may justly incur punishment when delivered orally to an excited mob assembled before the house of a corn-dealer.' " Deciding that what *Hustler* had done was not incitement, the court dismissed the suit.

This lengthy litany of cases was an imposing body of precedent. "I just don't see," said Felicia, "given the cases we read last week, that there is any likelihood any court would permit criminal or civil liability to be imposed against our hypothetical scientist, no matter how mad or malevolent he might be."

Kent Greenawalt, unable to restrain his teacher's impulses, intervened with a question. "But are those copycat cases really analogous to Rod's hypothetical?" he asked. Christine jumped in. "No, I don't think so. In none of those copycat cases can it really be said that the speaker is actually intending for the viewer or reader to go out and emulate the behavior. Take the *Hustler* case, for example. Whatever ugly things might be said about the publishers of *Hustler,* they clearly did not intend that the autoerotic asphyxia trick be imitated."

"That's true, isn't it?" I said to the class. "The whole point of the article was to warn people that this kind of sex with yourself could be dangerous."

"Yes," Christine continued. "But in your hypothetical, it seems to me that the scientist *expects and intends* at least some of its readers to blow up planes."

"We read another case last week that also bears on this," I reminded the class. "The *Progressive* decision." In the case I was talking about, *United States v. Progressive, Inc.,* the court enjoined *Progressive* magazine from publishing an article containing material on how the H-bomb worked. "Kent," I said, "there's probably no greater expert on these issues in the country than you. The precedent in the *Progressive* case seems to support the possibility of taking action against our mad scientist. Yet the long line of copycat cases seems to go the other way. What do you think is the right answer?"

"I'm not sure," he said, explaining to the class that it had been something he'd been struggling with. Perhaps the answer would turn on exactly what the mad scientist's "intent" really was, and whether it could be proven in court.

I took solace in his answer, not because it unlocked the key to the mystery, but because it made it clear to me that one of the smartest and most thoughtful scholars in the country was as perplexed by the problems as I was. If he had said "no way, you can't get the scientist," I'd have been worried. Instead, his answer was waffling, middling, ambivalent. I took that as an endorsement.

13

Soldiers of Fortune

Lawyers are trained to reason by analogy, to incessantly contrast and compare. In preparing our case, Howard, John, and I embarked on a process of thinking by analogy that lasted for months. One of us would discover a line of cases, excitedly sending them to the others. We'd then pick them apart, pro and con, trying to decide if they helped or hurt our position, how we could use them to our best advantage, or minimize their potential damage. One of the most interesting set of decisions with which we wrestled involved *Soldier of Fortune* magazine, founded by Peder Lund's former partner, Robert Brown. *Soldier of Fortune* had been sued three times in cases involving professional contract killers who placed ads in the magazine and were hired for hit jobs through those ads.

In yet another of the eerie coincidences that seemed to abound in our case, one of those *Soldier of Fortune* suits involved one of my own former law students from the University of Arkansas in Fayetteville. Doug Norwood had been a student in several of my classes at Arkansas. One day a professional hit man burst into Norwood's apartment intent on murder. The gunman had apparently been hired by an ex-paramour of Norwood's girlfriend. Norwood, a former cop, managed to avoid being shot, grabbed the would-be assassin, and tossed him off the apartment's second-floor balcony. Norwood became a hero, with a rush of media appearances, and even a story on "60 Minutes."

The hit man had been hired through an advertisement he had placed in *Soldier of Fortune*. Norwood sued the magazine and won, adding fortune to his fame. The judge in the case observed that Norwood was "not attempting to have [the] defendant enjoined from exercising its right to run advertisements such as those in question. Instead, he is simply asking that a jury, after a trial, award him damages for the consequences of those advertisements." In an interesting passage, the judge also questioned whether an assassin's ad qualified as the kind of "public debate" the First Amendment was designed to protect.

In another suit against *Soldier of Fortune*, called *Eimann v. Soldier of Fortune Magazine, Inc.*, however, the magazine prevailed. The son and mother of a murder victim in *Eimann* brought a wrongful death action under Texas law against *Soldier of Fortune* for publishing a personal service ad through which the victim's husband hired an assassin to kill her. The ad read: "EX-MARINES—67–69 'Nam Vets, Ex-DI, weapons specialist-jungle warfare, pilot, M.E., high-risk assignments, U.S. or overseas." The jury found for the plaintiffs and awarded them $1.9 million in compensatory damages and $7.5 million in punitive damages. Applying principles of Texas tort law, a federal appeals court reversed the jury's verdict, holding that to impose liability merely because the advertisement *could* reasonably be interpreted as an offer to engage in illegal activity would require a publisher to reject all ambiguous ads, a standard too burdensome on publishers.

Yet a third *Soldier of Fortune* case came from Georgia. In *Braun v. Soldier of Fortune Magazine, Inc.*, the court sustained a wrongful death suit against *Soldier of Fortune* arising from a more explicit "gun for hire" advertisement headlined "GUN FOR HIRE" by a self-described "professional mercenary" who promised discretion and privacy for body guard, courier, and other "special" jobs. The court in *Braun* held that the magazine could be held liable for running the ad, distinguishing the prior decision in *Eimann* by noting that in *Eimann* the ad was "facially innocuous," whereas in *Braun* the illegal conduct contemplated by the ad was apparent on its face.

Howard, John, and I booted this trilogy of *Soldier of Fortune* cases back and forth, debating how they fit into our suit. The key inquiry that emerged from them, we decided, was whether the illegal purpose of the advertisements at issue was apparent on the face of the ads. In *Braun* and *Norwood*, the illicit purpose of the speech was overt. In *Eimann*, however, the ad was more opaque. Applying the learning of these cases to our *Hit Man* suit, it seemed obvious that the how-to instruction in *Hit Man* fell more on the *Braun* and *Norwood* side of the line than the *Eimann* side. There was absolutely no ambiguity in the openly professed purpose of *Hit Man*, no ambiguity in its title, its preface, its beginning, middle, or end. Page by page, *Hit Man* was precisely what it says it was: a technical manual published for the independent contractor.

We knew that Tom Kelley and Lee Levine would attempt to diminish the importance of the *Soldier of Fortune* precedents. All of the cases involved advertising, a form of "commercial speech" that has historically received less protection under the First Amendment. But I didn't think commercial speech doctrines were what the cases were really about. If *Soldier of Fortune* had put the same information, including addresses and phone numbers, in a feature article it did on guns for hire, I was confident the decisions would have come out the same way, even though it wouldn't have involved advertising. *Soldier of Fortune* got nailed in *Braun* and *Norwood* because it was functioning as a middleman, putting the killer and the client together. *Hit Man* did much the same thing in reverse—instructing the killer how to find clients. Indeed, what Paladin did was worse than what *Soldier of Fortune* did. Not only did Paladin help assassins find clients, it trained the assassins on how to pull off the job.

14

Aiding and Abetting

Roger Reitzel's voice was so loud I had to hold the receiver a foot from my ear. " 'I don't want to sound critical of Professor Smolla, because he certainly has advanced the First Amendment ball significantly over the years, but the position he has advocated in this case is so extreme that it threatens to set us back light-years in the world of day-to-day First Amendment litigation.' So who is this scumbag Henry Hoberman?"

I laughed. Roger had seen a quote in a newspaper article entitled "Trading Places," sounding the increasingly familiar theme of Rod Smolla, double agent. This had become a popular motif, with headlines like the one in the Newport News *Daily Press:* " 'Turncoat' Walks Legal Balance Beam."

"He's a media lawyer. Like I *used* to be. From Baker and Hostetler, a Washington law firm. Hoberman and his partner Bruce Sanford, another big-shot media lawyer, are working with a coalition of media and journalism groups opposed to our suit. So basically, Roger, the deal is that I'll never work in this town again."

Roger laughed. "Well, hell, I tried to tell you."

"Right. You told me to *take* the case."

"So, are you getting reamed by everybody?"

"Not everybody. My mother is backing me."

• • •

I had known about the *Soldier of Fortune* cases when I was first approached by Howard and John to work with them on the *Hit Man* suit. But there was another line of decisions that proved to be enormously important that I had not known about. I'm sure we would have discovered them through the ordinary and often tedious processes of intensive legal research. But we were saved that toil by a tip we received from a lawyer in New York, who read about our suit in the *New York Times* and called us to give us some free help and advice.

The lawyer used to work for Consolidated Edison. It seems people are always coming up with ingenious ways to cheat the power company, such as rewiring their houses and short-circuiting power meters to steal electricity without paying for it. Apparently, somebody actually published some how-to guides on how to fleece the power company, which was sold in some kind of underground black market in New York. Consolidated Edison got wind of these pamphlets and asked its lawyers to do legal research into the question of whether it could hold the authors of the "how to steal electricity" guides legally liable. The lawyer who called us turned us on to a series of interesting cases.

"What do you think of them apples, Mr. Professor?" Howard asked. I could tell he was pumped up, always a perilous sign.

"Number one, I think these cases are great." I said. "Number two, I'm embarrassed and humbled. Here's this whole line of case law, central to all we're doing here, and I had no goddamn idea it even existed. If I was a doctor, it would be like finding out, after twenty years of practicing medicine, that there's an organ called a kidney."

"The suit is over, Rod. We just won!"

Well, I doubted that, but we sure as hell had been helped. For the first time we had our hands on precedent that seemed truly close to our own case. In *United States v. Barnett*, a federal court of appeals case from 1982 that came out of California, the criminal defendant, a guy named Barnett, was the publisher of an instruction manual on how to manufacture the illegal drug PCP, or "angel dust." Agents of the DEA caught a man named Hensley in the act of manufacturing PCP. Hensley was seated with the ingredients and a copy of Barnett's instruction manual open before him, which he was reading. Hensley obtained the defendant Barnett's instruction manual through an ad placed in the drug-culture magazine *High Times,* in which Barnett advertised a catalog of "available drug manufacture instructions." Hensley purchased the instruction manual for ten dollars and was using it at the time of his arrest. The publisher Barnett was prosecuted for aiding and abetting the manufacture of PCP and for using the mails to cause and facilitate the commission of the crime of attempted manufacture of PCP.

Like Paladin and Peder Lund, Barnett argued that the First Amendment insulated him from liability. The court in *Barnett* didn't buy it. All Barnett was doing, the court reasoned, was indulging in the simplistic logic that because the First Amendment protects speech, including the printed word, and Barnett's instruction manual used printed speech, it followed that the First Amendment protected Barnett's manual. The court called this a "specious syllogism" that "finds no support in the law," stating that the First Amendment "does not provide a defense to a criminal charge simply because the actor uses words to carry out his illegal purpose."

"What are they gonna say when you read the judge that quote?" Howard asked with a strutting bounce to his voice.

"Hammena, hammena, hammena," I replied.

The second case from our power company tipster was *United States v. Buttorff,* a 1978 federal court of appeals decision from Missouri. The *Buttorff* decision, it turned out, opened up for us a whole line of similar decisions from around the country, all involving the Internal Revenue Service and tax evasion. There is a cottage industry in the United States that exists for the purpose of putting out information on how to beat the IRS. Most of the tax advice is perfectly legal, involving such things as strategies on how to structure transactions to reduce tax liability, or the do's and don'ts for avoiding audits. There are also, however, a wide range of tax protest groups that put out literature and hold meetings on how to *illegally* beat the tax system. Sometimes these groups are engaged primarily in ideological propagandizing, arguing that the tax system is unconstitutional or contrary to Natural Law and should be resisted as a matter of civil disobedience. Sometimes, however, these groups go beyond that, actually training readers and listeners in the specific transactions that will, supposedly, allow one to break the law and avoid paying taxes without detection. The IRS, as one would expect, does not look kindly on these groups or their publications, and frequently prosecutes them for aiding and abetting income tax evasion. There were numerous federal cases involving such prosecutions. Sometimes the IRS won the cases, sometimes the tax protesters won. The common theme running through them was a distinction between abstract ideological advocacy and detailed illegal instruction. When the protestors had engaged in only ideological harangues against the tax system, urging others to resist and not pay taxes, the First Amendment protected their activity. When the protestors went beyond mere protest and into the realm of detailed training, they usually got convicted, and the First Amendment did not shelter them.

We did more research and uncovered several more helpful holdings. One case, *United States v. Mendelsohn*, was a prosecution against a publisher of a computer program used to instruct bookmakers on how to run an illegal gambling operation. The court sustained convictions for aiding and abetting illegal gambling, rejecting the defendants' First Amendment defense. We also found an interesting tax evasion case written by Supreme Court Justice Anthony Kennedy when he was still a federal court of appeals judge sitting in California. In that case, *United States v. Freeman*, Kennedy cited as precedent our two pet decisions, *Barnett* and *Buttorff*. Anthony Kennedy was prestigious, and a jurist with a reputation for valuing highly the protections of the First Amendment. If he approved of *Barnett* and *Buttorff*, that approval lent them extra weight and respect.

My favorite quotation, however, came from an opinion by Justice William O. Douglas. In modern times, Justice Douglas has been regarded, along with Justice Hugo Black, as among the few jurists who believe that the First Amendment is a virtual "absolute," that it permits no abridgement of freedom of speech of any kind. Yet in a well-known Supreme Court case, *Dennis v. United States*, Justice Douglas had made some observations that were highly encouraging to us. The case involved the prosecution of certain high-ranking officials of the American Communist Party for violating the Smith Act, a statute that made it a federal crime to "knowingly and willfully advocate and teach the duty and necessity of overthrowing and destroying the Government of the United States by force and violence."

The Supreme Court affirmed the convictions. I did not agree with the result, because I did not believe that the evidence in *Dennis* really supported the proposition that these Communists posed any genuine threat to our security. The Communists were persecuted for their beliefs, and for their propaganda, I thought, and the *Dennis* decision was a setback for the protection of civil liberties in this country. Justice Douglas dissented in *Dennis*, arguing eloquently that the defendants had been convicted for doing no more than teaching Marxist-Leninist doctrines. But Justice Douglas opened his dissent with this caution: "If this were a case where those who claimed protection under the First Amendment were teaching the techniques of sabotage, the assassination of the President, the filching of documents from public files, the planting of bombs, the art of street warfare, and the like," he wrote, "I would have no doubts. The freedom to speak is not absolute; the teaching of methods of terror and other seditious conduct should be beyond the pale. . . ."

John Marshall read the Douglas quote out loud at one of our strategy meetings. He read it well, with perfect emphasis. We all sat silently as he finished.

Presently, John said: "Techniques of sabotage, assassination, filching documents, planting bombs, the art of street warfare. William O. Douglas is describing Paladin Press."

15

"We Shook the World"

I was asleep when Howard's early morning call came. John had counseled me to get used to Howard calling while I was still in bed, just as John had gotten used to Howard showing up on his doorstep at 6:30 in the morning proclaiming that he'd unlocked the key to the universe.

"We shook the world!!" Howard boomed.

"Yes we did!" I counterboomed, rubbing my bleary eyes to clear the fuzz. "What the hell are you talking about?"

"Read the *Washington Post. We shook the world!* Call me back."

I traipsed to the street and retrieved the paper. The *Post*, in its editorial column, had described our suit, and then endorsed our position! The editorial writer recited some of the worst passages from *Hit Man*, as well as our allegations that the publishers had known and intended that it would be used to kill people. If we could prove what we had alleged, the *Post* asserted, the First Amendment should not protect Paladin, and we deserved to win. I wouldn't have said we shook the world exactly—it was one editorial in one newspaper—but it *was* the *Washington Post*, after all, patron of freedom of speech and press—and it was a needed shot of endorsement at a moment when the raucous bandwagon chorus was still loudly against us.

Over the next several weeks, as commentators and pundits and talk-show hosts began to process our arguments more fully, getting past the initial instinct that "in this country you just can't sue a book," the public discussion became much more balanced. Writing for the *American Lawyer,* the distinguished legal commentator Stuart Taylor, Jr., wrote, "I like my freedom of speech as well as the next fellow, but I'm with Smolla on this one. . . . A murder manual intentionally marketed to would-be contract killers (along with assorted fantasists and others) doesn't strike me as the kind of 'freedom of speech' that the framers sought to protect."

I was starting to think that maybe we really did have a chance.

• • •

Amiable adversaries at the beginning of the case, Howard and Lee Levine liked to kibitz, each believing he was gaining advantage by getting into the mind of the other. One day soon after our suit was filed, Howard and John called me after a long telephone conversation with Lee. "We got a surprise for you, my friend," said Howard. "It looks like you're going to be up to the plate a little earlier than we thought. They want to try the First Amendment question first, before any trial. That means you're going to be arguing this case at the front-end, not the back."

In putting our legal team together, it had always been assumed that my principal role would come at the end of the case, after the jury trial, when we were defending the jury verdict that we hoped to win. Howard and John were to play the lead role in the jury trial. Tom Heeney would serve as all-purpose backup. I would help with the trial, but take a back seat. I was the appeals man.

But what Tom Kelley and Lee Levine proposed to do was to reverse this process—essentially to put the appeal before the trial. The idea was for the two sides to agree to a formal Joint Statement of Facts, a document that would "stipulate" the facts for the court. Paladin Press would then file a Motion for Summary Judgment, addressing only the First Amendment issues. Kelley and Levine would claim that even if all the facts stipulated in the Joint Statement of Facts were true, they were still entitled to win the case outright, without a jury trial, because under those facts the First Amendment insulated Paladin from liability.

If we proceeded with this plan, it would be my job to argue the case for our side, first to the district judge to whom it had been assigned, Judge Alexander Williams of the U.S. District Court for the District of Maryland, and then to the appellate court, the U.S. Court of Appeals for the Fourth Circuit, located in Richmond.

"So what do you think?" Howard and John asked me.

"I've got two questions," I said. "First, is this a Trojan horse? Have they got some trick up their sleeve? Something we can't yet see? And second, do you have enough confidence in me to let this whole case rest on my shoulders on the front-end? If I lose in front of Judge Williams, or more important, at the Fourth Circuit, the whole show is over. Can you handle that?"

"We can absolutely handle having you argue the case," said John. "That's why we got you into this. It's just coming sooner rather than later. But I'm wondering about the Trojan horse."

"Why would they do this?" I asked. "What's in it for them?"

"I'm with ya," said John. "Why not drag us through discovery and trial for the next two years, make us spend hundreds of thousands of dollars, take their chances with a jury, and *then* appeal?"

"Because they know they're going to get hammered with a thirty-million-dollar verdict in front of jury, and that scares the hell out of them," offered Howard. "If they can get the case chucked early, why not?"

"And there's the 'First Amendment lawyer' mentality to factor in," I said. "There's this constitutional conceit you sometimes sense within the First Amendment in-crowd, a holy certitude that suits against magazines, newspapers, and publishers are always wrong, and in the end are usually doomed. First Amendment zealots start believing so much in the First Amendment that they can start to imbue it with an aura of invincibility."

"Tom and Lee *do* think they're invincible," Howard agreed. "I can tell that from talking to Lee."

"I think they may have this sense of obligation, almost, to get the First Amendment issue tried first, because in their minds there is just no way that, ultimately, they will lose this case," I elaborated. "If the First Amendment entitles them to victory, then it entitles them to victory early. It's almost a religious creed. That's how they think. We're just a motley ramshackle group of publicity-seekers who have filed a frivolous nuisance suit. They figure they are certain to win this case in front of an appellate court. So from their perspective, they have everything to gain by getting the First Amendment issue resolved up front. It saves their client a lot of money and makes them look like free speech heroes."

"I'll tell you this, Rod," Howard agreed, "you're right about one thing. Lee and Tom absolutely believe, with every fiber of their being, that they are right and you are wrong. You, personally, Rod Smolla, are wrong. They want to knock this case out. They want to knock you out."

"Yup," I said. "In the first round."

"To get this motion for Summary Judgment, they're going to have to concede in the Joint Statement of Facts all the main allegations in our complaint," John observed. "As long as we are intelligent in negotiating the wording of the statement, I don't see how they can sneak in a Trojan horse."

"Then let's get it on," said Howard.

16

Music from the Ten Commandments

W e set about negotiating the Joint Statement of Facts. What we wanted was an acknowledgment that Paladin published its books *Hit Man* and *Silencers* with the knowledge and intent that real criminals would use the books to kill people, and that James Perry had used these books to murder Trevor, Millie, and Janice. We would accept nothing less. What Tom Kelley and Lee Levine wanted was an acknowledgment that these books were also sold to people who would *not* commit crimes.

After a surprisingly swift week of negotiation, a statement was agreed upon. Each side got what it wanted, and thought it needed. The statement would become the single most important document in the case. Paladin conceded in the statement that it had "engaged in a marketing strategy intended to attract and assist criminals and would-be criminals who desire information and instructions on how to commit crimes," and that "in publishing, marketing, advertising and distributing *Hit Man* and *Silencers*, defendants intended and had knowledge that their publications would be used, upon receipt, by criminals and would-be criminals to plan and execute the crime of murder for hire, in the manner set forth in the publications." Paladin also conceded that "in publishing, distributing and selling *Hit Man* and *Silencers* to Perry, defendants assisted him in the subsequent per- petration of the murders."

In turn, we conceded that Paladin's "marketing strategy was and is intended to maximize sales of its publications to the public, including sales to (i) authors who desire information for the purpose of writing books about crime and criminals, (ii) law enforcement officers and agencies who desire information concerning the means and methods of committing crimes, (iii) persons who enjoy reading accounts of crimes and the means of committing them for purposes of entertainment, (iv) persons who fantasize about committing crimes but do not thereafter commit them, and (v) criminologists and others who study criminal methods and mentality."

"You can't always get what you wa-ant. But if you try sometimes, you just might find, you get what you need!" I'd always agreed with Mick Jagger, and I thought we'd gotten what we needed. The statement, in my view, faithfully captured the essence of the underlying reality in the suit. There was no doubt in my mind that Paladin did indeed knowingly and intentionally publish *Hit Man* to assist people in committing murder. To me, that was apparent on the face of the *Hit Man* book itself, and the Joint Statement merely confirmed it. I also accepted it as entirely plausible that Paladin sold the book to a lot of others who were not going to actually use it for a crime.

I believe that when this statement was agreed to, each side thought it had won the case. Paladin thought that once we conceded that some noncriminals had read the book, it was home free. We thought that once Paladin conceded that it had intentionally assisted in murder, it had forfeited whatever First Amendment protection it might have had.

"They stipulated in their bed," I said to Howard, "and now they must lie in it."

• • •

Paladin's insurance company originally took the position that it had no responsibility to insure or defend Paladin against our suit because the kind of intentional act of aiding and abetting murder that we had alleged was not covered by Paladin's insurance policy. Paladin actually had to sue its own insurance company to get it to agree to assume coverage. In a settlement agreement that resulted from that suit, the insurance company reserved the right to insist in the future that it would not have to pay any monetary judgment we might ultimately obtain against Paladin, but agreed in the interim to foot the bill for all of Paladin's attorney's fees.

From our perspective, this was a gloomy development. It seemed to guarantee that Peder Lund and Paladin would be able to draw on unlimited legal resources in fighting us. At the same time, if we were ever to actually win a damages award from a jury, it was questionable whether there would be any insurance proceeds to help cover it.

Paladin filed its brief first. Its submissions to Judge Williams were as remarkable for their physical heft as for their jurisprudence. Paladin's brief was accompanied by two handsome volumes of bound exhibits, meticulously indexed, cross-referenced, and labeled with color-coded tabs, including compilations of news clippings, literary references, and scenes from famous movies. *Hit Man*, Paladin maintained, was really was no different from thousands of other informational and artistic offerings in modern culture, and indeed in culture dating back hundreds of years. I could see in the brief the mountainous research and painstaking handiwork of Steve Zansberg and Seth Berlin, the lawyers who were supporting Lee Levine and Tom Kelley. I wasn't convinced, but I had to admire the elegance of the effort. Lee Levine's and Tom Kelley's law firms were laying on the premium presentation. And I was sure Paladin's insurance company was paying premium prices.

Howard was less admiring. He sent John and me a fax so angry I imagined my fax machine giving off explosion sound effects as my copy came sizzling over the wires. A full-blown Howard was exploding into the apocalyptic cybernight, composed in capped and bold profanity. Howard was proposing that we file a motion with Judge Williams to strike Paladin's handsome appendix. In the midst of his

17

Friends of the Court

At the same time that Paladin filed its briefs with Judge Williams, a consortium of various news organizations and First Amendment groups, represented by Bruce Sanford of Baker & Hostetler, filed a motion with the judge asking permission to submit an amicus curiae (Latin for "friend of the court") brief on behalf of Paladin. Such briefs are typically filed by public interest groups, government agencies, trade associations, political action committees, and other "special interest" organizations in high-profile cases that pose significant issues of law and public policy. The briefs serve a number of functions. Often, the special interest group will be able to offer the court factual information or policy perspectives that draw on its unique expertise and experience. From the perspective of the lawyers involved in a case, getting others to participate in supportive amicus briefs also increases the total amount of legal argument that can be set before a court. We were limited, for example, to fifty pages in our main brief, but if we could get amici on our side, additional and more elaborate arguments, taking more pages, could be brought to the court's attention. And finally, on a crass level, amicus briefs are a form of judicial lobbying that simply register with a court the vote of a particular group. If the organization or government agency that files the brief is prestigious or influential, the very endorsement of the group may carry some modest weight with a judge.

Amicus briefs have become commonplace in high-profile cases at the appellate court level. But they are relatively rare at the trial court stage. Bruce Sanford filed his motion asking for permission to file his amicus brief, and simultaneously filed a copy of the brief itself. Howard called me when Sanford filed his motion and accompanying brief, incredulous at Sanford's gall. "Is this *done*," he asked me. "You file your brief *before* the judge even grants you your permission?"

I explained that this is a common practice before appellate courts but that I hadn't seen it at the trial level. "People don't usually challenge the filing of amicus briefs," I said.

"Look," he said, "I don't give a rat's ass if that's the way the First Amendment gentlemen play the game. I think Judge Williams will see it the way I do. Chances are he's never even *seen* an amicus brief before in the short time he's been on the bench. He'll recoil at the pretentiousness of it all." This was Howard at his best. He'd been restless with the idea that there was this special set of clubby rules that the silk-stocking First Amendment guys played by, and had been chomping at the opportunity to say "Not in my case."

I agreed with him. "I suppose Judge Williams will grant the motion and accept the Sanford brief," I said, "but let's oppose it anyhow. I'm used to being very humble and respectful in front of trial judges, at least at the beginning, before you develop a rapport. If I were Bruce, I would have asked for permission first, and only filed the brief *after* it was granted."

• • •

"In *United States v. O'Brien*," I lectured to the class, "the Supreme Court held that the federal government could send a young man to jail for burning his draft card in protest against the Vietnam War. Yet we've already seen, in *Texas v. Johnson*, that the Supreme Court says that the First Amendment protects the right to burn the American flag. *I don't get it.* You can burn the flag, but you can't burn a draft card. Sheldon, I see you are in uniform today." William and Mary is close to many military installations, and I had several service persons in my class. Sheldon, a navy lieutenant, was a delightful student. "Sheldon, you can burn the flag but not a draft card. How can this be?"

"You're asking one of your trick questions," he answered, grinning. His wire-bristle hair was cut as flat as the top of the carrier on which he worked.

"When you're right, you're right, Sheldon. Can't fool you. So what's my trick?"

"The issue is not what is being burned. The issue is why the government seeks to prevent you from burning it. If I burn the flag, I cannot be prosecuted for flag desecration, because that would be censorship. The government would be penalizing me because it does not like what I am expressing through my action of flag-burning. But let's say I take the flag, and bring it inside a building, and now I light it up, in violation of the fire code. Now I imagine that I am prosecuted not for flag-desecration but simply for lighting a fire in a place where fires are prohibited. The First Amendment would not protect me because now the government's purpose would be unrelated to censorship. It would simply be fire prevention."

This was a superb start. I wanted to see if Sheldon could follow through. "But I still don't see why the government should be permitted to send somebody to jail for draft-card burning. I once had a draft card myself. And I was very much opposed to the Vietnam War." This had the students' attention. I never burned my card—though I did alter my driver's license once. But let's say I *had* burned it. Let's imagine that I was right there, standing with Paul O'Brien on the courthouse steps in South Boston, burning away. Wasn't it obvious that the reason O'Brien burned his draft card on the courthouse steps in South Boston was to protest the war in Vietnam?"

"It isn't O'Brien's reasons that matter," Sheldon responded. "It's the government's reasons. The government did not want guys burning their draft cards, because destroying a draft card would tend to obstruct the administration of the draft. Like Oliver Wendell Holmes said, the First Amendment does not give a person the right to shout 'Fire!' in a crowded theater."

"Actually, you *can* shout 'Fire' in a crowded theater, if there is one," I pointed out. "Which reminds me of a story about a friend of mine, a famous First Amendment lawyer named Richard Schmidt. Even as a kid, he once told me, he knew he would grow up to be a radical defender of freedom of speech, because as a young boy he loved to go into fire stations and scream *'Theater!'*"

• • •

Judge Williams set the date for oral argument on Paladin's Motion for Summary Judgment, and displaying his moxie and independence, refused to grant Bruce Sanford permission to file his amicus brief, unceremoniously striking the brief from the record. Howard was tickled, bubbling fits and giggles. "How much do you think old Bruce charged his clients for the brief that never got read!" Howard cackled, his eyes glazed in watery joy. "Judge Williams is sending the First Amendment boys a message. He's not going to be pushed around!"

"Maybe," I was more circumspect. "I suspect Bruce is embarrassed. On the other hand, whichever side wins in front of Judge Williams, there will eventually be an appeal. Bruce will have his amicus brief ready in reserve. And already paid for."

18

The Battle of Williamsburg

Howard, John, and I met in Williamsburg to dissect the brief Kelley, Levine, Berlin, and Zansberg had filed and to begin to construct our own response. I told Howard and John that I thought the other side had done an excellent job, and that we would really have to roll up our sleeves and concentrate to counter their arguments.

Howard and John were flabbergasted. They thought Paladin's brief was utter crap, and they were stunned that I would give it a favorable review. Howard was furious with me. "Your problem is that you still think like them. You have been with the First Amendment crowd so long, you can't shake their worldview. I don't think any objective person would see this brief of theirs as anything but total crap."

"But well-written crap," I said. "Look, I'm not saying they deserve to win. I'm not saying I buy their arguments. I'm just saying that to Judge Williams, this is going to read like a very well-researched, very persuasive brief. We can't just waltz in with a response filled with rhetoric and bombast and think it's going to bowl the judge over. The First Amendment is like magic with judges. They get hypnotized by it. If Judge Williams thinks this is a replay of *Jerry Falwell v. Larry Flynt*, if he thinks this is a suit persecuting Paladin because of its bad taste and unsavory views, we're screwed. All I'm saying is that they've done a good job of creating that impression."

We argued for the rest of the morning, and then got down to business. It was agreed that I would write the first draft of our brief, and that Howard and John and I would then tear it apart together, line by line, until we were satisfied with its content. It was a healthy process, and in the end we were all happy with our brief.

We pointed out to Judge Williams that Paladin spent a large part of its brief attacking its own book, trying to make light of *Hit Man* by dismissing it as whimsical and fictional. We countered by reminding the judge of the grave facts and macabre realities. Three innocent people were slaughtered. Paladin could not now disown the deadly seriousness of its own publication, dismissing it as braggadocio, fantasy, or fiction. The book explained how to locate, interview, and deal with clients, including suggestions on what to charge, stating that "Prices vary according to the risk involved, social or political prominence of the victim, difficulty of the assignment, and other factors. A federal judge recently brought a price of $250,000, for example. A county sheriff might bring $75,000 to $100,000."

In its brief, Paladin lampooned its own book and the assassin James Perry as if they were the gang that couldn't shoot straight. But that book and these murders were no joke. *Hit Man* was not some isotope, some tragicomic metaphor, it was the real thing, a murder manual marketed to murderers.

Paladin also made much of the fact that Perry did not follow all of the instructions in the book. Well, of course, we said, he didn't follow *all* of them—but tragically, he followed enough. Paladin's argument, in fact, had a perverse ring. The publishers of an instruction book on how to commit murder were now seeking absolution because the murderer who bought the book and followed the instructions failed to follow them properly, as if, somehow, for *that* reason the publisher should be free of responsibility. It was as if Paladin was arguing that had Perry only done a better job, neither he nor Paladin would have been caught. Indeed, this seemed to be the chill explanation of *Hit Man* itself, which stated that if the "advice and proven methods in this book are followed, certainly no one will ever know."

Paladin relied heavily on a federal case from Georgia, *High Ol' Times v. Busbee*, in which the court held that a Georgia "head shop" law, which made it illegal to publish information regarding illegal drug use, was unconstitutional. We countered by stating that *Busbee* was not a case in which the publisher had the same kind of deliberate intent as Paladin, and that the precedential authority of *Busbee* had been undermined by a later Supreme Court opinion that had sustained a "head shop" from Illinois.

Throughout the process of writing the brief, the *Brandenburg* case continued to haunt me. I went back and read the case again. After the famous sentence emphasizing the requirement that the speech "must be directed to inciting or producing imminent lawless action," the Court had quoted from an older case, *Noto v. United States*, a 1961 decision that had drawn a distinction between "the mere abstract teaching" of the "moral propriety or even the moral necessity for a resort to force and violence" and "preparing a group for violent action and steeling it to such action." If in *Brandenburg* itself the record had demonstrated that the leaders of the Ku Klux Klan rally did more than burn crosses and spout racist venom, but actually distributed material such as maps, diagrams, chemical formulas for bombs, travel arrangements, instruction on weapons selection, and specific killing techniques, surely that would have crossed the line from mere abstract advocacy to specific training and preparation. If, following those instructions, Klan members went out and committed murder, using the techniques distributed at the rally, and had later stupidly stipulated that in distributing their material, they *knew and intended* that the information would be used to kill, it was inconceivable to me that the Supreme Court would have reversed the convictions. To the contrary, the Court would surely have cited holdings such as *Noto*, and sent the Klan members traipsing to the penitentiary. This was our ticket. We needed to emphasis that *Hit Man* was not abstract teaching but was about preparation and steeling.

We also decided to include some general social policy arguments in our brief. As between the innocent plaintiffs who were ruthlessly murdered by an assassin following the defendants' instructions, and the nihilistic publishers who aided and abetted their murder through the dissemination of their murderous instructions, we argued, certainly it was the cold-blooded publisher, and not the innocent victims, who should bear the loss. This was a tort case, we wanted to remind the judge, and the body of First Amendment law most closely analogous to it was the law emanating from *New York Times Company v. Sullivan*, in which the Supreme Court held that in order for a public official to prevail in a libel suit arising from allegedly defamatory statements on issues germane to the public official's performance in or fitness for office, the plaintiff must prove that the defendant published the material with knowledge of falsity or reckless disregard for truth or falsity.

Paladin, we argued, admitted to fault exactly equivalent to that required by the *New York Times*. If the First Amendment permits defendants guilty of knowing or reckless misconduct to be held liable in tort for millions of dollars in damages when their publications cause injury to reputation and hurt feelings, then of course the First Amendment must permit parallel liability in tort when publications cause physical injury and death.

• • •

For several years I had been meeting once a month with three friends at something we called "the luncheon group." The friends were Bishop Walter Sullivan, the Catholic bishop for the Archdiocese of Virginia; Monsignor Charles Kelly, a priest who was the Catholic student chaplain at William and Mary and the bishop's close friend and confidant; and Professor James Bill, the director of the Reeves Center for International Studies at William and Mary and a renowned expert on foreign policy and the Middle East, particularly Iran. Walter, Charlie, Jim, and I would gather one afternoon each month for a couple hours of escape and camaraderie. We talked politics, philosophy, religion, and church policy; we gossiped about everyone from the president to the pope; we unwound, confided, and imbibed in simple friendship. I treasured these lunches. All three of my friends were remarkable people. Walter was one of the country's most liberal Catholic bishops. He was a humane, pastoral, compassionate, unpretentious man who had many times gone out on limbs to defend the role of women in the church and to reach out to gays and lesbians, letting them know that they were part of God's family and welcome in his church. Charlie was one of the Church's most respected intellectuals; he had directed the North American Seminary in Rome for years and was an inspiring preacher who drew huge student crowds for his masses. And Jim was one of my best friends. A passionate firebrand who often angered the State Department for speaking out to lambast American foreign policy in the Middle East, Jim was one of the few top-tier American foreign policy scholars to advocate closer relations with Iran and to urge American officials to see disputes in Iran with a greater understanding of Arabic traditions and culture. Jim had been diagnosed a few years before with Parkinson's disease, and one of the things the lunch group would often talk about was how Jim was coping with his illness, and the importance of trying to live a quality life and taking time for family and friends.

Arguments over the law often filtered into our conversations. I'd taken on a lawyer for the Catholic Cathedral in Richmond at which Walter and Charlie presided, helping to represent a consortium of Richmond churches that wanted to feed homeless persons on Sundays but were prevented from doing so because of a Richmond City zoning ordinance. But they were usually more interested in talking about *Hit Man*. The lawsuit became a frequent topic for our discussions. All three men were strong believers in civil liberties. But they were squarely with me on the *Hit Man* case. For them there was simply no plausible argument that the First Amendment's guarantee of freedom of speech encompassed the right to publish a murder manual. "Freedom of speech is fine and dandy," said the bishop, "but whatever happened to a sense of the or unsound—and 'repression' of political liberty lurking in every state regulation of commercial exploitation of human interest in sex." Much the same could be said of *Hit Man*. There was no harsh hand of censorship lurking in regulation of commercial exploitation in the market for training paid assassins. We decided to include a short section on obscenity in our brief.

19

Pieces of Silver

We finished our briefs and filed them with the court. There was nothing to do but sit back and wait for the oral argument in the case, scheduled for the third week of July. This lull had an unnerving effect on Howard. Fits of impish tweak repeatedly bubbled up and burst out of him in a constant flow of restless provocation. One of his most wondrous jewels was a fax to our opponents containing color-commentary on recent events. In it he described himself as the Dennis Rodman of the First Amendment, and bragged about having administered "an involuntary high colonic to Bruce (who is totally out of juice) Sanford and the boys at Baker & Hoffberg." His letter contained a multiple-choice question, asking "Which of the following will be of importance to the ultimate outcome of your pending motion? (a) Brandenburg (b) Zansberg (c) Kronenberg (d) The Hindenberg." Litigation life with Howard was like having Muhammad Ali in his brash years as your partner. Howard was walking narcissistic fibrosis, the textbook case of shirt-won't-fit-over-the-head disease. *The man is absolutely crazy*, I thought. *Bruce (who is totally out of juice) Sanford and the boys at Baker & Hoffberg? And Brandenburg, Zansberg, Kronenberg, the Hindenberg?* My law partner was Robin Williams on speed. I couldn't imagine myself writing a taunting letter to my opponent commenting on a brief. Howard did it every day, his mind racing at the speed of light, not bothering to run his ravings past me or John, or, God forbid, the straight-shooting Tom Heeney, tripping out like a spaced-out acid-head high on word puns without the slightest apparent concern over what impact his mad epistles might have, or even the slightest thought as to why he was launching these projectiles other than to amuse himself.

The problem was I couldn't get mad at him. He was having too much fun. Hell, *I* was having too much fun. No one had forced me into this cockpit. I just prayed the son of a bitch wouldn't get us all disbarred.

• • •

Our family vacationed that summer in Italy, staying in Barbarino, a tiny walled village in Tuscany, about thirty miles south of Florence, near Siena. In June, a few days before I was scheduled to present my *Hit Man* argument, I returned to the United States with my children, Erin and Corey. Exhausted from our flights as we drove out of Dulles Airport, we decided to check into a hotel near Tysons Corner rather than attempt to survive the three-hour drive south to Williamsburg. Famished, we ordered room service, took showers, and settled down to bed. Corey fell asleep the moment her head hit the pillow. Erin and I turned on the television. It was the opening ceremony of the summer Olympics in Atlanta. This was Erin's first real awareness of the Olympics. She was mesmerized by the spectacle. We sat up and snuggled together for three hours, watching the ceremony through sleepy eyes. I began to cry when Muhammad Ali lit the Olympic torch. I tried to explain to Erin who Ali was and why he was one of my heroes. It was yet another bond between Erin and me. She became totally absorbed in the Olympics over the next few weeks, and we watched endless hours of coverage together, making our own charts and graphs and posters of favorite events and athletes.

And then the killing bomb exploded in Centennial Park outside the Olympic Village. Erin wanted to know who the people were that planted such bombs, and why they did it, and how they learned how to put the bombs together, and what could be done to stop them.

• • •

I sat quietly at the plaintiff's attorney's table, gazing at the empty courtroom bench in the Federal District Courthouse in Greenbelt, Maryland. A federal marshal was posted sentry at the door to the judge's chambers. Lawyers, like athletes, handle the final few moments before a match is to begin in many different ways. Some work themselves into an adrenaline frenzy, psyching up, pumping up. But I get quiet and reflective, almost serene. That day I wasn't going over my opening lines or rehearsing my points—if I didn't know my case by now, I figured, I never would. I was focused and determined, staring at the vacant high-backed leather chair on which Judge Williams would soon be seated, and from which he would determine who won the first crucial round in our battle with Paladin Press.

I felt a gentle tap on my shoulder. It was Tom Kelley. "Rod, I'd like to introduce you to my client," he said nervously. Tom has a quiet demeanor and a somewhat mumbling voice, and I had to strain to hear him. I got up and walked across the center aisle with Tom to the defense table. Peder Lund, the proud and unrepentant publisher of Paladin Press, rose to greet me, puffing his chest as he extended his hand. "Professor Smolla," he said, his voice quavering with intensity. "I've heard a lot about you. I just want to know how many pieces of silver they paid you to take this case!"

The line was not well-delivered. It had the quality of being over-rehearsed, yet in a voice shaking so badly Lund could barely spit out his words. I shot Tom a look that said, *So this is why you brought me over here?* And then, not missing a beat, I smiled at Lund without uttering a word, dismissed his juvenile jibe with wave of my hand, and walked back to our side of the courtroom.

If Peder Lund thought he was clever at playing mind games, trying to disrupt my concentration moments before the hearing, his tactic backfired, for it was Tom Kelley who seemed chagrined and off-balance. Tom followed me back to my seat and whispered, "Rod, I'm sorry."

"Forget about it, Tom," I said. "It's nothing." And it was nothing. Lawyers can't always control what their clients do or say, anymore than they can always trust that their own clients are being straight with them. Yet while Kelley might have been upset at the amateurish timing of Peder Lund's remark, I suspect he more or less agreed with its substance. But I was well past that now.

I focused on what I knew of Judge Williams. He was brand spanking new to the federal bench, having only been recently appointed by President Clinton. Williams, an African American, had been a county prosecutor for many years before getting his judgeship. He had a reputation for being affable, charismatic, considerate, and eminently fair. He was supposed to be a commonsense and pragmatic sort of judge, not particularly interested in high theory or academic arguments.

The chambers door opened, and Judge Williams entered the courtroom, to the bailiff's cry of "God Save the United States and this Honorable Court!"

Kelley rose to speak first. He argued that *Hit Man* had plenty of redeeming value, saying that people who read it were as likely to be persuaded *not* to enter the profession of paid assassin as they were likely to be persuaded to become assassins. He claimed that there was no principled way to distinguish *Hit Man* from novels, movies, and television programs containing details about crime. Perhaps most important, he argued that contrary to all we had been saying, Paladin did not actually intend that its book be used by people to commit murder. Paladin merely knew that it was *possible* that a person would follow the techniques described and kill someone. But that was true of countless other novelists, crime writers, and moviemakers. Paladin's statement that it "intended and had knowledge" that its book would be used by murders, Kelley claimed, was really just "knowledge" that its book might be used by them, and only in that sense did they "intend" for it to be used. Finally, Kelley sounded his "the book is really just a big joke" theme. He recounted some of *Hit Man*'s dumber bits of advice and even tried to use the cover of *Hit Man*, with its ugly bright purple backdrop and cartoonlike caricature of a hit man in a yellowish suit, to make the point that no one could take the book seriously.

Kelley paraded through all of his points. Judge Williams interrupted a couple times to ask questions, but for the most part sat silently and listened. I'd seen Kelley speak before several times, and had always thought him very effective. Yet overall, to me, he seemed off as he presented his argument to Judge Williams. It was a workmanlike performance in which he made all the intellectual points he needed to make, efficiently and competently, but there was no spark, no passion to his presentation. He seemed to lack energy, to be a bit rambling and off-key.

"I can do better than that," I said to myself when it was my turn to approach the podium. It wasn't a thought born of vanity or mean-ego, but aspiration. My clients were sitting behind me. Howard and John and Tom Heeney were with me at the counsel table. Everyone was depending on me. And I didn't want to let them down.

And if energy levels counted for anything in court, I wouldn't have. I started the argument at a high-intensity pitch, and for thirty minutes, never let down. This was not a case, I told Judge Williams, in which we sought to engage in censorship. We were not inviting a jury to punish Paladin and Peder Lund because their book was revolting, disgusting, or morally repugnant. This suit was not about taking sides in the marketplace of ideas; indeed, it is not about ideas at all. This suit was about recompense for physical injury and death. Paladin, I told Judge Williams, was perfectly free to publish *Hit Man*. But it was not free to escape compensation for the catastrophic injury it helped cause.

I took umbrage at Kelley's argument that Paladin had not really intended that people would use *Hit Man* to commit murder, an effort that I dismissed as wholly disingenuous. Paladin had stipulated that it "intended and had knowledge that their publications would be used, upon receipt, by criminals and would-be criminals to plan and execute the crime of murder for hire." How could Tom Kelley now get up and attempt to engage in "spin control" over that stipulation? Paladin had used two terms, "intended" and "knowledge." The two words did not mean the same thing. This was a Motion for Summary Judgment, I reminded Judge Williams, and we, the parties trying to take our case to a jury, were entitled to all inferences in our favor. If there was any doubt in the judge's mind as to the meaning of Paladin's professed "intent," we were the ones entitled to the benefit of that doubt. I pounded on the many precedents we had cited in our brief, particularly cases in which people had been prosecuted for assisting in crimes. "But those are not tort cases, those are criminal law cases, aren't they, Mr. Smolla?" Judge Williams interjected.

I acknowledged that the judge was correct but insisted that it made no difference, arguing that the same First Amendment principles would apply to both criminal and tort cases. If it is permissible to send someone to prison for providing information that aids and abets crimes, it is certainly permissible to hold someone civilly liable in tort for the same type of conduct. I also gave Judge Williams a hypothetical problem. Imagine, I said, that someone called Paladin Press's sales office and was actually dumb enough to say to the sales operator, "I want to go into the business of murder for hire. I have a client who is interested. I have the courage, the motivation. But I need some additional technical know-how, some coaching. Have you got anything in your catalog that will help me?" And imagine, I said to Judge Williams, that the Paladin operator goes through the catalog, saying, "Well, let's see what we've got, ummm, bomb-building, how to dispose of dead bodies, let's see—oh, here we go, *Hit Man: A Technical Manual for Independent Contractors*." And the caller says, "Perfect, just what I need!" And Paladin sends the caller the book. Now imagine the FBI has caught the whole phone call on tape. If the caller goes out and follows the instructions in the book and kills somebody, is there any doubt, in those circumstances, I asked Judge Williams, that Paladin would be liable for aiding and abetting murder? None. It's an easy case. I argued to Judge Williams that there was no moral and legal difference between what I had just posed in that hypothetical and what Paladin Press had admitted to in the suit. Paladin knows and intends, I explained, that some of its callers are ordering *Hit Man* for the same reason as my hypothetical caller: to use the book to plan and carry out murder for hire. Paladin just doesn't know which *particular* order happens to match with real murderers. It knows some of the checks it is cashing are from murderers using the book to kill. It just can't separate the checks that come from killers and those that come from fantasizers. But that inability to match check to killer surely makes no moral difference. And it should make no legal difference either.

I thought the argument before Judge Williams had gone well enough. But that bubble was burst when the judge decided to give us his preliminary reflections before leaving the bench. He began by paying almost gushing compliments to both Tom Kelley and to me for our arguments. The briefs and arguments had been exceptionally thoughtful, he said, and had helped him considerably with this very difficult case. But the more he talked, the more it became obvious that he had already made up his mind.

"Mr. Smolla," Judge Williams said, "I have read this book *Hit Man*, and I find it disgusting and reprehensible, but the First Amendment protects many things that we find revolting, and I don't see how your lawsuit can proceed in light of the First Amendment."

•　•　•

Howard, John, and I gathered afterward with the family members at a hotel restaurant. Elaine, Marilyn, and Gloria were especially sweet to me. But their gracious congratulations could not mask the deep despondency all of us felt. Although I knew Howard was seething inside, he did a remarkable job of counseling our clients. An aspect of Howard I had not before seen emerged, an ability to touch and console people on a very human level. "Don't worry about it," he told the families. "We are in a long war. This is just one battle. There will be many more. We may lose this round. If we do, we will appeal. We did the right thing to file this suit. You did the right thing. No one can guarantee results. No one ever knows for sure how a jury or a judge will rule. But I still believe, and John and Rod believe, that we are right in this case, and that we deserve to win."

No one was much in the mood for food, and I had a long drive back home to Erin and Corey. I hugged Elaine, Marilyn, and Gloria as we left. They were teary-eyed. "I know this is terrible for all of you," I said. "Having to dredge up all these facts, and relive all of this horror yet again. John and Howard and I are going to do absolutely everything we possibly can to win this case. I just want you to know that it is an honor to represent you."

20

You Are Cordially Invited to

Watch Us Eat Crow

The cycle of life continued. Fall arrived in Williamsburg. The Williamsburg Montessori School began its year in a freshly remodeled facility, opening a new classroom for elementary school students. With other parents, I had worked long hours during the week before the new school's opening day, helping to paint bookshelves and assemble playground equipment. I was bursting with pride when Erin walked in and saw her splendid new classroom for the first time.

Law school classes were also beginning. I was teaching a heavy course load, with classes in "Constitutional Law," "First Amendment Law," "Law and Religion," "Mass Media Law," and "Civil Rights Litigation." As always, I found my students endearing, sometimes razor-sharp and sometimes hopefully lost, occasionally crabby, but usually enthusiastic and amiable, at times cynical, but often filled with dreams and the promise of American life.

If it was fall by the academic calendar, the climate was still summer. The cool changes of autumn had yet to arrive, and we were still crackling in heavy August heat. It was August 30, and I was driving in that heat, sweating because the air conditioner on my Jeep Cherokee had gone on the blink, when the call from Howard came on my cell phone.

"We lost," Howard said, with no preliminaries. "I just got the opinion. It's about thirty pages long."

"How bad?" I asked.

"I want you to read it first, before you hear my reactions."

I asked Howard to fax the opinion to the law school, where I was heading. He was already getting calls from the press asking for comments. We agreed that our sound-bite party line should be simple: We were disappointed but planned to appeal.

I read Judge Williams's opinion as it came off the fax machine, a page at time. It began on a very curious note. There was no such thing, he held, as a civil tort for aiding and abetting recognized under Maryland law. Thus, wholly aside from the First Amendment, Judge Williams was throwing out our suit on the grounds that cases such as ours are not permissible in Maryland. This was a shocker, for two reasons. First, both sides had agreed that the only issues placed before Judge Williams in the Motion for Summary Judgment were issues of First Amendment law. Neither party had briefed or argued anything on Maryland's law of torts. So the judge's decision on this issue was reached entirely on his own, catching both sides by surprise. Second, we had assembled solid case law that made it absolutely clear that Maryland *did* recognize the tort of civil aiding and abetting.

Hit Man, Judge Williams reasoned, fell within no recognized "exception" to the protection of the First Amendment. There could be no liability against *Hit Man* under the *Brandenburg v. Ohio* standard, he reasoned, because the book simply did not incite imminent lawless action. "Nothing in the book says 'go out and commit murder now!'" Judge Williams wrote.

I read the decision and digested it, reacting with equanimity. Perhaps it was because I had expected to lose, given the judge's comments at the end of our oral argument, and had prepared myself for the loss.

I called Howard and John. We walked through the opinion, analyzing it paragraph by paragraph, line by line. Because Judge

Williams's First Amendment analysis was so mechanical and straight-forward, it posed no special problems for us as we thought about our appeal. He had simply accepted all of Tom Kelley and Lee Levine's arguments, and rebuffed all of ours. On appeal we would make our arguments again. We'd try to make them better, and more convincing, but we'd still make them.

But Judge Williams's decision on Maryland law threw us for a loop, tossing a crazy wild card into the litigation and threatening to wreak havoc and confusion on appeal. "We want a clean case, a clean *First Amendment* case, in front of the Fourth Circuit," I said to Howard and John. "We don't want to have to jack around arguing Maryland law. Hell, the Fourth Circuit could decide to do something quirky like certify the state law question to the Maryland Court of Appeals. Then we'd be delayed for a whole year, bogged down on Maryland tort law. It would be a nightmare."

"Well, Judge Williams got the Maryland law question flat-out wrong," said John Marshall. "I'm looking at the cases, right here in front of me. You remember, Rod, the *Halberstam* decision we talked about a long time ago."

Fortunately, John had researched the Maryland law point months before and had sent me a thick file of cases. For hundreds of years, it has been a basic axiom of criminal and tort law that someone who provides assistance or encouragement to another person in the commission of a crime or a tort may be held responsible as an "aider and abetter." Maryland had a long history of recognizing this concept, and had, only a year before, approved of the result in a fascinating case involving the murder of Michael Halberstam, the brother of writer David Halberstam. In that case, the court held that someone who merely provides information to another that is used to perpetrate a murder may be held civilly liable for aiding and abetting that murder. Somehow, Judge Williams or his law clerk had overlooked these precedents.

"You know what we should do, gentlemen?" Howard interrupted. "We should be nice about this. The judge obviously made a simple mistake here. I doubt it's a mistake that would cause him to change his ruling, but you never know. Let's bring it to his attention, immediately, in a polite and respectful way. We file a short Motion to Reconsider. We say that we didn't realize that the judge wanted briefing on Maryland state tort law, and so we negligently failed to supply him with cases demonstrating that Maryland recognizes suits such as ours. Here are the cases. Please reconsider your ruling in light of these. Then, he does what he does. If he sticks with the same outcome, we have a cleaner case for appeal. If it causes him to change his mind, we've turned defeat into victory."

We liked Howard's strategy, and followed it. Judge Williams seemed tremendously appreciative of our move. I believe he was relieved that his mistake had been brought to his attention before we took our appeal. He actually called Howard to thank him for alerting him to the Maryland cases. He then issued a revised opinion. The revised opinion was exactly like his first version, but it took out the passages stating that aiding and abetting was not recognized under Maryland law. Our little maneuver had saved the judge some embarrassment and streamlined the case. But it had not changed the sober reality that the only federal judge to consider our suit had thrown it out of court. If we could not get that decision reversed on appeal, our case was over.

•   •   •

I wrote a simple congratulatory note to Tom Kelley and Lee Levine immediately after receiving Judge Williams's decision, complimenting them on the fine work they had done. While I hoped to get the result reversed on appeal, I admired the highly professional and effective effort that had gained them the victory before Judge Williams.

Howard also wrote a note to Kelley and Levine, a little different from mine. It contained a dictionarylike compendium of definitions

21

The Splits of Lawyering

The fall and winter months were spent preparing our appeal. We had three tasks to undertake. First, we had to write our brief. Second, we had to approach and encourage various outside groups who might be on our side of the legal and policy issues in the case to consider filing amicus briefs in support of our position. And third, we had to prepare and practice for the oral argument.

Of the three members of our team, Howard was far and away the least distracted by other tasks, a fact that was at once a blessing and a curse. John had a very busy law practice of his own, with a heavy load of other clients and cases. I had my teaching, a busy schedule with kids, speaking engagements and publishing deadlines, and other cases of my own to worry about. In two of the talks I gave that year, one at Yale and one at Washington and Lee University, I explored some of the moral and ethical dilemmas of being a lawyer, dilemmas that I'd often found especially poignant in my work on the *Hit Man* case. I presented to the Yale and the Washington and Lee students pieces of a play I had written entitled *The Trial of Oliver Wendell Holmes*, in which a modern lawyer, lying in a coma, is asked in a dream to defend the famous Justice Holmes, who is on trial for his "immortality." We then talked about the legal profession and issues of morality and ethics.

Lawyers in America, I noted, often complain about the cultural image of the profession. Movies, novels, public opinion polls, and lawyer jokes reveal a pervasive cultural doubt about whether the legal profession is honorable and the justice system just. At its worse, lawyers are seen as shysters and crooks and the justice system as a variant of organized crime. Under this view, lawyers routinely bribe juries, manufacture or destroy evidence as their needs require, suborn perjury, force or alter documents, and generally "do what it takes" to win, service their clients, and earn large fees.

But while any sensible person understands that corrupt lawyers and judges certainly do exist, the poor cultural image of lawyers does not stem primarily from a belief that most lawyers and judges are actually criminals. The poor image instead comes from a widely shared sense that there is something intrinsic in the American legal system and intrinsic in the American concept of what it means to be a lawyer that tends to drain the system and its participants of moral sensibility. The problem with the legal profession is not that it is affirmatively immoral, but that it is passively amoral. The problem is not that Americans believe that lawyers are liars, but that they believe that lawyers do not tell the truth.

The classic response of the profession to all of this, I told the students, is that the people just do not understand. The American Bar Association attacks the portrayal of lawyers as sharpsters in movies and television programs as cheap, unfair sensationalizing that undermines public confidence in the integrity of the legal system. Even lawyer jokes are seen as corrosive, for they reinforce the false cultural perception that lawyers are mostly scorpions and vipers.

In defending itself, the profession argues that what the movies and lawyer jokes fail to show us are all the attorneys who devote themselves to championing the rights of the poor and oppressed, who dedicate themselves to the preservation of civil rights and civil liberties, who labor tirelessly to ferret out frauds and charlatans, who take on clients and causes for no compensation, all because they believe it is the right thing to do. The legal system is adversarial, and all who attempt to navigate it need and deserve vigorous representation. There are strong ethical rules that govern this adversarial system, and most lawyers strive earnestly to stay within the bounds of those rules. Ethical concerns are prominent within the profession, and disciplinary boards police violations conscientiously. We are a robust people with a robust justice system, but we should not confuse aggressive lawyering with immoral or amoral lawyering. To be sure, most lawyers are trained to pursue the interests of their clients with a certain single-minded focus, but this is a good thing, not a bad one, and ultimately draws from the same competitive ethos that animates all other sectors of the free-enterprise economy.

The legal profession's defense of itself is, on the face of it, highly credible and seemingly persuasive. But if so, I asked the students, why has it done so poorly in the court of public opinion? The one thing lawyers are supposed to be good at is making a convincing case. Yet lawyers seem to have lost this one. How can this be?

There is a temptation, of course, for lawyers to dismiss their collective bad image as simply that: an image problem. If image is all that is at stake, the problem may be an annoyance, but it is hardly grave; attorneys are presumably tough enough to weather jokes and sleazy dramatic portrayals.

But I wondered, I told the students, if perhaps there was more at work. Perhaps, in the dissonance between image and reality, something was revealed. Perhaps the gap between the noble ideal of the law as an honorable profession and the popular perception of the law as something less was worth plumbing for what it may uncover about the nature of lawyering and the currents of modern culture.

A major shortcoming of the legal profession's defense is that it requires a vision of the big picture and a sense of the long run. Big picture and long run defenses are never as gripping as the indictment immediately before us. Lawyers often seem immoral or amoral because we are focused on behavior in a particular case, in which it appears that the machinations of the lawyer, the clever moves and vigorous advocacy, caused the system to reach the "wrong" result.

The profession's response is structural: We must look not at the result in this case, but rather at society's dependence on the adversarial system as the only reliable long-term test of truth.

The weakness of the "big picture" defense, I suggested, exposes an ambivalence many Americans may have about the adversarial system itself. On one level, our adversarial system is quintessentially American. We do not rely on public opinion, conventional wisdom, orthodoxy, or consensus to decide the outcome of legal disputes, but instead employ professionally trained advocates to vigorously represent the opposing sides and battle it out. In defending freedom of speech, Oliver Wendell Holmes wrote that "the best test of truth is the power of the thought to get itself accepted in the competition of the market." The same might be said of how we test for truth in the legal system, placing our reliance on the power of a proffered fact or argument to gain ascendency in the legal "marketplace" of juries and judges.

No juror or judge can *know* if O. J. Simpson committed murder. No juror or judge can *know* to an omnipotent certainty that Paladin Press really knew and intended that its book *Hit Man* would be used by real people to commit murder. The best we can do is allow the criminal prosecutors (or in a civil suit such as our *Hit Man* case, the plaintiffs' lawyers like John, Howard, and me) to contest the evidence to the hilt, leaving juries to decide matters after weighing the presentations of both sides. To many this may seem as American as it gets, as American as the Old West, presidential debates, or the National Football League. Few would express admiration for a lawyer who is an outright crook, bribing judges and witnesses, but many Americans do express admiration, at least with a wink and a nod, for the lawyer who is "sharp" if not an actual sharpster, the lawyer who can bend the rules or stretch the rules or tweak the system to secure a win despite long odds. While many Americans were upset by the jury's acquittal of O. J. Simpson, seeing it as a breakdown of the legal system and a triumph of appeals to racial identity, many others not only delighted in the verdict but hero-worshiped

Simpson's lawyer Johnny Cochran as someone who truly seemed willing to do whatever was required to secure victory. In a culture that revels in contest, it is only natural that rewards go to those who win. Vince Lombardi said that winning isn't everything, it's the only thing. And George C. Scott, in his famous film portrayal of General George Patton, exclaimed that "all real Americans love a winner, and will not tolerate a loser."

Holmes wrote of the marketplace of ideas: "It is an experiment, as all life is an experiment." Holmes had no doubt of the wisdom of experiment, and certainly no doubt of its constitutional pedigree; reliance on the open marketplace, he claimed, was "the theory of our Constitution."

Yet this linkage between the adversarial system, the faith in the marketplace, and the Constitution does not solve the mystery of the legal profession's bad image, I suggested to the students, but rather services to deepen it. American lawyers may plausibly contend that their adversarial mode of operating is not just a good idea, it is an idea embedded in the Constitution itself. With all this going for them, why do they still do so poorly in defending themselves? If Howard Siegel and others like him are such magnificent advocates, why is it, as the poet Carl Sandburg wrote, that the hearse-horse snickers as it carries the lawyer away?

Perhaps, I told the students, there are clues to the causes of the poor image of the profession to be found in exploring the recurring conflicts that lawyers confront within the adversarial system, and the toll exacted by those conflicts on the human struggle to find value and meaning in life. A modern lawyer is constantly forced to engage in "splits" in life, splits that are fully justifiable morally and function-ally necessary if a lawyer is to fulfill his or her societal function. But these splits may come at a price. They may take their toll on the psychological well-being of the individual lawyer. They may take their toll on the cultural image of all lawyers.

The very act of representation can create ethical tensions. When I represent another, I speak not entirely in my own voice for my own reasons out of my own conviction, I speak on behalf of the interests of another. Once I signed on to represent the families of Janice Saunders, Trevor Horn, and Millie Horn, I was no longer a moral free agent, at liberty to say whatever came to mind about their case. When I spoke I no longer spoke solely in the voice of Rod Smolla. I spoke in the voice of representative and advocate.

This is, at its core, an eminently honorable exercise, perfectly natural and functionally necessary; society could not work without it. But doing this all the time—constantly speaking for others rather than for oneself—has its consequences. On a subtle level, speaking always and only for others tends to slowly corrode authenticity. Many of the traditional pejoratives aimed at lawyers capture this. The lawyer is a "mouthpiece" or "hired gun." He or she has no personal moral gyroscope but merely takes on whatever cause is at hand, believing in whatever the client needs to be believed in. A lawyer can become an actor, always playing a role, with no authentic self discernible to others, and at its most destructive, no authentic self discernible to the self.

The split of representation may cause corrosion even when one generally agrees with the interests of one's clients. Far less subtle, however, is the "split of doubt," the infamous conflict that arises from being placed in the position of having a duty to energetically advance the interests of a client whom the lawyer, at some inner level, believes is in the wrong. At its most dramatic, this occurs when a criminal defense lawyer strives with unchecked vigor to secure the acquittal of a defendant that the lawyer believes is guilty. Very few practicing lawyers have not been asked the question, at some point in their lives, "How can you lawyers defend people you know are guilty?" It doesn't matter that the lawyer answering the question specializes in tax, bankruptcy, real estate, or immigration law; it doesn't matter that he or she may never have represented a criminal defendant in his or her life, or even set foot in a courtroom. At certain visceral levels, all lawyers are lawyers, all lawyers are Johnny Cochran, urging "If it doesn't fit, you must acquit," all lawyers are challenged to explain, in cocktail party conversations, in lectures before the Rotary Club, in family gatherings at Thanksgiving, "How can you lawyers represent people you know are guilty and get them off on technicalities?" After a glass of wine or two, the questioning may get sharper and more righteous, with the interrogator invariably adding, "*I* could never do that!"

Now, lawyers, to be sure, are well-trained to field these questions. They repeat the stock answers, explaining how every person is presumed innocent until proven guilty, how the Constitution guarantees criminal defendants the assistance of counsel, and how there is an important distinction between factual guilt (well, yes, he did stab her) and legal guilt (it was not proven beyond a reasonable doubt that he stabbed her with premeditation). But these explanations are typically met with snickers and even deeper self-righteousness. These systemic answers don't entirely wash with the nonlawyer public. And indeed, there is a general suspicion that they don't so completely wash with lawyers themselves—at least, they would not wash if lawyers could be given a truth serum and made to say what they really think. Many people just can't accept that lawyers do not feel at least some qualms about defending the clearly guilty. How can they not?

Another important split is the compartmentalization of persona. This is not a phenomenon unique to lawyering, but lawyering implicates a constant and often intense version of it. I call this the "role of role," and it is a constant consideration in moral and ethical behavior. A person might say, for example, "Let me offer you this advice. I'm not speaking as your doctor now, but as your friend." This sentence pattern gets repeated in endless permutations. I'm not speaking as your lawyer now (or your teacher, or as any professional role we might substitute), I'm speaking as your friend (or your spouse, or your parent, or some other social or familial role we might substitute).

What are we to make of the role of role? Is it a positive or a negative thing that we are often tempted to give different answers to questions, or behave differently in resolving ethical conflicts, based on the role we are in at the time? On one level, the answer must be that these differences in behavior are justified. We must accept the role of role, if roles are to mean anything. The clearest example of this involves confidentiality. One of the defining characteristics of many official roles is that one is made privy to information that one is supposed to keep in confidence. The priest and the penitent, the psychological counselor or medical doctor and patient, the lawyer and client all have relationships of confidentiality imposed by ethical tradition and legal rules.

Yet even here there is a price to be paid. Sometimes one's intuitive ethical response to a problem will vary dramatically depending on what "hat" one is wearing. If you can look in the mirror and plainly see only one hat on your head, you will usually be fine. But vision may become blurred or doubled by a crisis; it may become difficult to see clearly what hat it is that is on one's head, or even more disorienting, one may seem to see two hats at once. Moving in and out of different personas too quickly can cause a person to get the psychic bends. Lawyers are not immune from this disease; like other professions in which the role of role is dominant, they may get sick from rushed decompression.

Finally, I told the students, there was a new, emerging split within the profession, a growing divergence between the ideal of the lawyer as a combatant and the ideal of the lawyer as a facilitator of resolution. This was a split, I suggested, that may ultimately prove to be a positive for the profession.

In a fiercely adversarial system, lawyers may come to see their role as that of warriors who are trained to seek the unconditional surrender of the adversary. Much of the current momentum toward the exploration of different forms of alternative dispute resolution, however, is animated by a different vision of the lawyer: the lawyer as a mediator, a problem solver, a facilitator of resolution. Now the goal is not to crush the enemy but to work with the other side, looking for a settlement that all can live with and that allows the real business of life to move forward.

The skills of reaching resolution are not necessarily the same skills as those that make for dominating an adversary. The ability to see the world from the other side's perspective, to make realistic assessments of one's own needs, to massage disputes in the search for common ground, to maintain lines of communication and dialogue—all help in reaching satisfactory settlements. These talents and affinities do not always coexist peacefully with such attributes as tenacity and gamesmanship, qualities that are often seen as more likely to produce litigation victory. As lawyers increasingly are called upon by a restless society to play the role of problem solver and dispute resolver, the intensity of some of the more corrosive splits may, at least for a lucky few, abate. Some lawyers may find themselves engaging in a more holistic version of legal practice, with the side-benefit of living less split and more whole professional lives.

As a warrior-lawyer in the battle against Paladin Press, I struggled with these conflicts. I also labored to keep my relationship with Howard and John on the beam. There were still times when Howard's ego got to me. Midway through our case, Howard and John joined forces on another suit, a class-action case alleging that a popular psychic hotline was a fraud and a ripoff. When Howard called me for some preliminary advice on the case, I wondered what his agenda really was. Did he really think the world needed a lawsuit against telephone psychics? Or was he in it for the publicity and ego-rush? I disclosed that I had just been involved in a suit defending a psychic. My client was a "spiritualist" author from New York who wanted to sign copies of her latest book and conduct readings, using spiritualist cards, for clients in Norfolk at a psychic and spiritualist bookstore, for which she charged seventy dollars a session. A Norfolk ordinance made all palm readings and fortune-telling for money illegal. Working with the Virginia ACLU, I filed suit against the city of Norfolk, claiming that my spiritualist client had a First Amendment right to ply her trade.

When I told Howard about this suit, I could sense his dismay. He obviously thought I was the one who was half-cocked, and that my suit was an affront to his debunking litigation. "No," I insisted, "our two suits are different. In my case, my client sincerely believes in what she does. To her, she is practicing religion. You may think it's hokum. But why is her faith, which she can connect to the universal potential inside each person, any harder to believe than Moses parting the Red Sea?" I knew this was not going to persuade Howard, for I doubted he had much faith in Moses either. "People are entitled to believe what they cannot prove," I said. "But your suit is different. You're actually claiming that the psychic hotline folks are complete frauds. That they hire actors to tell fortunes, and don't believe, themselves, in what they are doing. That's arguably different."

I was trying to placate Howard and smooth the waters, if not part them. If he thought I was dumb to be defending psychics, I thought he was dumb to be suing them, but I kept my opinion to myself. Maybe his suit was about ferreting out fraud, but it seemed a trifle goofy to me—like the prosecution of Santa Claus in *Miracle on 34th Street.*

22

Trying to Please Morris Dees

It is no more true that familiarity breeds contempt than that opposites attract or like forces repel. Human chemistry is too complex to be reduced to the aphorisms of physical science. The tripartite chemistry of Howard, John, and me had remained reasonably stable despite Howard's occasional mercury-pops of ego. But we'd been shaken by our loss, and the shaking had made us all more volatile.

The first signs of a serious schism in the dream team appeared as we sat down to write our brief for the Fourth Circuit. In an early strategy session, Howard casually volunteered to write the first draft, noting that he was far less busy than either John or I. John seemed immediately enthusiastic about Howard's suggestion, though he was low key about it. I had the sense they had rehearsed the scene, even the low-key part.

"I thought things worked pretty well the way we did it for Judge Williams," I said, meeting casual with casual. "With me writing the first draft, and then all of us tearing it apart and rebuilding it."

"Well, that's fine," Howard jumped right in.

"Good," I replied, hoping that was enough said.

It wasn't, "Though I think there's something that *I* can bring to this," Howard added, with an undercurrent of cynical provocation.

"Now don't misunderstand me, Rod, when I say this: I think there's a way I have of putting things that can grab a judge, that can make a judge sit up and pay attention. I know you think that I'm a wild man, and that I don't have the polish to write an appellate brief. But I can be very effective when I need to be."

"It's true, Rod," said John, in a voice too thin to mask his mutinous intent. "I've seen Howard in front of judges. You haven't. All the craziness we see, he keeps it entirely in check—at least for the most part—and when he does explode, it's always for a reason."

So, it was out. I was a marionette about to be caught in a snare of strings. I lashed at the lines. "You know, Howard," I said, "I think you and I have been friends from the very beginning, and we've never been afraid to say what we were thinking."

"Absolutely," he said. "If we ain't past that by now, we got real problems."

"So here's what I'm thinking," I said. "I think you're on an ego trip and it's interfering with your judgment about what is in the best interest of our clients." My tone was moderate, but this was a mean-spirited goad, and a part of me regretted it as I said it.

John tried to break in, but I fought him off, directing my comments to Howard. "I'm thinking that the two of us are more alike than either of us ever really lets on," I said, trying to control my swelling rankle. "The image is that you are the trial lawyer, the practical guy, the street fighter who likes to get down and dirty and butt heads and kick ass. And I'm supposed to be the intellectual, the professor, the polite and genteel one who likes to dabble in these cases, but always as the gentleman litigator. My head's in the clouds, with a lot of ivory tower theory; you're the *real* lawyer."

Howard grinned. John grinned. Neither contradicted me. "But here's my take," I continued. "Howard, you're a lot more of a theorist than you let on. Both of you are. You're just as smart as me, you can analyze a case as well or better than I can, and Howard, particularly, is as likely, maybe even more likely, to build elaborate conceptual arguments, with wheels on wheels, to try to make a point. On the other side of the coin, I ain't no pointy-headed intellectual who's afraid of a fight. I can be as tough and as tenacious an advocate as either of you. I've never pulled a punch in this case and never will."

"We know that," Howard, his face dissolving into softer focus. "No one doubts that for a second."

"The problem with you and me, Howard," I said, "is that we both crave approval. From everybody, and especially from each other. From the day we first talked, you've wanted to impress me with your smarts. You've wanted me to know you're an intellectual, too. And from the first day, I've wanted to impress you that I'm also a real lawyer, with common sense, and practical judgment, and the ability to make persuasive arguments in court. Well, let's stop trying to impress each other. I've got no problem with you helping to draft the brief. I've got no problem with you drafting major portions of it, even the majority of it, if that's what we decide. You're the captain of the ship, I've always said that. I take my orders from you. But here's the story as I see it: I *am* a damn good appellate lawyer. Not a professor pretending to be an appellate lawyer, a *real* appellate lawyer. And the number one loyalty we *all* have, our number one duty, is to our clients. John has strengths, you have strengths, I have strengths. Right now, at this stage of the case, we're in the realm of my strength. I respect you, and any sentence you write, any paragraph you write, any whole twenty-page section that you write that is the best we are possibly capable of, collectively, should go directly into the brief. I have no ego in this thing. I really don't. But you gotta be careful that you don't either. Why don't you draft every argument you can think of that you believe should be included? I'll do exactly the same thing. We'll then take everything you've written, everything I've written, and anything John decides he wants to write, and we'll sit down, and shmooze and argue and kibitz and fight and wrestle like we always do, picking and choosing the best from each, and mold it into a coherent whole?"

My speech seemed to clear the air. If it wasn't a full truce, it was at least a temporary cease-fire. We talked more and reached a compromise. It turns out that there were really just a few pet issues that Howard wanted to make sure were included, and included with his spin. That was fine with me. It was decided that I would draft about two-thirds of the brief, working on the sections that dealt with the main First Amendment arguments and with *Brandenburg*. Howard would draft the portions dealing with the facts, and with concepts of aiding and abetting.

●   ●   ●

If we were tense over the brief-drafting, we were amicable over amici. Howard and I worked together on the amicus brief angle, trying to recruit allies to our cause. I think we were largely searching for legitimacy. We knew that Tom Kelley and Lee Levine had already lined up a number of groups to join as amici against us, and that Bruce Sanford already had the brief-that-never-got-filed ready and waiting for the appeal. We knew Bruce and other amici would attempt to paint our suit as offbeat and experimental, not to mention an affront to the First Amendment. If respected public interest groups, or a significant government agency, were to file a brief supporting our position, we would not feel so marginalized. There was strength in numbers. We'd taken a whipping in the decision of Judge Williams, and needed a shot of confidence.

My first "pitch" for amicus support was to the attorney general of the state of Virginia. Jim Gilmore was the Virginia attorney general and was running as the Republican candidate for governor of Virginia. Gilmore had made "victim's rights" a central plank in his platform, and had come to the law school at William and Mary to deliver a speech on victim's rights. A friend of mine at William and Mary, Professor Walter Felton, was one of the top lawyers in Virginia and a person who had been active in the Attorney General's Office over the years. Walter was both a professor and a government attorney, serving in various capacities in Virginia state government, as a manager of the state's commonwealth attorney's counsel, as a deputy

attorney general, as a senior counsel to the attorney general, and ultimately, as legal adviser to the governor. Walter offered to introduce
me to Attorney General Gilmore for a "private audience" in which I
could describe our case to him, and see if he would be interested in
directing his office to file an amicus brief on our behalf. The meeting went well, and went nowhere. Gilmore was cordial and sympathetic, but the minute he got wind that it was a book publisher we
were suing, he backed off. "No, no, you can't do that," he said. "You
can't sue the media for these things. First Amendment."

Our next try was Morris Dees, the well-known civil rights and
criminal defense lawyer, and his group the Southern Poverty Law
Center. Dees and his center had made a name for themselves going
after extremist hate groups, like the Ku Klux Klan and members of
the militia movement. He'd managed to bankrupt the Klan in a case
in which he'd established that its members had conspired to aid and
abet murder. Howard called Dees, and talked to him and to one of
his legal policy assistants at the center. They were highly supportive
of us, and said they might well be willing to file an amicus brief on
our behalf, though at the moment they were swamped with work and
were not sure they had the time or resources to write one. As
Howard was courting Dees, by happenstance I got invited to appear
on a PBS talk show that originated in Nashville called "Freedom
Speaks," a half-hour weekly program that focused on First Amendment and press issues. The show was on the *Hit Man* case, and Morris Dees was also going to be one of the guests. My job was to
buttonhole Dees behind the scenes and try to convince him to join
our case.

At the studio in Nashville, I found Dees to be a captivating presence. He is strikingly handsome, folksy, and charismatic, a natural
southern storytelling raconteur who charms everyone he meets.
Dees was chatting up the technicians, the receptionists, the producers, the other guests, the people bringing in the sandwiches and
Cokes, everyone. They called me in first for makeup, and I came out
of the makeup room as I always do when I go on television, feeling

caked up and embalmed and uncomfortable from all the prim and powder they pile on. Finally it was Dees's turn to be called into the makeup room.

"No ma'am," he said, with a melodic drawl. "I believe I'll pass. I believe I'm just fine as I am." The aide was speechless. Apparently no one had ever refused makeup before. I was slack-jawed. I didn't know you could do that. Just say no, and make them film your own face! I was envious. We walked onto the studio set. About a hundred people were in the live audience to watch. Damn if Morris Dees didn't deviate, and walk right into the studio audience and begin to press the flesh, like a politician on the stump. "Hello, ma'am," he smiled to an elderly woman with blue-gray hair in the front row. "I'm Morris Dees. Now what brings you here on such a fine afternoon?" They had to drag him up to his seat in front of the camera. It was all genuine, I felt, and all effective. Throughout the show, Dees always had the audience with him, clapping at his points, laughing at his jokes and stories.

I finally got him alone after the program, as we were waiting for a lunch to be served for us. (This was not the usual talk-show regimen. "Freedom Speaks" was an unusually high-class operation. You got picked up at the airport in a limo, whisked to the studio, and fed a nice meal afterward.) Dees was as charming to me one-on-one as he had been to everyone else he'd met during the gig. At first we talked about the Unabomber, Ted Kaczynski. Dees told me he had almost landed the appointment as Kaczynski's lawyer. He was disappointed, because he was certain he could have gotten Kaczynski off—at least off the death penalty, with the insanity defense. Then he turned to Timothy McVeigh and the Oklahoma City bombing. He'd been approached, he said, about bringing a suit a lot like ours against the *Turner Diaries*, the novel that had supposedly inspired McVeigh. He decided against it, though, because he was convinced that under the First Amendment, no court was going to allow the families to sue a novelist.

"What about our case?" I asked. "Do you think we have a chance?"

"Well, you heard what I just said on the show," said Dees. "I completely support y'all. But privately? Candidly? I do believe you're gonna lose."

"Maybe we'd have a better chance if the Southern Poverty Law Center would assist us with an amicus brief."

Dees was noncommittal. It was a worthy cause, he said, but he left such decisions to his deputy. The problem was time and resources. They were all overworked and stretched thin. I took it as a polite no, which turned out to be correct. The center never filed a brief.

While I was experiencing repeated rejection, Tom Kelley and Lee Levine were getting most of the freedom-loving universe as we know it lined up to support Paladin Press. Bruce Sanford finally got to file his previously rejected opus, on behalf of ABC, Inc. and Walt Disney Company, America Online, the Association of American Publishers, the Baltimore Sun Company, the E.W. Scripps Company, the Freedom to Read Foundation, the Magazine Publishers of America, the McClatchy Newspaper Company, Media General (publisher of the *Richmond Times-Dispatch*), Media/Professional Insurance, the National Association of Broadcasters, the Newspaper Association of America, the New York Times Company, the Reporters Committee for Freedom of the Press, the Society of Professional Journalists, and the Washington Post Company. A host of well-known lawyers, including many people I'd worked with, signed this brief "Of Counsel," including Alan Braverman of ABC, Randall Roe of AOL, Bruce Rich of the Association of American Publishers, Teresa Chmara of the Freedom to Read Foundation, Kenneth Richieri and Slade Metcalf of the Magazine Publishers, Debra Foust Bruns of McClatchy, George Mahoney of Media General, Chad Milton of Media/Professional Insurance, Henry Baumann of the National Association of Broadcasters, Rene Milam of the Newspaper Association, George Freeman of the New York Times Company, Jane Kirtley of the Reporter's Committee, and Mary Ann Werner of the *Washington Post*.

Douglas Winter, another Washington lawyer, filed a brief against us on behalf of the Horror Writers Association. Arthur Spitzer of the American Civil Liberties Union of the National Capital Area, Dwight Sullivan of the American Civil Liberties Union Foundation of Maryland, and Robert O'Neil and J. Joshua Wheeler of the Thomas Jefferson Center for the Protection of Free Expression at the University of Virginia filed a brief against us. Bob O'Neil was a particularly good friend. We'd been allies on many projects and in many forums, often serving together on boards and advisory committees.

If I were thin-skinned, I would have been punctured, for the list of our opponents was long and it was personal. I'd done work as a lawyer for many of the companies and organizations on the list, and many of the lawyers who signed the briefs on their behalf were friends and colleagues with whom I'd dealt harmoniously over the years.

But my skin was plenty thick. What interested me was intellectual substance. Was there anything in these amicus briefs that I thought would turn the heads of the judges, and clinch the case against us? I found nothing. They were well-written and well-researched, if at times a little overblown in rhetoric, but that was common in amicus briefs, including many I had written myself. I found in them, however, no theories, no precedents, no clever new legal points that we had not previously heard and previously grappled with. The briefs were good for Paladin and bad for us, but not devastating. There were no knockout punches.

Indeed, on one level, I began to wonder if maybe the avalanche of amici might hurt Paladin more than help it. If there was any one theme that came through with resounding resonance in these briefs, it was that there was no principled way to distinguish Paladin's murder manual from countless other forms of expression, including mystery and horror novels, crime books, news presentations on crime, television programs, and movies. We'd heard all this before, of course—it was one of the main arguments Paladin had presented to Judge Williams.

But in my heart, I still didn't believe the argument rang true. Sure, Judge Williams had bought into it. But I had this faith, or at least hope, that a new group of three appellate judges, seeing the case with fresh eyes, would find the argument transparent and lame. A murder manual just wasn't the same as a Tom Clancy novel—in its lethal potency, in its detail, in its encouragement, in its *intent*. I began to wonder if, as more groups joined the fray to pile on and try to bury us, the more an appellate court might just step back and say, "Hold on here, enough is enough!"

In the end, we did end up with at least some amici support. David Crump, a law professor at the University of Houston Law Center, filed an amicus brief as an individual. Crump had previously written an article for the *Georgia Law Review* entitled "Camouflaged Intent: Freedom of Speech, Communicative Torts, and the Borderland of the *Brandenburg* Test." In his amicus brief and his article, Crump advanced a notion he called "camouflaged intent." In a scholarly and engaging presentation, Crump argued that the First Amendment should not protect incitements to violence that are intended but artfully disguised. It was a short but clever brief, and we were happy to have it.

An attorney from Washington, D.C., named Neal Goldfarb, who specialized in defending the rights of crime victims, filed a long and exhaustively researched brief on behalf of the National Victim Center, the Stephanie Roper Foundation, and the Victim's Rights Political Action Committee. When he initially filed his brief, it contained ninety-four footnotes. The clerk of the court for the Fourth Circuit actually rejected the brief, citing the court's rule against excessive footnoting. It was the first time I'd ever heard of a court actually sanctioning a lawyer for a footnote violation. Goldfarb responded with a motion complaining that the clerk was wrong, and touting the utility of footnotes in briefs. This was another first for me—a brief about footnotes. In the end, Goldfarb filed an amended version of his brief—with fewer footnotes this time—and the clerk accepted it. Goldfarb argued forcefully that Paladin's conduct really could not be distinguished from "garden variety" aiding and abetting of crime, and that it deserved no special First Amendment protection.

We had pretty much given up on getting any additional support in the case when serendipitous coincidence once again intervened, this time in the form of one entity that we knew could very well cause the judges of the Fourth Circuit to sit up and take notice: the U.S. Department of Justice.

The call came in late December from a Justice Department lawyer named Marty Lieberman. The Justice Department, he explained, was very interested in the question of whether federal law currently did prohibit the publication and dissemination of information providing instruction on how to make destructive devices such as bombs, dangerous weapons, or weapons of mass destruction that might be used by terrorists or other criminals to commit acts of terrorism and violence. The Oklahoma City bombing, and proposed new legislation by Senator Dianne Feinstein dealing with this issue, had caused Attorney General Janet Reno to ask a special task force of lawyers and policy advisers within the Department of Justice to prepare a report on this subject. The report would deal with the degree of public availability of such dangerous information in various media, including books, magazines, pamphlets, and material available on the Internet. The report would then look at the extent to which such information has facilitated the manufacture and use of explosives and other weapons in terrorist and criminal activity, and the likelihood that such material would assist in such terrorist and criminal activity in the future. The report would then canvass existing federal law to determine the extent to which it did or did not make such publication and dissemination illegal, and further explore the possible need for new federal legislation to fill in gaps in the present coverage of those laws. Finally, the report would turn to constitutional issues, examining the extent to which the First Amendment placed restrictions on the power of government to enact and enforce such laws.

"We've been heavily researching this entire area, and have been following your case closely," said Lieberman to me. "We're very interested in what will happen to Judge Williams's decision when it reaches the Fourth Circuit."

I couldn't believe what I was hearing. This was potentially an enormous break for us. If the Justice Department was interested in our case, and supportive of our position, and willing to come out publically in an amicus brief and say so, it would give us an extraordinary boost at a time we were much in need of one. By coincidence, I was scheduled to be in Washington, at the Department of Justice, in just a week. The solicitor general, Walter Dellinger, had invited me to come up for two sessions to help prepare him to argue cases that were pending in the Supreme Court: *Clinton v. Jones*, involving the question of whether Bill Clinton enjoyed any special presidential immunity from Paula Jones's sexual harassment suit, and two companion cases, *Washington v. Glucksberg* and *Vacco v. Quill*, raising the issue of whether the Constitution prohibited the government from enacting legislation preventing physician-assisted suicide. The solicitor general is the third-highest-ranking member of the Department of Justice, and the lawyer who represents the government of the United States in all litigation pending before the U.S. Supreme Court. The Solicitor General's Office also manages appeals and amicus briefs filed by the United States in federal courts of appeal. Walter Dellinger had been appointed by President Clinton to succeed Drew Days, who had vacated the office to return to teaching at Yale. Walter and I were good friends. He had been acting dean at Duke Law School when I was a student there. I was a visiting professor at Duke in 1992, and during that visit Walter and I had cemented our friendship. Walter joined the Clinton administration immediately after Clinton's election, serving as a legal policy adviser in the White House and later in the Department of Justice. I'd jumped at his invitation, first because I was flattered that he would invite me to help him, and second because it gave me a rare opportunity to have an "inside look" at the solicitor general's preparation for two historic cases. I told Marty Lieberman that I would be in Washington to help with Dellinger's preparations, and asked if I could stop by his office as part of that trip. Coincidences continued to compound. Lieberman, it turned out, was also a friend of Dellinger's, and had also been asked to assist in preparing the Paula Jones and assisted-suicide cases.

Lieberman was not going to be in Washington that week, however, because of surgery scheduled for a family member.

So Lieberman and I conducted our business on the phone. The Justice Department was considering the possibility of filing an amicus brief in *Rice v. Paladin Enterprises*, he disclosed, but it sounded as if the department probably would not file such a brief. Instead, he said, the department would probably simply complete its report, and rely on that as its sole public comment on the issues our case presented. Lieberman did not want to disclose the contents of the Justice Department's report before it became public, and I did not press him for any "sneak preview." He also wanted to be "neutral" in our litigation, and to that end told me that he wanted to contact Tom Kelley and Lee Levine and let them know that the Justice Department was preparing a report. I encouraged him to do that.

Lieberman then proceeded to pick *my* brain. The report, he said, was still a "work in progress," and he was interested in my views, as a First Amendment scholar, of the questions posed by the report. I asked him if he'd read the brief we'd submitted to Judge Williams in the *Paladin* case. He had read the briefs, he said, and had found them very helpful in preparing his report. We then spent a long time on the phone kicking the issues back and forth. He was particularly interested in two federal criminal cases that involved prosecutions under a little-known federal statute passed in 1968, at the height of national ferment over the Vietnam War, that dealt with training persons for the purpose of advancing "civil disorder." The law stated that

> Whoever teaches or demonstrates to any other person the use, application, or making of any firearm or explosive or incendiary device, or technique capable of causing injury or death to persons, knowing or having reason to know or intending that the same will be unlawfully employed for use in, or in furtherance of, a civil disorder which may in any way or degree obstruct, delay, or adversely affect commerce or the movement

of any article or commodity in commerce or the conduct or performance of any federally protected function . . . Shall be fined not more than $10,000 or imprisoned not more than five years or both.

In the only two federal cases that had ever construed the meaning of this statute, the courts held that it did not violate the First Amendment. Lieberman was extremely bright and thoroughly professional. I'm sure I learned more law from him than he did from me.

The conversation provided us with an enormously important morale boost. For the first time, we had some concrete proof that our suit was not as idiosyncratic and off the wall as our adversaries had constantly painted it. This was something we had always believed, and said to ourselves, but when you are fighting a battle against formidable opponents with powerful allies, largely isolated and on your own, your own voices can start to blare hollow. Marty Lieberman and the Justice Department had not given our case any imprimatur. We did not know if the U.S. government was on our side or if it would even take sides. But we did know that one of the best legal minds in the Department of Justice, after long research and arduous analysis of the issues we had been struggling with, seemed to be very much on our "wavelength." I had found Lieberman fully comfortable and conversant with every argument I made, every case I cited. He didn't quibble or fuss with any of my conclusions. The questions he asked, the observations he made, seemed simpatico. I came away from our conversation feeling that he and the Department of Justice were talking our talk and walking our walk.

23

Winds of Coup d'État

Howard and I finished our respective portions of the draft of our Fourth Circuit brief and sat down with John, as arbiter and arbitrator, to attempt to meld them into a harmonious whole. The process turned out to be easier than any of us had expected. Howard and I just beat each other for an hour, and once that was out of our system, settled down and completed the brief.

The fight, as always, was over *Brandenburg*. We continued to struggle with whether *Brandenburg* should be the centerpiece of the brief or shunted aside in favor of emphasis on aiding and abetting. Howard liked the aiding and abetting argument. For him the case was a simple syllogism:

Paladin aided and abetted murder.
Aiding and abetting murder is a crime.
Crimes are not protected by the First Amendment.
Paladin is not protected by the First Amendment.

"*Brandenburg v. Ohio*," Howard kept insisting, doesn't have anything to do with this case." John agreed with him. "The first time I talked to you, you made me read *Brandenburg*. Well, I never told you this, but I read the case, and I said to myself, this case doesn't have a thing to do with our lawsuit. I never told you that before. I should have. I was right then and I'm right now."

For me, the case was not that simple, and it was a dangerous strategy to present it to the court of appeals as if it were. "There is just no way that three federal judges, confronted with this case, are going to decide it without a long and complex discussion of *Brandenburg v. Ohio.*"

"That's because you still just don't get it!" Howard screamed at me. "You're still too much of a First Amendment maven! You still think like all of them!"

"Howard, settle down. *You're* the one who just doesn't get it. I'm not saying that *Brandenburg* should govern this case. I'm not saying that *Brandenburg* is the right standard for the court to apply. I'm not saying we are doomed to lose because of *Brandenburg*—although I might point out that we did lose because of *Brandenburg* in front of Judge Williams. What I *am* saying is you can't just blow the case off! It's a United States Supreme Court decision, goddamn it! One of the most famous First Amendment cases in history. And to ninety-nine percent of the lawyers who know something about the First Amendment, their first reaction is that we are going to lose because *Brandenburg* is against us. Now, *we* know that it's not against it. We know that the better view is that it should not be applied in our case at all. We know that even if it is applied, we should still win. All I'm saying is that it takes a lot of thinking, a lot of arguing, a lot of explaining to get to that point. I am damn sure that if we win this case in front of the Fourth Circuit, you are gonna see thirty goddamn pages worth of *Brandenburg* discussion. If you think the court is going to say, this is a crime, this is aiding and abetting, case over, class dismissed, boom, boom, boom, boom, boom, in two pages, you're crazy!"

I pulled a Howard as I said all this, stalking around, pounding the bookshelves, pointing and yelling. Howard was so pissed he had to leave the room.

"I've gotta find the john," he sneered, and stalked away.

When we were all back in the room, John cut the compromise. "Why don't we just sit down with the drafts and see where it takes us," he suggested. We tried it, and discovered that our disagreements were more matters of tone and emphasis than substance. Even the tone and emphasis were actually closer than we'd thought. It had something to do, I think, with my "let's stop trying to impress each other" speech, though I'm not sure that the psychology worked quite as expected. The material that Howard drafted was generally more restrained and analytical than predicted. The material that I drafted was generally more biting and acerbic than predicted. John is a superb editor, largely because he is brutally honest. He cut Howard's hyperbole, he punched up my theory and policy, and in the end we arrived at a brief we were all satisfied with. Aiding and abetting and *Brandenburg* got equal time. Aiding and abetting went first.

•   •   •

It was March in Williamsburg, a beautiful spring. Daffodils, azalea, dogwood, and rosebud blossoms scented the air. Our briefs were filed. The clerk of the court notified us that the date of oral argument would be May 7. It was a time of waiting, a time of rumbling, a time for the skittish winds of coup d'état.

Howard and John participated in a program on our case at American University. The program was a moot court in which Howard argued the case for our side and my friend Bob O'Neil, of the Thomas Jefferson Center in Charlottesville, argued the case for Paladin Press. The panel of judges were law professors from the American University Law School. Bob O'Neil is a renowned First Amendment scholar and an estimable figure in higher education. Among many positions, he had been president of the University of Wisconsin and president of the University of Virginia. Howard was thoroughly pumped up for the moot court. He came away from the exercise as high as kite, screaming about how he had whipped Bob O'Neil's ass. I could see it building. What he really wanted to do was whip mine.

Howard sent me a videotape of the argument. I watched it the night I got it, and he called me before I went to bed. "You see what I did?" he told me. "I grabbed 'em by the balls. That's what we've gotta do, grab 'em by the balls." I felt Howard grabbing.

The next morning, John Marshall called. He didn't have his usual candor. He hemmed and hawed and stumbled and mumbled for about ten minutes. "Did you watch Howard's argument?" he asked. "Were you comfortable with the way he did that? I tell you, I was there, and I've never seen anything like it. He just totally annihilated O'Neil."

I assured John that I was totally comfortable with Howard's argument.

"We just want to make sure you were comfortable with the way he presented things," John repeated lamely. "It's just . . . well, I've seen Howard in court many, many times. He's just a master. I know you think he's crazy, but he's not that way in court."

I'd heard all this before. "So what is going on here, John, is that you and Howard want to depose me. You want Howard to do the oral argument instead of me. You want to take the case away from me."

"Yes, we do."

I felt a Howard forming inside me, yearning to be set free. I let it out. "Well, it's *my* case and Howard is not getting it without a fight. I can do a better job than Howard. I can whip Howard's ass. So you want him to argue? Let him prove he can do better. So Howard does a moot court one day and suddenly thinks he's a regular goddamn Clarence Darrow. So let's do another moot court, this time with both of us. I'll argue. Then Howard can do his again. We'll get a neutral group of experts to judge us. Some lawyers, some professors, maybe a retired judge. We'll have our own moot court–off. Winner gets the case."

John agreed. I think he might have been surprised that I'd fought back so vehemently. A minute later Howard called. Howard was elated. He'd been trying to tell me for several days, but hadn't been able to. Neither had John. Now it was all out in the open, and they were both relieved. And they were delighted by my reaction. They liked the fact that I'd come out swinging. I was too livid to join in the merriment. "I'm gonna whip your ass" was all I could say.

The next day Howard sent me a fax. "Please read this letter slowly and assume that I am leaving nothing unsaid," it began. This was an easy enough assumption. He was writing to express his hope that the air had cleared. "We are both good at what we do," he wrote, "and we have completely different styles. Neither of us is going to screw this case up and it is simply a question of who gets us the better edge. We both trained hard and we both want to fight the big fight. That's a good thing. I took a back seat before and if need be I will take it again. I understand that you feel that my song and dance routine won't cut it in the 4th Circuit. You may be right. But there are times when I tell myself that my song and dance routine is exactly what is driving this case."

Driving us off a cliff, I thought.

"I am sorry if your feathers are a little ruffled," Howard concluded. "This isn't about our respective feathers. My feathers have been ruffled plenty of times since this thing started. You ain't exactly dainty when you think I am going off in the wrong direction."

No, I ain't exactly dainty. And I'm still going to whip your ass.

•   •   •

Necessity may be the mother of invention, and discord the provenance of peace. We set up our moot court competition. In the intense preparation for it, we invented new and better answers to the questions we knew the judges would ask, and in that process of invention, became friends again. But if the competition was now friendly, it was no less fierce. The argument would be held at William and Mary, my home "court," and would be judged by several of my law professor colleagues and a local lawyer, a friend named John Tucker, who had successfully argued many appeals, including victories in the Supreme Court. Having cooled our tempers, Howard, John, and I agreed that we would not delegate the job of selecting the lawyer to present the argument to outsiders. I would argue, Howard would argue, we'd listen to the critiques of the others, and the three of us would decide among ourselves. If Howard voted for himself and I voted for myself, Johnny would be on the spot. But that's why he got the big bucks, if ever he got them.

I was never more primed for any argument in my life. I stole the best lines from Howard's American University videotape, and wrote more good lines of my own. I stood before the panel of mock judges and let them fire questions at me for ninety minutes. Howard and John both sat on the bench themselves as judges. For ninety minutes I stood at the podium and was grilled. I fielded every brilliant and insightful question, every serious and searching probe, every smart-ass and cutesy trick the moot crew could dream up.

When I was done, Howard was the first to speak.

"You're the man," he said. There wasn't a hint of duplicity or regret in his voice. "You did a great job. It's your case. There's no reason for me to argue. We're one team, with one focus. Let's just concentrate on winning."

I was ecstatic. I was also impressed. The truth is that it probably would have made no difference whether Howard or I had ultimately been our choice. Our voices were different, our accents, our gestures, our word-choices. But our arguments would have been the same. I knew it was eating at Howard not to be making the argument. He was a racehorse, and he had a passion to run. The thing was, so did I.

• • •

The week before the oral argument, the Department of Justice released its report to Congress. Bearing the cumbersome title "Report on the Availability of Bombmaking Information, the Extent to Which Its Dissemination Is Controlled by Federal Law, and the Extent to Which Such Dissemination May Be Subject to Regulation Consistent with the First Amendment to the United States Constitution," the fifty-three-page document bore out my intuition that

Marty Lieberman had indeed been on our wavelength. As we expected, the report made it clear that the dissemination of information on criminal activity such as bombmaking is a substantial social problem, and "will continue to play a significant role in aiding those intent upon committing future acts of terrorism and violence." The report specifically addressed *Rice v. Paladin Enterprises*. Although couched in diplomatic terms, the bottom line was clear. Early in the discussion of our case, the report stated simply, "we think that the district court's First Amendment analysis in *Rice* is, in some respects, open to question." Echoing our analysis of *Brandenburg*, the report drew a distinction between the "mere abstract teaching" of the "moral propriety" of and the act of preparing and steeling others to unlawful action. Then came a sentence in footnote sixty-three of the report that, for us, said it all, succinctly and bluntly: "The district court in *Rice v. Paladin* thus erred in concluding that the *Brandenburg* standard applies to speech 'which advocates or *teaches* lawless activity.' As we explain in the text, the constitutional analysis can differ quite a bit depending on whether a case involves the 'advocacy' or the 'teaching' of lawless activity." It was the sweetest footnote I'd ever read.

And there was more. In a long and thoughtful discussion, the Justice Department examined the issue at the crux of our suit: whether a publisher that knows and intends that its materials will be used for a criminal purpose, but does not know specific readers who will use the material for specific crimes, may nevertheless be held culpable for this more "generalized" aid to crime. The report noted that there were few precedents directly on point, but observed that the *Barnett* and *Buttorff* decisions were "consistent with the conclusions we reach." In a passage that I wanted to gild in gold and wear stitched on my suit for my appearance in court, the report then stated: "At the very least, publication with such an improper intent should not be constitutionally protected where it is foreseeable that the publication will be used for criminal purposes; and the *Brandenburg* requirement that the facilitated crime be 'imminent' should be of little, if any, relevance. Accordingly, we believe that the district court in *Rice v. Paladin* erred insofar as it concluded that *Brandenburg* bars liability for dissemination of bombmaking information *regardless* of the publisher's intent."

Throwing one stale and crusty bone Paladin's way, the report acknowledged that it would often be very difficult to prove a publisher's intent. In the *Hit Man* case, the report noted, the publisher claimed that its audience included many noncriminal readers, such as authors, readers who enjoyed fantasizing about crimes, readers who simply wanted to learn more of criminal methods, criminologists, and law enforcement personnel. But a publisher who, like Paladin, attempted to maximize sales by marketing to criminals and would-be criminals, the report concluded, could still be found guilty of impermissible intent. Quoting Justice Oliver Wendell Holmes, the report observed that it is fair to assume that items are designed for unlawful use when they are "offered for sale in such a mode as purposely to attract purchasers who wanted them for the unlawful [use]."

The Justice Department had not filed an amicus brief. It had done better than that.

Lee Levine and Tom Kelley filed a motion asking for the opportunity to file additional briefs with the Fourth Circuit addressing the positions taken by the Justice Department in its report. The court granted the motion, and Paladin filed a ten-page brief attempting to do damage control.

There are times when nothing speaks so eloquently as silence. We decided to say nothing. We filed a short statement commending the Justice Department's report to the court and stating simply that the report spoke for itself.

24

Appellate Incitement

Iwas up early on May 7. I was only going to Richmond, an hour away, but I always felt sad leaving Erin and Corey, even for just a day. The girls were still sleeping as I bent over their beds to kiss them. I backed my jeep out of the garage and then stopped it and walked back into the house. My eyes were moist as I went back into the girls' bedrooms, and kissed each of them again.

• • •

The U.S. Court of Appeals for the Fourth Circuit has its headquarters in an imposing granite courthouse occupying a full city block on the corner of Tenth and Main Streets in downtown Richmond. The court consists of fifteen federal appellate judges who hear cases in "panels" of three judges. The panels are randomly selected, and the lawyers arguing a case do not know who the three judges on his or her panel will be until the morning of the oral argument.

I was in the court clerk's office on the first floor at eight o'clock, the minute it opened, to officially sign in for the argument. As always, the courthouse staff were unbelievably solicitous and hospitable, like I was checking into a four-star hotel. We were assigned to the "Red Courtroom," on the fourth floor, the same courtroom in which I had argued Peggy McCrerey's case. I took that as a bad omen. The three judges on our panel were William W. Wilkins, Jr., Karen J. Williams, and J. Michael Luttig. I took that as a good omen.

John and Howard arrived minutes after I did. John took one look at my suit and winced. Bad omen. Howard just laughed. "What, you trying to dress like a hit man? Are you here to argue the case or rub somebody out?"

"I try to educate you yokels, but it's hopeless," I said. "These are the finest clothes from the capitals of Europe and the New South. We got a good panel. Michael Luttig's on it. We've got the fourth case of the morning, which means we'll probably not start until about noon, but the clerk says we have to be in the courtroom at nine when the first case is called."

John studied the assignment board posted on the clerk's counter. "Wilkins, Williams, and Luttig," he said. "What do we know about them?"

A courthouse staff member overheard John's question. "If you want to visit our library on the fourth floor, right next to the courtroom you'll be in, we have a notebook that contains profiles of all our judges. You're welcome to go up and look through it." Man, these people were nice. We went upstairs and pulled out the notebook. It contained biographies on all the judges, excerpts from the major opinions they had written in the past, and a compendium of "reviews" from lawyers who practiced regularly before the court. We avariciously skimmed the entries for Wilkins, Williams, and Luttig.

I actually knew a bit about Judge William Wilkins. I had argued a case before him once before, and been lucky enough to win it. The case involved David Baugh, a well-known Richmond criminal defense and civil rights lawyer with a booming voice and mesmerizing presence. Baugh and a client he represented had filed charges of unethical conduct against a Virginia state judge before the state's Judicial Inquiry and Review Commission, the board that adjudicates ethics charges against state judges. Under the commission's rules, all of its proceedings are confidential, and neither Baugh nor his client were permitted to tell anyone that he had brought the charges against the judge, or to describe to anyone the nature of his complaint against the judge. The commission had been "sitting" on Baugh's complaint for over a year, and Baugh was frustrated. He wanted to find out what was going on with his complaint, and he wanted to "go public" with his accusations. But if he did so, he risked ethical proceedings against himself, and even criminal prosecution for violating the commission's secrecy law. So Baugh filed a federal lawsuit, with the support of the Virginia ACLU and a very able Richmond lawyer named Gerald Zerkin, arguing that the secrecy provisions violated the First Amendment. They lost at trial, and I was asked to handle the appeal in the Fourth Circuit. I argued that while the state of Virginia could choose to conduct its inquiries into the ethics of judges in secret, it could not silence citizens and lawyers who brought complaints against judges from speaking out publicly about their charges. "Mr. Baugh and his client," I told the court, "could make photocopies of their complaints and post them to the courthouse door, like Martin Luther nailing his remonstrances to the door of the cathedral, and there is nothing the state could do about it. This is not the world of Franz Kafka, where public proceedings are conducted in secret and citizens who enter those proceedings are forever silenced." The Fourth Circuit panel agreed with this argument and reversed the lower court. Judge Wilkins wrote the opinion giving us our victory. I remembered Judge Wilkins as being very polite, but also very pragmatic and astute in that oral argument. Of course, anytime a lawyer get's a victory from a judge, there is a tendency to remember him as astute.

Judge Wilkins was fifty-five and came from South Carolina. He had gone to Davidson College and the University of South Carolina School of Law, where he was a star student, and editor in chief of the *South Carolina Law Review*. Active in politics, Wilkins was close to Senator Strom Thurmond, working as the state director for Thurmond's Senate campaign in 1972 and working again on Thurmond's campaign in 1978. Wilkins was the first Republican in South Carolina to be elected to the post of "solicitor," a prosecuting attorney, since Reconstruction. Thurmond sponsored Wilkins's initial appointment to the federal bench by President Reagan in 1981. Four years later, Reagan appointed Wilkins to the position of chairman of the U.S. Sentencing Commission, the seven-member panel empowered by Congress to set the sentencing guidelines used by federal judges in criminal cases. Chairing the commission proved to be a prodigious task. In his eight-year tenure, the commission promulgated sentencing guidelines for over eight hundred federal criminal offenses, and trained some eighteen thousand judges and criminal justice employees involved in the federal sentencing process. The work of the commission was often politically super-charged, requiring that Wilkins mediate between conservative and liberals on issues such as the death penalty, the severity of sentences, and white-collar crime. Despite Wilkins's own tough conservative law-and-order views, he often lead the commission toward moderate positions, bowing to political realities and the need to govern through consensus. In 1986, he was rewarded for his hard double-duty work as a sitting federal judge and Sentencing Commission chairman by being elevated to the U.S. Court of Appeals. He was approached by the Reagan White House in 1987 to determine if he would consider becoming the new director of the FBI, but refused. When Robert Bork's nomination to the U.S. Supreme Court foundered, Strom Thurmond strongly pushed Wilkins for the vacant Supreme Court post. Wilkins was a finalist for the high court nomination, but did not get it.

Judge Karen Williams, age forty-five, was another South Carolina native. She had gone to Columbia College and then the University of South Carolina School of Law, where she had been a top student and member of the *Law Review*. She had been in private practice for twelve years, and very active in bar association and civic affairs in the state, before being nominated in 1992 by George Bush to the U.S. Court of Appeals. She had a reputation as a bright, solid, moderate conservative who tended to ask intelligent questions from the bench, but was respectful and restrained in her demeanor.

If Wilkins and Williams seemed to be cut in the classic mold of moderate Republican conservatives, with judicial personas that were even-tempered and composed, the third member of the panel, Michael Luttig, age forty-two, had quite a different reputation. Luttig had gone to college at Washington and Lee, and law school at the University of Virginia. After graduating from law school in 1981 he worked for a year as an assistant counsel in the White House under Fred Fielding, counsel to President Reagan. He then clerked for Judge Antonin Scalia on the U.S. Court of Appeals for the District of Columbia, before Scalia was elevated to the Supreme Court. Luttig went on to clerk for Chief Justice Warren Burger on the Supreme Court, beginning a long and close relationship with the chief justice. After his clerkship, he stayed on for a year as a special assistant to Burger, and he retained close personal and professional ties to Burger for the rest of Burger's life. Luttig went into private practice for four years at the prestigious firm of Davis, Polk, and Wardell, and then began his career with the Justice Department, where he rose quickly to the highest echelons, serving as a close adviser to Attorney General Richard Thornburgh, and later Attorney General William Barr. In 1991, President Bush nominated Luttig to the U.S. Court of Appeals. After his nomination was confirmed by the Senate but before Luttig had been sworn in as a judge, the controversy over the nomination of Clarence Thomas to the Supreme Court erupted, with the allegations of sexual harassment by Anita Hill. Luttig played a prominent role in advising Clarence Thomas and the White House in its counterattack on Anita Hill. On the court of appeals he was regarded as a staunch conservative who was particularly tough on criminals, cut in the mold of Supreme Court Justice Scalia: brilliant, fiery, animated, passionate, and mercurial, a jurisprudential buzz saw.

By the time we finished perusing the biographical reviews, Howard, John, and I were pumped with adrenaline. We still had a half hour before our clients were scheduled to arrive, just as the court would be calling its first case of the morning. I suggested that we leave the building and walk across the street to the Ukrops deli, which had a coffee and breakfast counter popular with lawyers who had business at the federal courthouse. We were chattering about the judges we'd drawn. On the basis of ten minutes of reading, Howard was spinning out deep psychological profiles. "Luttig is gonna be the key," he said. "He's a Scalia. You've gotta appeal to his law-and-order side, not his libertarian First Amendment side." I complimented Howard on his genius.

John laughed. "Isn't this fun?"

It was fun, and we were loose. As we crossed the street we spotted Tom Kelley, Lee Levine, and Peder Lund walking together toward the courthouse. Even from a half-block away, I could see they were stiff and uptight.

"Look, there they are," I said, holding back the urge to point. "Is it my imagination or is that the grimmest-looking group I've ever seen?"

Howard nodded. "We didn't tell you: We spotted them last night in the hotel restaurant. Nobody was smiling. Lund looked miserable. He was not a happy camper."

• • •

"Oyez, oyez, oyez! All rise! The United States Court of Appeals for the Fourth Circuit is now in session. All persons having business before this Court are admonished to draw nigh and lend their attention. God save the United States and this Honorable Court."

We stood as Judges Wilkins, Williams, and Luttig entered the courtroom and took their seats on the bench. I sat in the back row of the courtroom, next to Michael Saunders, Tom Heeney, and Howard. Elaine, Marilyn, and Gloria sat in the bench in front of us, with John. The clients had arrived just a few minutes before, very nervous, and everyone seemed anxious to just get seats in the courtroom and watch the morning's proceedings.

Wilkins was the most senior judge on our panel and, given his prestige and experience, was the person on whom I focused my principal attention. But Wilkins said very little throughout the morning, leaving most of the questioning to his colleagues, Karen Williams and Michael Luttig. There were three cases scheduled before ours, with up to one hour allotted to each, but the first two cases took up only twenty minutes each. We would be starting early. Several of my friends who had promised to come and watch had not yet arrived—I had told them I didn't think our case would be called any earlier than eleven—and I was worried they might miss the argument entirely if things kept moving so quickly. But the next case took nearly the whole hour. It involved the Jim and Tammy Fae Bakker scandal over the Praise the Lord Club. The question was who would bear the losses from the financial debacle, and though I couldn't follow all the legal issues, it seemed to turn on whether people who invested with Jim and Tammy were motivated primarily out of a desire to make money or a desire for religious salvation. The lawyers in the case were colorful, and the questions from the judges brisk. *They're warming up for our case*, I thought.

My friend John Tucker arrived, and my friend David Savage from the *Los Angeles Times*, and several law students from William and Mary. The seats in the courtroom were filling up with lawyers and reporters and law clerks interested in the case. The Jim and Tammy saga ended, and Judge Wilkins called for the next case on the docket, *Rice v. Paladin Enterprises, Incorporated.*

"May it please the Court, I am Rodney Smolla. I represent the appellants Vivian Rice, Marilyn Farmer, Tiffani Horn, and Michael Saunders." I made eye contact with all three judges. Michael Luttig shifted forward in his seat, like he was ready to interrupt my introduction. "This is not a case about the First Amendment rights of Paladin Press," I continued. "This is not a case attacking Paladin for unpopular ideas. This is not a case attacking Paladin because it is unsavory. This is not a case about opinion. This is a case about the knowing and intentional providing of informational assistance to aid and abet a crime. This is—"

"Do you think it's a case of the mere provision of information?"

Michael Luttig interrupted. It had taken him about thirty seconds to pop his first question.

I answered that it was a case about providing detailed information with the intent that it would be used.

"So when you read the book," Luttig asked, "that's *all* you see there in the instructional manual?"

"If you were to read the book, Your Honor, just *alone*, there would be a fact question as to whether or not there was intent, a fact question as to what the intent behind providing the book would be."

"Focusing now just on the text of the book?"

"Yes, Your Honor."

"You think it is just a mere instructional manual?" Luttig's voice was rising. He seemed impatient. Something in my answers seemed to be agitating him, but I could not figure out what.

"It *is* an instructional manual," I repeated firmly. "If your question is whether it contains some kind of advocacy, or ideology, or political thought, our position is that it does not. It is a how-to instructional manual. That is *manifestly* what it is." There, I thought, that's clear enough.

"It is *nothing more* than an instructional manual?"

Well, I guess it wasn't clear enough. I tried again. "There *are* a couple of sentences in the book that sort of have a pep-talk quality. 'Yes, you too can be a hit man. Being a hit man fulfills a valuable role in society. If you follow these instructions, you will be able to go out and do it.' "

"You only found a couple of sentences to that effect?"

"Pardon me, Your Honor?" I felt myself stumbling.

"You only found a couple of sentences to that effect?"

He's trying to crucify me, I thought. He's trying to make *Hit Man* into some kind of political tract, some kind of ideological manifesto, protected by the First Amendment. He's trying to nail me to the burning cross of *Brandenburg v. Ohio*. He's doing just what I warned Howard and John they would try to do. Well, I won't give in. "The manifest character of the book, Your Honor, is instruction. 'This is how you go through the process of murder for hire, step by step.' Certainly it is *not* an ideological presentation."

"So you agree with the district court that it is an instructional manual?"

I knew this was a trick question. But I didn't know what the trick was. Feigning confidence, I answered, "I do agree with the district court, Your Honor, that it is an instructional manual. The key to our case is that if it is an instruction manual, that makes this an assistance case, sufficient to constitute the crime of aiding and abetting."

"That principle seems limitless," said Luttig, almost shouting. "If all they are doing is merely providing information, that strikes me as the core of the First Amendment."

Ah, that was the trick. And I was getting murdered. I tried to shift the ground. "It would be limitless," I said, nodding, "but for the limiture of the intent." I actually said "limiture," which I don't think is a word. Luttig just stared blankly at me. I glanced at Judges Williams and Wilkins, who I had not looked at for several minutes. They also stared blankly. I had to make a move. "The intent here, Your Honors, is powerful." I purposefully looked directly at Wilkins and Williams, sending a signal that I was not going to let Judge Luttig set the agenda. "This book was intended to be used by criminals to commit the crime of murder. It was marketed to a subset of readers who were criminals who desire information on how to commit the crime. Paladin knew and intended this. That is the extraordinary stipulation—"

Luttig interrupted. Yes, he would set the agenda. "Well, it wasn't *simply* a stipulation that it was intended for criminals or would-be criminals, was it?" There was outright anger in his voice. Something I was doing was royally pissing him off, and I was clueless as to what to do about it. "The stipulation," Luttig continued, "was that the book was intended for a cross-section of society that *included* criminals and would-be criminals. If your case rests solely on that intent, and if you concede this was instructional only, you come close to giving away your case."

There was movement behind me. I glanced to my left and saw Gloria Maree being escorted out of the courtroom. She was weeping. I was at rock-bottom. I was getting knocked out in the first round, knocked out so badly that one of my clients was leaving the courtroom in tears. I tried again to fight back. There may have been multiple intents, I argued, but it was sufficient that *one* intent of the publisher was to aid and abet murder. I cited the tax cases, and the *Barnett* case, I argued that the "copycat cases" were not applicable, and I maintained that Paladin could not attempt to "sanitize" its stipulation on intent by now claiming that intent did not really mean intent. Luttig interrupted me constantly during this presentation, challenging every point I made. I was convinced that he had made up his mind to rule against us before he had ever walked out onto the bench. He hated our case; he hated me. The only chance I had to win was to convince Judges Wilkins and Williams. And so far they had not said a word. I decided to play the terrorism card. "Other courts have held," I said, "in applying a federal law that makes it a crime to provide information on how to make a bomb or a gun for the purposes of civil disorder, that as long as the intent is established, there is no problem under the First Amendment."

Again Judge Luttig interrupted. "So I assume then that you would concede that this is not a steeling a group to action case within the meaning of the *Noto* decision?"

I gave the answer that Howard and John had been pounding into me for weeks. Like a programmed robot, I responded, "This is not a *Brandenburg v. Ohio* type of advocacy or 'steeling a group to action' sort of case. This is an 'information' case."

I thought Judge Luttig was going to jump over the bench and throttle me. He leaned over the edge of the bench with a look of abject disgust. "That is absolutely incredible!" I was being destroyed. I shot a glance at Howard. He was staring at me urgently, sending me some kind of telepathic signal. He shook his head slightly, as if to say no. I was missing something—something he was seeing and I was not.

"Your Honor, I—"

"I find it absolutely incredible that you would concede that!" Luttig interrupted again.

And then I saw it. He found it "absolutely incredible that I would *concede* that." He used the word *concede*. It was my *concession* that bothered him! He didn't want me to concede the point. He was my friend, not my enemy! Judge Luttig is my friend, tra, la, la, la, la! I could still turn this around. I smiled at him. "In that case, Your Honor, I won't concede it."

The courtroom exploded in peels of laughter. I glanced at Judge Wilkins, who was smiling. Judge Williams was actually laughing, as if to say, "Good for you."

Judge Luttig, however, did not seem to see the humor. I still had work to do. What I suddenly realized was that we had been talking past one another. He thought we could win under *Brandenburg v. Ohio*. What made him mad was my apparent concession that under *Brandenburg* we would lose. I had been so programmed by Howard and John to insist that *Brandenburg* did not apply that I had missed the gift Judge Luttig was offering me. I now had to backtrack, accept the gift, and lie prostrate before him. Above all, I could not be a smart-ass. Looking intently at Luttig, I stated calmly, "Your Honor, I don't mean to be flippant—not at all. We have strenuously argued before the district court and this court that *if* the *Brandenburg* case is to be applied—*if* this court believes that this case should be analyzed against the backdrop of the incitement line of cases—then we are entitled to win. We do not concede the *Brandenburg* issue. We merely believe that the closer analogy is the line of cases involving aiding and abetting. But if that is wrong, and *Brandenburg* is applied, we still win, because the stipulation says that this book would be used upon receipt by murderers to begin to plan and execute the crime of murder for hire."

Judge Luttig, for the first time in the argument, did not appear angry with me. He wasn't exactly happy, but at least he wasn't angry. "But now that you've told me that it's not 'steeling a group to action,' then it seems like your *Brandenburg* claim fails."

He was giving me a second chance. This time I was not going to blow it. "Your Honor, on page thirty of Paladin's brief, in the footnote, Paladin admits that this book was produced to advocate illegal activity as a form of resistance to government."

This was an apparent contradiction with what I had said before, and Luttig jumped on me. "You told me to the contrary. You told me it was mere instruction."

It was time to lay prostrate before the gods, sacrificing myself for the good of my client. "Your Honor, I apologize for that," I said, with full humility and sincerity. And I meant it. "I didn't mean to mislead you. Let me retract what I said." This was a dicey gamble. Could I pull this off gracefully? I took a glance at Howard. He was dying slow deaths. I plowed forward. "Your Honor, there *is* an element of incitement. I referred to it before as the pep-talk quality of the book. That is the quality of the incitement, if you will. The point of *Brandenburg* is to protect people who engage in advocacy on matters of public concern, because we don't want to punish them merely because of the unsavory nature of their positions. There has to be a close nexus between that abstract advocacy and the teaching of illegal activity for there to be liability."

Luttig looked perplexed. "That is your case? That to the extent that there is anything more than instruction, it was mere abstract advocacy?"

Another trick question. But this time I understood the trick. "To the extent that there is *more* than mere instruction, Your Honor, there is *encouragement*." I had finally hit on the right word. "That is how I would describe it, Your Honor. Encouragement, not abstract advocacy."

"But that's not what you've been saying, at all." Yup, he was right about that.

"Your Honor—"

"Now, you better figure out what your argument is. Because you've got a question of whether it is mere abstract advocacy or whether it is advocacy to action. Now, if I understand my own syllogism, you lose."

This was the moment of truth. I had to figure out my argument, now or never.

"No, Your Honor. Respectfully, we win. If, in *Brandenburg v. Ohio*, when the members of the Ku Klux Klan had been conducting their rally, they had passed out copies of this *Hit Man* book, there could have been liability. That would have crossed the line. That would have been exhortation. There would have been the providing of assistance."

"See, I don't know about that," said Luttig. His manner was thoughtful now. We were getting down to the intellectual point that genuinely concerned him. "There is that statement in *Brandenburg* about abstract advocacy—"

I interrupted him. This is something appellate advocates are taught never to do, but Luttig and I had been boxing each other for twenty minutes like college sophomores in a late-night bull session, and I felt I'd earned the right. I did not want the court to look at *Brandenburg* in isolation, but to view *Brandenburg* as part of a century-long tradition of Supreme Court cases. "Your Honor, in the long line of cases that led up to *Brandenburg* and in numerous cases since the Supreme Court has talked about the distinction between political advocacy and providing actual assistance, in which the speech is part and parcel of the crime, an instrumentality of the crime."

For the first time, Judge Williams asked a question. "How can the mere handling of this manual—considering your response to Judge Luttig's questions—how can the mere handling of this manual make a difference? How does that provide the incitement to imminent unlawful activity?" she asked.

I was pleased to have another member of the court step into the fray. "Your Honor," I said, "the text of the manual would be the only predicate for the incitement."

"So then you are saying that the text of the manual *is* incitement?" Judge Williams asked.

"The text of the manual lacks ideological or political advocacy," I replied. "But it does contain exhortation and urging and encouragement to go out and engage in the business of murder for hire. This is not a case involving political discussion, among members of the Communist Party, say, or a civil rights group."

"This is the problem," said Judge Luttig, chiming back in. "As I understand it, the flaw in your argument is that you conclude from that fact that the book is not protected."

"We are arguing that if this case is *outside* of *Brandenburg*, it is not protected," I said.

"Tell me your argument if it is *inside* of *Brandenburg*," countered Judge Luttig, "because so far you haven't made one."

I argued that the *Brandenburg* standard was met because of the stipulation that Paladin knew and intended that the book would assist criminals. But Judge Luttig was not satisfied, and we went back and forth for several more minutes. Judge Luttig continued to press me on how criminal instructions could amount to incitement. As I saw it, the case was now getting narrowed down to the meaning of one word. "Judge," I said, "I guess we're now down to what the word *incitement* means."

"I don't think there's a great debate over that issue. I certainly understand the argument that their instruction was intended to incite."

I felt that I had almost won Judge Luttig over, but had still not quite pushed the right button. I had this sense that, deep down, we were in agreement, but there was some kind of hangup over language, some way I was phrasing things that was still bothering him. Once again, I was humble. "Your Honor," I said plaintively, "I don't want to mis-state things, and make a concession that I don't intend to make."

"Well, that's the risk of appearing," he chided. The courtroom burst into laughter. It was his turn to be the comedian.

I let the laughter roll through the room and subside, and then tried again to clarify our position. At most, I argued, there were one or two sentences in the entire book that could qualify as "political."

The idea that it is permissible to take justice into one's own hands for personal retribution was, in a sense, a political idea. At this, Judge Williams broke in again. "Is that not the whole ideology this whole book promotes?" she asked. "That you can take the law into your own hands and get revenge and retribution in the way in which you want to?"

"Your Honor, by analogy to what the Supreme Court has said in the obscenity area, a quote or two from Voltaire does not turn otherwise obscene speech into literature. Overwhelmingly, *Hit Man* is a how-to instruction manual, with a few sprinklings of political statements." A light on the podium went on, indicating I had only a few minutes remaining. The half hour of argument had blitzed by in the blink of an eye. In my summation I canvassed several points that I had not been able to develop during the argument, particularly the *Soldier of Fortune* cases. Judge Williams and Judge Luttig interrupted several times again, seeking clarification of my positions. They seemed more sympathetic toward the end, like they knew they had put me through an ordeal and that I had weathered their blasts. Judge Wilkins then broke in, speaking for the very first time, to tell me that my time had expired.

I returned to my seat. John whispered that the argument had been brutal, but that I had done a great job of coming from behind. Howard nodded in agreement. "You were terrific, congratulations," he whispered. But I didn't feel terrific. I didn't think I had lost— things *had* gone better toward the end—but I didn't think I had won either. I still had my rebuttal coming up, after Tom Kelley finished his argument. One more chance to try to score points. I focused intently on Kelley, and on what I should say during my rebuttal.

"May it please the Court," Kelley began, "I am Tom Kelley for the defendant-appellee Paladin Press. This is a case in which a plaintiff for the first time seeks to hold a book publisher liable for the act of the reader without applying *Brandenburg v. Ohio.*"

"What did *Barnett* do?" asked Luttig. Kelley seemed stunned to have been interrupted so quickly.

"*Barnett*, Your Honor, involved a motion to suppress evidence." This was a weasel answer and I knew it wasn't going to satisfy Michael Luttig, the Judge from Hell.

"I *know*," said Luttig adamantly. "But there's no question that *Barnett* was ruling on exactly the issue we have here, is there?" *Yes! Don't try to fool Michael Luttig, Tom.*

"I disagree, Your Honor. In *Barnett*, the defendant was offering to sell instructions on how to manufacture drugs, of no use to really anyone except someone that wanted to manufacture drugs illegally—"

Luttig interrupted, in a tone sterner than anything he had given me. "That is not a difference relevant to our discussion," he sneered.

"Well—"

Luttig interrupted again, "Does it make a difference to impose liability on a publisher if there is instruction to engage in illegal activity?" Luttig asked in a demanding voice. "I don't understand your opening statement!"

You only gave him ten seconds to try and get out his opening statement, you crafty bastard. And now you're nailing him with the very argument I had been trying to make for half an hour! You agreed with me all the time! I love you, you crafty bastard! I love you!

"Well, the problem—"

"You don't *mind* us following *Barnett?*" Luttig interrupted. He wouldn't let Kelley get two words out.

"I do mind—"

"Okay, why?"

Kelley paused and took two steps backward, away from the podium. He crouched downward, putting on his glasses and bending over to peer at his notes. He actually seemed to shrink in size. Luttig's palpable animosity was wilting him, physically, before my very eyes. I actually felt bad for him, one lawyer to another.

"Let me explicate my answer," he said softly. *The "let me reason with you" approach. Good luck, buddy.* "In this case we are dealing with a mass-distributed book—"

"So also in *Barnett*," Luttig insisted. *Like I said, good luck.*

"Well, Your Honor, you have submission of a recipe to someone. It's hard to imagine the person has any use for it but to manufacture drugs without a license?"

Luttig held up his copy of *Hit Man* and waved it toward Kelley. "In contrast to *this* book?" he said, sarcastically. *Yeah, Tom! In contrast to that book?*

Kelley noted that it was stipulated that there were "all kinds of lawful uses" for *Hit Man*, and that it had been sold to some thirteen thousand people, and that law enforcement officers and people interested in crime were among the readers.

"Just because the publisher says that doesn't make it so," Luttig snapped. He wasn't going to let Kelley get away with anything. "I don't think there is any question that the author intended it for the sole purpose of assisting criminals or would-be criminals." I could not believe what I just heard. Chills were running through me. I grabbed Howard by the forearm and squeezed it, afraid to take my eyes off Luttig for a second. Luttig may have given me a hard time, but it was nothing compared to what he was doing to Kelley. Luttig was incredulous that I had said that the *Hit Man* book was not incitement. In Luttig's mind, *every page* of the book was incitement. Suddenly, as he pilloried Kelley, it all became clear.

Luttig held up the book again, staring Kelley down, referring to him as "you," as if Kelley himself had written and published *Hit Man*. "You begin with the dedication of the book." Luttig began to read from the book. " 'To those who think, who dare, who do, who succeed.' " Luttig looked at Kelley again, and continued, "You go on to exhort people to take the law into their own hands. You talk about moving up the ladder of success by killing people. You talk of the rendezvous with destiny, and about how you kill people once and then repeatedly." Luttig read from the book: " 'The next time,' the author says, 'you don't even need a reason to kill. And after you've killed, you realize what morons—*morons*—others are, because *you're superior.* You've taken charge of your life. You have killed once. Now you can kill repeatedly.' " Luttig stared down from the bench at Kelley. "And why?" Luttig asked. He flipped to another page in *Hit Man*. As he did so I focused intently on the copy of the book he was holding. It was dog-eared and well worn, stuffed with self-stick notes. Luttig continued reading: " 'You realize you don't even need reason to kill.' " He looked back at Kelley. "Why?" he demanded, and without waiting for an answer, continued from the book, " 'Because you're a *man* now.' " Luttig looked up. "Without a doubt you've proved to society that you're a man," he said, paraphrasing the book. "It's forward-looking," he said. "It contemplates not just one killing but repeated killings. And the final paragraph of the book says what?" Judge Luttig began to quote from *Hit Man*, but *without looking down at the text*. My God, I thought, *he's got the damn book memorized!* "It says that you've met the challenges. You've met the new frontiers. There are none left to conquer, now that you've learned how to kill and kill repeatedly. The argument that this is mere instruction is frankly not even plausible."

The courtroom was absolutely silent. I could not move from my chair. I had never seen a judge so viscerally enveloped in a case. Tom Kelley tried to recover control of his argument. "Your Honor," he said, "the last sentence says something to the effect that 'maybe someday you'll write a book about this.' I suggest that sentence culminates unavoidable signals throughout this book that this is a matter of fantasy and not fact."

I knew this was a mistake the moment Kelley said it. Treating *Hit Man* as fantasy was not going to sell to this judge.

"Let's read the last sentence," Judge Luttig mocked. " 'Then some day, when you've done and seen it all, when there doesn't seem to be any challenge left or any new frontier left to conquer, you might just feel cocky enough to write a book about it.' "

"Your Honor—" Kelley tried to break in, but Luttig would not let him.

"Now you may or may not have a First Amendment protection," Luttig lectured, "but you can't argue that it is nothing more than an instruction manual."

Kelley replied that what I had described as words of "encouragement" did not amount to "incitement."

Judge Luttig then spoke the single most important sentence of the hour: "I'm not sure that the words *he* used are either," he said, "but I'm fairly certain that the words *I* read are."

The moment Judge Luttig spoke that sentence, I finally saw his full hand revealed, and I knew what I had to say when I got up for rebuttal.

Kelley, meanwhile, struggled to survive twenty more minutes of judicial torture. He would get a sentence, or more often a fragment of a sentence, out, and Judge Luttig would jump all over him. Luttig had *Hit Man* virtually committed to memory. And any statement Kelley made to try to characterize *Hit Man* as benign or as mere fantasy or entertainment would be met by a barrage of counterexamples from Luttig. "I'm not just making these passages up," Luttig admonished. "It's the sinew of this book. The *sinew*. What happened is that the district court seemed to just read it as an instruction manual, without ever understanding the book itself."

Kelley claimed that *Hit Man* was really no different than a Tom Clancy novel. Luttig jumped all over him, stating that Tom Clancy, John Grisham, and other popular authors do not encourage the reader to go out and kill for the fun of it. Kelley then argued that the written word, alone, could never amount to incitement, or to "steeling someone to action." Luttig was incredulous, repeatedly hammering at Kelley to explain why the written word could not have this effect. Kelley responded by claiming that *Hit Man* contained "too many contrary signals," alerting the reader that the reader must make his or her own judgments and decisions before actually killing someone. This wasn't even close to incitement, Kelley insisted. Judge Luttig was entirely unimpressed, rebuffing Kelley with more quotes from the book.

Judge Williams then entered the discussion, asking Kelley what his view was as to the meaning of Paladin's stipulation that it intended that the book would be used by real criminals to commit murder. Was Paladin admitting to "civil intent," she asked, or to "criminal intent"?

Kelley responded by stating that mere "civil intent" would not be enough, under the First Amendment, to hold Paladin liable. His answer seemed to equate "civil intent" with mere "knowledge" that the book could be used to assist in murder. This did not seem to sit well with either Judge Williams or Judge Luttig. Since Paladin had stipulated to "intent," they both asked, why shouldn't a jury decide what level of intent Paladin possessed when it published the book? Kelley's only response was that the stipulation meant merely "knowledge" or "civil intent." This set Judge Luttig off on a blistering counterattack. "You've changed the intent stipulation," he charged. It was obvious that Judges Luttig and Williams saw Paladin's maneuver the same way we saw it—as stipulating to one thing and then trying to "spin" the stipulation afterward.

The red light went on, indicating that Kelley's argument time had expired. Judge Wilkins, again speaking for the only time, thanked Kelley and excused him from the podium. I rose for my two minutes of rebuttal, knowing exactly what I wanted to do.

• • •

"May it please the Court, I'd like to focus in my brief rebuttal time on the passages that Judge Luttig read, and make our position exactly clear.

"Yes. The passages read by Judge Luttig constitute incitement.

"Yes. The passages constitute 'steeling someone to action.' "

I looked directly at Judge Luttig. "Judge, I think in my colloquy with you, when I heard you use the word *incitement*, I was thinking of that term as the buzzword for 'political advocacy.' "

Judge Luttig beamed and leaned back in his chair, exhaling with a huge sigh of relief. He seemed to suddenly relax, as if some terrible knot had been loosened. "Yes!" he said, "I think you were." He was giving me absolution.

"Your Honor, I shouldn't have resisted your characterization. We use this phrase *aiding and abetting*. It is a famous common-law term that falls trippingly off the tongue. But it actually consists of two distinct concepts. *Aiding* is the provision of assistance. *Abetting* in providing encouragement."

Judge Luttig smiled and nodded affirmatively, encouraging me with his body language.

"We ought not be penalized because Paladin engaged in both aiding and abetting," I argued. "The provision of detailed information, when coupled with the element of encouragement, makes the information more lethal, not less lethal."

"I thought that's what you were trying to argue," said Judge Luttig.

"And," I continued, "it is perfectly consistent with both tort principles and the First Amendment to say that in there can be sufficient detailed information to constitute aiding and abetting, and also sufficient encouragement to satisfy the *Brandenburg* standard. Above all, if there is any element that is a close call in this case, if the outcome turns on the characterization of any of these elements, then the case should be remanded for further amplification, discovery, and trial before a jury. Thank you."

I sat down. I took a quick glance backward, at my clients, the members of the families. They were smiling. Everyone in the courtroom rose as the judges got up from the bench and filed down to the counsel table, shaking the hands of all the lawyers.

• • •

We gathered for the debriefing at a restaurant a few blocks from the courthouse, The Tobacco Company. The restaurant was built in an old tobacco warehouse building, and was decorated like a cross between a fern bar and a bordello. We had a private dining room on the second floor. All of the family members were there, along with Howard, John, Tom Heeney, and me.

Janice Saunders's husband, Michael, was filled with enthusiasm. For the first time, I believe that he really believed. "You did a great job," he said to me. "And by the end, I thought the judges were completely on our side."

Gloria, who had been escorted from the courtroom weeping when I was at the lowest of the low, smiled through tears. "I couldn't take it anymore, Rod. I had to leave. Then someone came outside and told me that things were getting better for us. I came in and heard you at the end. It lifted my heart."

"You were strong," said Elaine. "You stood your ground and weathered the storm. I was proud."

Several reporters and other lawyers dropped in, including David Montgomery from the *Washington Post* and David Savage from the *Los Angeles Times*. The mood was euphoric. The lawyers tried to be restrained in the presence of the clients, cautioning that one can never tell what a court will do, and that it is dangerous business to try to predict how an appellate judge will rule on the basis of the questions they ask as oral argument. But this had been no ordinary oral argument, and we could not conceal our now-soaring expectations. The fate of the case seemed clearly to lay in the hands of one indomitable judicial presence, Judge J. Michael Luttig. And unless he was the best actor since Jack Nicholson, it seemed almost certain that he wanted to rule our way.

25

The Search for the Hunch-Producers

There is a school of American legal thought known as legal realism," I lectured to the class. "The American legal realists were a group of elite intellectual judges, lawyers, philosophers, and law professors, many with ties to Yale, Harvard, and Columbia, who set out in the 1920s and 1930s to attack much of the conventional wisdom about the nature of law. Supreme Court Justice Oliver Wendell Holmes was the judicial grandfather of the school, and among its greatest luminaries were law professor Karl Llewellyn, New Dealer and later Supreme Court Justice William O. Douglas, and federal judges Joseph C. Hutcheson, Jr., and Jerome Frank. Today you read excerpts from their readings. Who can tell me what the realists were all about?"

I called on Burt. "The realists argued that lawyers should divorce law and morality," he said.

"That's right," I said. "They argued that the legal system was highly fluid and quintessentially human, filled with passion, prejudice, quirks, and uncertainty. Intellectual deduction, detailed analysis, and convoluted doctrines and concepts were not really what law was all about, law was much more practical and earthy. To understand 'law,' you really had to understand people, including their biases and emotions as well as their minds. Lawyers should thus be realists, focusing on how real-world judges and juries and bureau-crats actually behave, and not be so concerned with high-fallutin rules, dense vocabulary, or sweeping generalizations. The legal scholar Roscoe Pound, a forerunner of the realists, thus talked about the difference between 'law in the books' and 'law in action.'

"Oliver Wendell Holmes, in an address he delivered on the occa-sion of the dedication of the new law school building at Boston Uni-versity on January 8, 1897, explored these themes with particularly poetic imagination. His speech was later published in the *Harvard Law Review* under the title 'The Path of the Law.' In this famous essay, Holmes argued that the 'primary rights and duties with which jurisprudence busies itself are nothing but prophecies.' Now Burt, this is a disturbing idea that Holmes seems to be advancing. What exactly, is he saying here?"

"He's debunking legal rules," said Burt. "Legal rules, such as the notion of a 'legal duty,' Holmes was arguing, do not really exist any-where. They are simply predictions."

"Excellent," I responded. "You might say that in Holmes's view, a lawyer is like a weatherman. Tomorrow's weather does not exist. The meteorologist merely *predicts*, using satellite photos, barometric readings, computer models, and accumulated scientific experience, what the weather system is *likely* to do tomorrow. Depending on the conditions, weather predictions may be more certain or less certain. Holmes claimed that law was, in an important sense, not that much different from weather. Ultimately, when a lawyer advises a client on whether or not to engage in certain conduct, citing a 'legal rule' to guide the client's behavior, the lawyer is doing nothing more than making an educated guess that if his or her client behaves in a certain way, and the matter is later litigated in court, the court will enforce against the client certain consequences. The scholar Karl Llewellyn, in an influential article published in the *Columbia Law Review* in 1930, built on this point by talking about 'paper rules,' and how the task of the lawyer is to determine how far the paper rule is real, and 'how far merely paper.'

"Now, let's see if we can work through this with a concrete example," I continued. "Burt, try this. Let's say you are a lawyer in a child custody dispute, representing the parent with primary custody over the children—the mother, let us assume. Let's imagine that she comes up to you in your office one day and asks you, 'What will happen if I attempt to move with my children to another city, so as to frustrate my ex-husband's ability to regularly visit the children?' What is the legal rule, the mother insistently asks. 'Am I allowed to pick up stakes and move wherever I want? Or will my former spouse have the power to block my move?' How would you go about advising her, Burt, if you were a lawyer who followed the gospel according to Oliver Wendell Holmes?"

Burt paused for a minute and thought. "Well, I guess," he began tentatively, "Holmes would say that the smart lawyer will caution his or her client that there 'is no legal rule.' All the lawyer can do is 'predict'."

"Yes. And Burt, we know you're going to be a smart lawyer. So what are you going to say to your client, looking at you with beseeching eyes?"

"I guess I would say to her, something like, well, the legal standard—the paper rule—is what the courts call the best interest of the children. Courts usually interpret that standard as heavily favoring the active and ongoing involvement of both parents in the children's lives. If you have no strong reason for making this move, a court might well not permit you to relocate with the children. If you attempted to do so, the court might shift primary custody to their father. There are several prior judicial decisions in this state, and sometimes courts have allowed such relocation moves, sometimes they have not, depending on such things as the motivation behind the move and the nature of the relationship between the children and their noncustodial parent."

"Now, Burt, frustrated by this ostensible waffling, your client protests, 'You mean that's the best you can do? "On the one hand, this, on the other hand, that?" What about morality? I am the children's mother! I was awarded primary custody! It seems immoral to keep me from making this move. *I* should be the one who decides these important matters in their lives.'

"Now what are you going to say, Burt? Or what would Holmes admonish you to say?"

"I think Justice Holmes might want me to utter a chilling warning to my client. 'Look,' I would probably tell her, 'we're not talking about morality here. We're talking about the law. People have different views of morality. Some might not see it your way at all. They might see you attempting to separate the kids from Dad as the real immorality. The point is that it's not your view of right or wrong that matters, it's the judge's. Now I know the local family court judge before whom this case has been assigned. I know how she thinks. I know how she feels. And she will not look kindly on this move. I suggest you don't try it.' "

•   •   •

We waited for the Fourth Circuit to render its decision, and as we waited, I contemplated the character of Judge Michael Luttig. He was a captivating puzzle, and I became engrossed in learning more about him. I was not driven by some impatient rush to anticipate his ruling—I had given the argument my best and was at peace, content to set the case aside and let it simmer with the court. Rather, I was propelled to learn more of Luttig for all the reasons I have always been propelled to learn more about the law. Here was a complex and brilliant man, who at moments had seemed almost possessed by some jurisprudential demon, some querulous law-god, and that law-god now possessed me, bedeviling me to learn more.

Judge Michael Luttig, indeed, was the archetype the American legal realists may well have had in mind. The realists' concentration on the psychology of the judge seems entirely natural to us at the end of the twentieth century, but earlier in the century it ran contrary to all legal orthodoxy. Judges were not thought of as highly subjective human beings, but as objective arbiters of some objective body of doctrines reified as "The Law." In a wonderfully impish piece published in the *Cornell Law Quarterly* in 1927, a distinguished federal judge from Texas debunked the stately image of judging by talking about a famous jurist, "a man of great learning and ability," who after hearing an especially difficult case "announced from the Bench that since the narrow and prejudiced modern view of the obligations of a judge in the decision of causes prevented his resort to the judgment aleatory by the use of his 'little, small dice,' he would take the case under advisement, and, brooding over it, wait for a hunch." Hutchinson wrote of the "judicial hunch," something he contrasted with the austere image of the judicial mind as a cold logic engine, describing how in his own life as a judge he would often "hunch out" a decision, seeking out the "still, sad music of humanity," reading the briefs, viewing the evidence, listening to the competing arguments of the lawyers, and waiting for "that sixth sense, that feeling, which flooding the mind with light, gives the intuitional flash necessary for the just decision." Judge Hutchinson wrote that it was the cultivation of this "tiptoe faculty of the mind," the feels and hunches, that ultimately made for the best judges and lawyers, and indeed, even the best gamblers, detectives, and scientists.

Judge Jerome Frank wrote in a similar vein in a powerful book published in 1930 entitled *Law and the Modern Mind*. If the law consists of the decisions of judges, Frank reasoned, and the decisions of judges are based largely on "hunches," then whatever produces the judges' hunches makes the law. The interesting question, then, is what are the hunch-producers? Drawing on the science of psychology, Frank argued that one must look at the individual judge's past to find out. "His own past," Frank wrote, "may have created plus or minus reactions to women, or blonde women, or men with beards, or Southerners, or Italians, or Englishmen, or plumbers, or ministers, or college graduates, or Democrats. A certain twang or cough or gesture may start up memories painful or pleasant in the main." Frank thus pushed "realism" to its extreme—to understand the law one had to understand the modern mind—indeed, if a judge, one's *own* mind. Frank himself underwent a rigorous regimen of Freudian psychoanalysis in 1927 to better unlock and understand his own prejudices.

As I pursued the enigma of Michael Luttig, I felt myself swimming through the cross-currents and whirlpools the realists had left in their wake.

It was obvious to me that Judge Michael Luttig had done much brooding over *Rice v. Paladin Enterprises, Inc.*, before I ever walked to the podium on the day of our oral argument. He had well-formed hunches about the just outcome of the case before I or Tom Kelley had spoken a word in open court. What were those hunch-producers?

•　•　•

People who become federal judges are usually accomplished and sophisticated players in legal, civic, and political circles. Very few people become federal judges by sheer dint of intellect or legal ability. Instead, they rise to the elite status of a federal judgeship by working their way up various ladders of success, influence, and visibility. Michael Luttig was in this sense typical. He had punched tickets in high places—at the White House, in private legal practice, and in the Department of Justice. For twenty years Chief Justice Warren Burger had been a special friend and mentor. When the chief justice died in 1995, Luttig delivered the most personal of the eulogies at his funeral, describing an incident in London in which the formidable cast-in-Hollywood chief justice with the thick white mane had entered a street brawl in London to save a person being beaten up by five men with fists and sticks, and recalling Burger's passions: his love of history, the Constitution, good wine, sculpture, and above all his children, grandchildren, and his wife, Elvera, who had died the year before. When it was revealed that Warren Burger had decided to leave his papers to the College of William and Mary rather than the Library of Congress, it was Luttig who spoke for Burger and his family, stating that the decision was based on the chief's special affection for William and Mary, and not any disdain for the Library of Congress.

I found Luttig's obviously deep affection for Warren Burger intriguing. Burger relished the pomp and circumstance of the Supreme Court, and the history surrounding the Constitution. He retired from the Supreme Court to become the chairman of the Constitutional Bicentennial Commission. Despite his relatively stiff and gruff public persona, in private moments he could be a gracious and engaging man. While Warren Burger was a conservative, he was no radical. He often took moderate and conciliatory positions on issues such as affirmative action or separation of church and state. It was interesting to me that Michael Luttig, who on the surface seemed much more of a firebrand than the chief justice, would be so personally close to him. On some levels Luttig seemed more like his other judicial mentor, the free-spirited Antonin Scalia, than the reserved and dignified Burger. Watching Antonin Scalia in oral argument, one always got this sense of joy about him, this "I just love this job" sense of sheer exuberance. Justice Scalia was famous for his gregarious persona, particularly his loquacious antics at oral arguments, stinging advocates with piercing questions and tricky hypotheticals, dominating the room like a judicial stand-up comic, playing to the crowd, jibing his colleagues on the bench, treating the events like rollicking intellectual festivals. Michael Luttig, like Scalia, had dominated our oral argument. But I could also see the Warren Burger in Michael Luttig. He was intellectually aggressive, yes, and he was passionate, but there was still a reserve of sorts. Or maybe, to be more precise, there was the palpable absence of joy.

Michael Luttig was now a judicial animal, but he had once been a political animal. Luttig was a central player in the Clarence Thomas nomination. When Oklahoma law professor Anita Hill came forward and testified that she had been sexually harassed by Thomas when he was her superior at the Equal Employment Opportunity Commission, White House and Justice Department lawyers advising Thomas decided to go on the offensive, aggressively attacking Anita Hill, attacking Democratic members of the Senate Judiciary Committee, and charging that Thomas was the victim of a racist "lynching." The strategy was devised and orchestrated by President Bush's legal counsel, C. Boyden Gray, and by Michael Luttig, who was still in his post at the Justice Department as assistant attorney general and director of the Office of Legal Counsel.

Luttig lead the research effort into Anita Hill's past, trying to raise doubts about her credibility. At the time, Luttig had already been nominated by President Bush to his position as a federal judge on the U.S. Court of Appeals for the Fourth Circuit, and the Senate had confirmed the nomination. But he had not yet taken his oath of office, and thus was technically not yet a federal judge, but still a member of the executive branch, holding his assistant attorney general's position. Liberal law professor Laurence Tribe of Harvard hit hard at Luttig for his participation in the Thomas matter, stating in the *New York Times* that it was "unprecedented for a judge to take such an active, behind-the-scenes role in the confirmation of a nominee for another judicial seat." Tribe argued that it made little difference that Luttig had not yet been sworn in, because "as soon as he was confirmed, people began to view him as a judge, and the first visible thing he did was to take sides in the battle over another Federal seat." Yale Law School professor Geoffrey Hazard stated that while technically Luttig did nothing wrong, "the better course would have been the one taken by the vast majority of nominees, who exercise every precaution to avoid even the slightest appearance of political partisanship as soon as they are nominated."

The Justice Department, however, staunchly stood by its man, stating that the department had specifically asked that Luttig delay taking his oath of judicial office so that he could stay on to assist with the Thomas hearings. And Rex E. Lee, Jr., a highly respected conservative legal scholar, president of Brigham Young University, and former solicitor general of the United States in President Reagan's Department of Justice, argued that Luttig did the right thing. "His obligation was to his client," Lee argued. "He still owed a duty to his superiors in the Justice Department and the Administration."

If this formal résumé of Michael Luttig was enough to document his impeccable conservative credentials, it wasn't entirely satisfying. Being a "conservative" did not necessarily dictate how one would view the legal issues in *Rice v. Paladin*. The free speech questions in the case were complex, and did not break down easily into any knee-jerk "conservative" or "liberal" labeling. And many conservatives, including Luttig's former boss Antonin Scalia, could be powerful defenders of the First Amendment. Above all, Michael Luttig's formal résumé did not account for how profoundly he had internalized the issues in our suit. As he had talked about the very sinew of the book *Hit Man*, the case had seemed to enter and possess Luttig himself, becoming a very part of him.

There had to be more, I thought. And there was. As I researched Luttig's past, I stumbled on an extraordinary coincidence. This was not the first time, I found, that Judge Luttig had ruled on a Fourth Circuit case involving murders committed with the aid of "recipe" information. The other case involved a man named Robert Russell, a former marine convicted of murdering his wife, Shirley Gibbs Russell, by following the instructions on a computer file containing twenty-six steps to carry out a murder, including "what to do with the body," "alibi, excuse from work," and "how to do I kill her." The case was extraordinary because it was based entirely on circumstantial evidence. Shirley Gibbs Russell was a marine captain at the Quantico Marine Base. On March 4, 1989, she disappeared, and was never seen again. Her body was never found. There were no witnesses to any crime. No murder weapon was recovered—indeed, there was no physical evidence of any kind indicating what the murder weapon or method of murder even was. The government's theory was that Russell, who had recently been discharged for disciplinary reasons, shot his wife behind the ear with a .25-caliber pistol while the two were in a storage shed adjacent to their quarters, and then dumped her body into a mine shaft in Pennsylvania. The government argued that Russell saw his wife as a symbol of the marine corps, which he had come to hate, because she was regarded as a star in the corps, on the way to a promotion to major, while Russell was being drummed out. There was evidence that Robert and Shirley's marriage had been stormy, that Russell had often been unfaithful, that he had physically abused his wife, and that he had been the last to see her alive. But the main evidence leading to the conviction was the computer instruction file, which the government labeled a "recipe" for murder. Russell's mother had testified that her son was an aspiring writer, and the computer file was his outline for a novel. The jury obviously did not buy this explanation, and despite the wholly circumstantial nature of the case against him, found Russell guilty.

Russell appealed his conviction. Michael Luttig wrote the Fourth Circuit opinion for a unanimous three-judge panel stating that the evidence against Russell was "substantial" and "more than sufficient" to sustain his conviction and life sentence. There was no strict legal requirement, Luttig wrote, that the victim's body be recovered, and the chain of circumstantial evidence, including the murder "recipe," was more than enough to support the jury's verdict. The Russell case was an astounding coincidence and, I thought, a significant one. Judge Luttig had seen first hand, in the Russell case, that people really did follow written blueprints and recipes in carrying out murders. He understood that such information could be lethal. The finding of such information in a defendant's possession could play an integral role in his prosecution and conviction. To be sure, there were no First Amendment issues in the Russell case. It was simply a very unusual criminal law decision. But the factual parallels to *Hit Man* and the murders committed by James Perry were obvious. It seemed likely that the Paladin suit would trigger Judge Luttig's memory of the Russell case, and on some subliminal level that had to help us.

But the significance of the Russell case was soon overwhelmed in my journey through Judge Luttig's past by a discovery of an event so hideous and tragic that it demeans human dignity to label it "coincidence." The moment I found it I was filled with loathing and self-disgust. *How could I not have known about this? How could I not have heard this story before. I argued this case in front of this man without knowing of this horror from his past.* But I could not have known Judge Luttig would be on our panel, I thought, trying to defend myself, and I could hardly be expected to research the personal histories of every sitting Fourth Circuit judge. Yet still, I felt somehow ashamed, chagrined, humbled, awkward. For now I understood Michael Luttig's arduous contempt for the book *Hit Man*, understood his angry impatience with me, understood his brazen ridicule of Tom Kelley's lame efforts to pass the book off as light spoof.

Michael Luttig's own father had been murdered.

On the night of April 19, 1994, John and Bobbie Luttig, the parents of Michael Luttig, were driving to their home in Tyler, Texas, near Dallas in their Mercedes-Benz, when three teenagers in a red Ford Probe began to tail them. The three men—Donald Coleman, eighteen; his brother Cedric, twenty; and Napoleon Beazley, seventeen—wanted to steal the Mercedes. As the Luttigs pulled into their garage, Beazley and Coleman rushed from the Ford Probe with a pistol and a sawed-off shotgun. John Luttig was shot through the head as he stepped out of his car. Bobbie Luttig survived by feigning death and rolling under the Mercedes. The three men backed the Mercedes over Bobbie and out of the garage and drove it several blocks before deciding it was too dangerous to keep it. They abandoned the stolen car and fled in their Ford.

Two months later the men were arrested and charged on federal counts of carjacking, illegal possession of a firearm, and illegal possession of a short-barreled shotgun, and state counts of murder and aggravated battery. The Coleman brothers were convicted on the federal charges. (Beazley, a minor at the time of the crimes, was not charged in the federal indictment.) The sentencing hearing for the Coleman brothers took place on January 18, 1995, before Senior Federal District Judge William Steger at the federal courthouse in Tyler. Under the provisions of a new federal law, the Violent Crime

Control and Law Enforcement Act of 1994, the victims of violent crime, or their relatives if they are killed, incapacitated, or a minor, are entitled to appear in court "to make a statement or present any information in relation to the sentence." Michael Luttig, a sitting federal court of appeals judge, stepped out of his official role and appeared before another federal judge at the sentencing hearing to speak for his murdered father and his devastated family. In a vivid and heart-rending statement, he recounted the hideous and tragic event that had forever changed his family's life, and the indelible scars it had left behind. He was making his statement, he explained, because he felt he owed it to the public and to the other victims of violent crime who either "stand silently by, or who speak and are not heard." In poignant detail, he then described what it had been like to have his father violently stripped from his life, the "horror, the agony, the emptiness, the despair, the chaos, the confusion, the sense—perhaps temporary, but perhaps not—that one's life no longer has any purpose." He described the horror his mother suffered as she feigned death and crawled under the car, knowing that her husband was dying only a few feet away, he described the disorienting grief and disbelief of the first moments when he and other members of his family were informed of the killing, he recounted the crushing anxiety and trauma of the public trials, trials in which he listened to the tape of his mother's call to 911, hearing the terror in her voice as she reported that her husband had been murdered, trials at which he listened as the autopsy report was introduced, explaining how the bullets had entered his father's skull, penetrated and exited his brain, and traveled through his shoulder and arm, trials at which he heard testimony as to how long his father might have been conscious and aware of what was happening, trials at which he learned that the .45-caliber gun used to murder his father was "basically a cannon," trials at which he saw photographs of his father lying in the driveway in a pool of blood.

Although his father and his father's family were the victims, Judge Luttig explained, they felt an inexplicable sense of guilt and embarrassment, as if they were somehow responsible for this ugliness that had entered their lives. Above all, Judge Luttig described the abiding sensation of emptiness that he felt in murder's wake, "the sickening sense that it all ended some time ago," and that he was "but biding time."

I was overcome as I read Judge Luttig's statement for the first time. I didn't give a damn what impact the loathsome murder of John Luttig may have had on his son's ruling in my case. I didn't think about winning or losing, or the First Amendment, or the psychology of the judicial mind.

I read Michael Luttig's statement and I wept, one human to another, for his loss, his dignity, his love. All I could think about were my own kids, Erin and Corey, and what it would be like for them if I were violently killed, or what it would be like for me if, in the greatest horror of the universe, I were ever to lose either of them. I was haunted by Michael Luttig's terrible and beautiful words, haunted by how much they reminded me of the feelings I had heard Elaine and Gloria and Michael express, haunted by the memory of Gloria actually walking out of my oral argument before Judge Luttig, because the stress of reliving the events and perhaps *not* being vindicated in our suit was too much to bear. There was an immediate human connection, a virtual bond, between the families of the victims in *Rice v. Paladin Enterprises* and this federal judge who would adjudicate their suit. It was a bond of empathy, of common remorse, of shared tragic experience.

As Judge Luttig's words washed over me, and I slowly calmed down, I tried to place this dreadful revelation in more analytic perspective. I wondered whether Judge Luttig could be objective in considering our case, or other cases involving violent crime. Undoubtedly he was a brilliant man, and undoubtedly he took seriously his oath of office and his obligation to render impartial justice. There is something about a person putting on a judge's robe and sitting up on a high bench that can cause all of us, even seasoned lawyers, to forget that judges are just human beings. Their lives may be as fractious and divided as any of ours, their emotions as deep and overwhelming, their hearts as striped and broken. I understood that Judge Luttig probably struggled, mightily and constantly, to keep his emotions in check and under control, to cross-examine his own motivations and impulses, to swim against the vanquishing flood tides of memory.

Yet he was only human, and when a case before him triggered some flashback to the night of his father's brutal demise, it had to affect him, perhaps consciously, perhaps only subconsciously, but it had to affect him, and when it did, he would have to summon all his will and self-control to remain objective. I suspected that Tom Kelley and Lee Levine harbored the unspoken wish that Luttig would have recused himself from sitting on the case, stepping down because of his father's murder. But my instinct was that Judge Luttig was right to remain on the case. Judge Luttig, I believed, knew as well as any judge alive that the net sum of life's experiences, its triumphs and tragedies, inevitably influence a judge's perspectives and attitudes. To disqualify a judge merely because a case conjures unpleasant memories would be to disqualify a judge for the sensitivity that makes the law feeling and human, instead of rote and mechanical. The question was whether Judge Luttig had the self-awareness to struggle for objectivity, and the self-discipline to achieve it. From what I had observed, he had both.

Reading his moving words, my first impulse was to try to communicate with him in some simple way—to drop him a card, or just call him and say I'm sorry, I hadn't realized, it all must have been terrible, it must still be terrible, and I admire your fortitude. But such a simple human gesture, a brief moment of reaching out, as innocuous as a comforting handshake or pat on the shoulder, was of course out of the question. He was a judge deliberating a case in which I was an advocate. It would have been unethical for me to contact him. And even were it not a violation of the cannons of ethics, it would have seemed contrived or calculated to him, for how could he be sure it was sincere and not manipulative. So in my own private way I made my contact through the mystic ether that connects us all, offering a simple prayer that he and his family might achieve some closure and peace in their lives.

But any such peace, I knew, would take a long time, as it had already taken such a long time for the families of Millie, Trevor, and Janice, and as I replayed our oral argument in the sad dim light of what I now knew, I could feel, for the first time, exactly how and why it was that he found the book *Hit Man* so profoundly fraught with death. When Michael Luttig spoke that day for his dead father and grieving family, he also spoke for something larger. He said it, in his opening words: "I also owe this to the other victims of violent crime who either stand silently by, or who speak and are not heard. . . . I owe it to the public." As Michael Luttig first read the text of *Hit Man*, he must have thought of his own father's killers. Kids. Punks. Buzzed-up on a violent thrill ride, thinking they were big men with their big guns, ready to massacre for a Mercedes, superior, feeling nothing, steeled to kill. And now here was this book, and its every page, its very *sinew*, he repeated from the bench, was calculated to make people think exactly that way, to become killing machines, above emotion, above all awareness or contrition for the destruction, havoc, and sorrow they will reek. District Judge Alex Williams had read the book, but never really grasped its essence, Judge Luttig had said. And neither, I realized, had I—not in the way Judge Luttig had grasped it. *It's fun to kill! It's easy to kill! You can make money, get women, and be master of the universe! Follow these easy instructions! Rise to the challenge! Feel the high! And feel nothing for the mark! Feel nothing for those left behind! Feel nothing, but your own superiority!* That was what the book said. That was its sinew. Page after page. It was not just an instruction manual. It was not just abstract advocacy. It was training. It was steeling to action. That's how it read to someone whose own life had been touched by violence. That's how it read to the families of Millie, Trevor, and Janice. That's how it read to Michael Luttig, who since his father's murder had been haunted by the sickening sense of biding time.

26

Rocky Weren't Just Another Bum

W e waited six months for the court of appeals to render its decision. We waited six months, and then it came. The opinion of the U.S. Court of Appeals for the Fourth Circuit in *Rice v. Paladin Enterprises* was announced on November 10, 1997. It was sixty-five pages long, and unanimous. Its author was Judge Michael Luttig. The opinion began to print on my fax machine minutes after it was released by the clerk's office in Richmond.

Judge Luttig's opinion opened with five pages of quotations from *Hit Man*, without comment or amplification, selecting many of the books most brazen and curdling passages. The families had alleged, he noted, that in publishing *Hit Man* Paladin had aided and abetted James Perry in his commission of the murders of Mildred Horn, Trevor Horn, and Janice Saunders. The record, he wrote, amply supported this allegation. Judge Luttig observed that in "soliciting, preparing for, and committing these murders, Perry meticulously followed countless of *Hit Man*'s 130 pages of detailed factual instructions on how to murder and to become a professional killer." Perry, for example, followed many of the book's instructions on soliciting a client and arranging for a contract murder in his solicitation of and negotiation with Lawrence Horn. Cautioning against the placement of advertisements in military or gun magazines, as this might prompt "a personal visit from the FBI," *Hit Man* instructs that "as a beginner" one should solicit business "through a personal acquaintance whom you trust." James Perry offered his services as a professional killer to Lawrence Horn through Thomas Turner, a good friend of Perry's and Lawrence Horn's first cousin. *Hit Man* contains instructions to request expense money from the employer prior to committing the crime, advising the contract killer to get "all expense money up front." The manual goes on to explain that this amount should generally range from five hundred to five thousand dollars, depending on the type of job and the job location, and that the advance should be paid in cash. Prior to commission of the murders, Lawrence Horn paid James Perry $3,500 through a series of wire transfers using phony names. *Hit Man* instructs that the victim's personal residence is the "initial choice" location for a murder and "an ideal place to make a hit," depending on its "layout" and "position." James Perry murdered the Horns at their place of residence. *Hit Man* instructs its readers to use a rental car to reach the victim's location. The book tells the reader to "steal an out-of-state tag" and use it to "replace the rental tag" on the car, explaining that "[s]tolen tags only show up on the police computer of the state in which they are stolen." James Perry stole out-of-state tags and affixed them to his rental car before driving it to the Horns' residence on the night of the murders.

Hit Man instructs the reader to establish a base at a motel in close proximity to the "job site" before committing the murders. On the night that he killed Mildred and Trevor Horn and Janice Saunders, James Perry took a room at a Days Inn motel in Rockville, Maryland, a short drive from the Horns' residence. *Hit Man* instructs that one should "use a made-up [license] tag number" when registering at the motel or hotel. James Perry gave a false license tag number when he registered at the Days Inn on the night of the murders. *Hit Man* instructs that a "beginner" should use an AR-7 rifle to kill his victims. James Perry used an AR-7 rifle to slay Mildred Horn and Janice Saunders.

Hit Man instructs its readers, Judge Luttig noted, on where to find the serial numbers on an AR-7 rifle, and instructs them that, prior to using the weapon, they should completely drill out these serial numbers so that the weapon cannot be traced. James Perry drilled out the serial numbers of his weapon exactly as the book instructs. *Hit Man* instructs in explicit detail, including photographs and diagrams, how to construct, "without [the] need of special engineering ability or machine shop tools," a homemade, "whisper-quiet" silencer from material available in any hardware store. James Perry constructed such a homemade silencer and used it the night he murdered Mildred and Trevor Horn and Janice Saunders.

James Perry also followed many of *Hit Man*'s instructions on how to commit the actual murders, Judge Luttig explained. The manual, for example, instructs its readers to kill their "mark" at close range, so that they will "know beyond any doubt that the desired result has been achieved." The book also cautions, however, that the killer should not shoot the victim at point-blank range, because "the victim's blood [will] splatter [the killer] or [his] clothing." Ultimately, the book recommends that its readers shoot their victims from a distance of three to six feet. James Perry shot Mildred Horn and Janice Saunders from a distance of three feet. *Hit Man* specifically instructs its audience of killers to shoot the victim through the eyes if possible, stating that "[a]t least three shots should be fired to insure quick and sure death. . . . [A]im for the head—preferably the eye sockets if you are a sharpshooter." James Perry shot Mildred Horn and Janice Saunders two or three times and through the eyes. Similarly, James Perry also followed many of *Hit Man*'s instructions in concealing his murders. *Hit Man* instructs the killer to "[p]ick up those empty cartridges that were ejected when you fired your gun." Although Perry fired his rifle numerous times during the murders, no spent cartridges were found in the area. *Hit Man* instructs the killer to disguise the contract murder as burglary by "mess[ing] the place up a bit and tak[ing] anything of value that you can carry concealed." After killing Mildred and Trevor Horn and Janice Saunders, James Perry took a Gucci watch as well as some credit cards and bank cards from Mildred Horn's wallet. According to the police report, a few areas of the Horns' residence appeared disturbed or slightly tossed, and a rug and cocktail table in the living room had been moved. *Hit Man* instructs that, after murdering the victims, the killer should break down the AR-7 in order to make the weapon easier to conceal. James Perry disassembled his weapon after the murders, in accordance with these instructions. *Hit Man* instructs killers to use specified tools to alter specified parts of the rifle. The author explains that the described alterations will prevent the police laboratory from matching the bullets recovered from the victims' bodies to the murder weapon. James Perry altered his AR-7 in accordance with these instructions. *Hit Man* also instructs the killer to dispose of the murder weapon by scattering the disassembled pieces of the weapon along the road as he leaves the crime scene. After killing Mildred and Trevor Horn and Janice Saunders, Perry scattered the pieces of his disassembled AR-7 rifle along Route 28 in Montgomery County.

After reviewing these facts, Judge Luttig turned to the philosophy underlying the First Amendment, explaining that the "right to advocate lawlessness is, almost paradoxically, one of the ultimate safeguards of liberty." Advocacy of violence, revolution, and murder, Judge Luttig understood, must fall within the ambit of the free speech principle: "Even in a society of laws, one of the most indispensable freedoms is that to express in the most impassioned terms the most passionate disagreement with the laws themselves, the institutions of, and created by, law, and the individual officials with whom the laws and institutions are entrusted. Without the freedom to criticize that which constrains, there is no freedom at all."

Nevertheless, Judge Luttig agreed with our claim that *Brandenburg* was never intended to cover situations in which the speech goes beyond the bounds of abstract advocacy and into the realm of providing specific instruction that aids and abets another in the commission of a criminal offense, drawing a sharp distinction between mere "abstract teaching" and more concrete preparation and instruction to aid and abet crime. At the very least, he held, we were entitled to a jury trial under the *Brandenburg* standard, reasoning that the stipulations entered into by Paladin—stipulations that Judge Luttig labeled "extraordinary" and "astonishing," were sufficient to avoid summary judgment.

As page after page of the opinion continued to spit out of my fax machine, I felt increasingly overwhelmed by a combination of euphoria and disbelief. Every argument large and small, every citation, every ringing quotation, every footnote, every philosophical point, factual assertion, legal distinction that we had made to the court surfaced somewhere in the opinion. Judge Luttig had even reached back into the brief I had written in the original argument before Judge Williams to quote a passage that we had not even included in our brief before the court of appeals: *"Hit Man* is not political manifesto, not revolutionary diatribe, not propaganda, advocacy, or protest, not an outpouring of conscience or credo. . . . It contains no discussion of ideas, no argument, no information about politics, religion, science, art, or culture . . . it offers no agenda for self-governance, no insight into the issues of the day." This was a passage we'd actually kept out of our appellate brief, worried it was a bit overblown. But Judge Luttig, who'd done the extraordinary homework of reading not merely what we'd submitted to his court but everything we'd submitted to the trial court as well, obviously found it persuasive.

Judge Luttig played particular havoc with what I had come to call the "Tom Clancy" argument, the refrain constantly repeated by Paladin and its many supporters who filed amicus briefs that there was no way to distinguish a murder manual from literary thrillers, real-crime books, news accounts, television programs, or movies that included graphic descriptions of crimes. "Paladin," wrote Judge Luttig, "joined by a spate of media amici, including many of the major networks, newspapers, and publishers, contends that any decision recognizing even a potential cause of action against Paladin will have far-reaching chilling effects on the rights of free speech and press. That the national media organizations would feel obliged to vigorously defend Paladin's assertion of a constitutional right to intentionally and knowingly assist murderers with technical information which Paladin admits it intended and knew would be used immediately in the commission of murder and other crimes against society is, to say the least, breathtaking."

Breathtaking, he wrote. *Breathtaking*. Judge Luttig's written opinion reflected the same intense internalization of the book *Hit Man* that had revealed itself in our oral argument. If I had never witnessed an oral argument so intense, I had also never read so intense an opinion. Judge Luttig painstakingly dissected the *Hit Man* manual, chapter by chapter, page by page. Summarizing that prodigious effort, Judge Luttig concluded: "Paladin's astonishing stipulations, coupled with the extraordinary comprehensiveness, detail, and clarity of *Hit Man*'s instructions for criminal activity and murder in particular, the boldness of its palpable exhortation to murder, the alarming power and effectiveness of its peculiar form of instruction, the notable absence from its text of the kind of ideas for the protection of which the First Amendment exists, and the book's evident lack of any even arguably legitimate purpose beyond the promotion and teaching of murder, render this case unique in the law. In at least these circumstances, we are confident that the First Amendment does not erect the absolute bar to the imposition of civil liability for which Paladin Press and amici contend."

I was on the phone with Howard and John the minute I'd finished reading the opinion. All three of us were oddly calm. It was a stunning victory, not so much in its result as in its utter and complete annihilation of Paladin's position. But none of us were hooting or screaming, not even Howard. We couldn't quite digest it. Maybe we couldn't quite believe it. We called the families. It was emotional, tearful, a gush of relief and release. "We still have a long way to go," I cautioned. "They'll try to take it to the Supreme Court."

• • •

Howard and his wife, Jackie, often communicated with their teenage children, Adam and Samantha, through e-mail. The day after the victory in the Fourth Circuit, Howard sent them an e-mail letter. Adam had asked Howard how much money he had made in the case. Howard tried to explain that money wasn't the point, using the movie *Rocky* as his metaphor. Rocky was a corny movie, Howard conceded, but a great one. "Rocky was basically a bum," he wrote, "but he was a bum in the same way we all are bums." Rocky was one of the little people on a planet of 6 billion other little people. With that math, it sometimes feels like what we do doesn't matter very much. But Rocky caught a lucky break. He just happened to be in the right place at the right time, and got his shot at the champ. Howard described to his kids what he thought was the best scene in the movie, when Rocky is in bed with Adrian, and tells her that he knows he can't win, but that "Nobody's ever gone da distance with Creed. If I can do that—if I'm still standin' when the final bell goes off—then I'm gonna know, for da first time in my life, dat I weren't just another bum from the neighborhood."

That, Howard explained, was what was important to him about our victory against Paladin Press. "Everybody gets a shot at one time in their life to be Rocky," he wrote. "It doesn't have to be before a crowd or on the 'Larry King' show. It could be the meat guy at the Giant who is told to put bad hamburger out for the customers so the company can save money. He decides not to obey orders and loses his job. Or it may come when somebody gives you the opportunity to get away with something that you know is wrong. Sometimes other people find out that you stood up and sometimes you are the only one who knows. Rocky didn't care if the crowds were cheering. He had to know in his heart that, when he got the chance, he took his best shot. And that's what he did. What was important was what he got to think of himself."

27

The Supremes

Paladin's first maneuver following its loss was to petition the entire Fourth Circuit to rehear the case en banc, before the full complement of all fifteen Fourth Circuit judges, a petition that was swiftly and summarily denied. That left Paladin only one recourse, a petition for certiorari seeking review of Judge Luttig's decision in the U.S. Supreme Court. Once again supported by numerous amici, Paladin asked the high Court to review the Fourth Circuit's judgment. Paladin's petition in the Supreme Court tried to capitalize on the intensity of Judge Luttig's opinion, attempting to marginalize it as extremist and outside the mainstream of First Amendment thinking. Judge Luttig, they argued, had flouted and warped *Brandenburg*. Reprising the Tom Clancy shuffle, they again claimed that the terrible flaw in Judge Luttig's opinion was that it would now open the floodgates for suits against every conceivable genre of legitimate expression.

Unlike the monumental power struggles and intellectual battles we'd had in putting together the Fourth Circuit brief, the drafting of our Supreme Court brief was entirely placid. John and Howard were already looking ahead to the trial. Their trial lawyer's blood was running hot, and the Supreme Court petition seemed like nothing but a pitiful and final act of desperation by Paladin. Howard and John were content to leave the Supreme Court work to me. It was but a mopping up operation, a prelude to the final and real battle, the run for the real money and the real vindication, in front of a jury good and true.

Our Supreme Court brief was largely a defense of Judge Luttig and his opinion. We argued that the defining theme of Judge Luttig's opinion was not merely what *Hit Man* did *not* contain—any serious political or social discourse—but on what it *did* contain. *Hit Man* could not embrace any plausible claim to being mere "abstract teaching" of the "moral propriety" of murder. As Judge Luttig had accurately recognized, *Hit Man* was precisely what it claimed to be, a "technical manual" published "for" the "independent contractor." *Hit Man*, we told the Supreme Court, was steeped in detailed step-by-step instruction, including engineering specifications, photographs, diagrams, charts, sample maps, checklists, formulas, suggested prices, information on selection of weapons, methods for altering weapons and ammunition, killing techniques, travel arrangements, instructions on appropriate garb, money-laundering methods—all the protocols, particulars, and minutia of contract murder from *A* to *Z*, punctuated page by page with exhortation and encouragement intended to prepare and steel the criminal for action.

•   •   •

Our victory in the court of appeals spawned a new flurry of media interest. Our case was moving on the same time-track as President Clinton's Monica Lewinsky scandal, and talk-show hosts, with quicksilver ingenuity, would often slide from asking me or Howard a question about our *Hit Man* case into queries about Paula Jones, impeachment, or perjury. In one episode of "Equal Time," when asked for the legal definition of "sexual relations," Howard opined that technically the term could be understood as limited to coitus, but admonished men in the viewing audience not to try that defense at home. I caught one of Howard's appearances while channel-surfing one evening. He was railing against Bill Clinton's lawyer in the Paula Jones case, Bob Bennett, claiming that Bennett's attempt to get the case thrown out on a motion for summary judgment was a stupid strategy and would only embarrass the president when the judge ruled against him. I called Howard after the show to compliment him on his bulldog tenacity. He was strangely ambivalent, almost depressed. He was wondering if he should hang up his pundit's spikes.

"It's no fun anymore," he said. "It's a chore."

"Howard, I went through the same thing several years ago. I had been on a book tour, and appeared on the same kinds of shows. Once they get you in the Rolodex, they call you all the time. And you're flattered, and your friends and family are all excited, for about a week or two. Then it becomes ho-hum. I was using words like confetti, throwing them out to dazzle and delight, without any depth, any thought, any reflection. It was all a game. It's still fun to appear on television from time to time, when I really have something to say. But the problem with being a regular is, you become a regular."

I could sense the titanic struggle within him. Howard never met a camera he didn't mug for, and to give up stardom was a major act of introspection. "Hell with it," he said. "I'm gonna quit. You're absolutely right. When we get back from Colorado, I'm pulling out."

• • •

James Perry and Lawrence Horn had been successfully prosecuted for murder by two highly regarded Montgomery County prosecutors, Bob Dean and Teresa Whalen. Whalen was a senior assistant state's attorney who had worked as a prosecutor for Montgomery County for twelve years; she was the highest-ranking woman attorney in the office. Bob Dean, another seasoned prosecutor with over twenty years' experience in the office, was her senior. Following the Perry and Horn trials, Dean was appointed to the top position in the office, becoming the Montgomery County state's attorney after his old boss and mentor, Andrew Sonner, a popular politician who had served as the county's state's attorney for a quarter century before being elevated to a judgeship on the Maryland Court of Special Appeals. Both Whalen and Dean were tough and accomplished lawyers. Dean especially had a reputation as a by-the-book guy, a trim, athletic workaholic, a no-nonsense straitlaced prosecutor. The Perry and Horn convictions were major accomplishments for them both. But there was more going on between them than prosecution.

On May 9, 1997, two days following our oral argument in the Fourth Circuit, Teresa Whalen was fired by Bob Dean in a whirlwind of scandal. The troubles began when other lawyers in the State's Attorney's Office came to work one morning and found a voice mail message waiting for them in which the voice of Teresa Whalen was heard discussing in embarrassing detail a relationship with Dean. The chagrined Whalen suspected that the tape had been made by her boyfriend, a Montgomery County police sergeant named Michael Mancuso. A distraught Whalen called her friend Lieutenant William O'Toole, another police officer on the force, to discuss problems in her relationship with Mancuso. When O'Toole arrived at Whalen's home, she told him she'd found an electronic monitory device attached to her phone line. O'Toole told Whalen he would have to report the incident, because it was possible Mancuso had used county surveillance equipment to illegally wiretap her phone and then to put the embarrassing message on the voice mail of her colleagues.

A few days later, however, Whalen told the police that she did not want to pursue the matter, and would not participate in any criminal prosecution of Mancuso. The whole matter was an embarrassing personal domestic relations incident, and she wanted it quietly dropped. The same day, she took a paid leave of absence, leaving a note for Bob Dean that said, "I am physically and emotionally unable to continue to work in the environment that you have created."

Two months of negotiations between Dean and Whalen then ensued. Dean wanted Whalen to sign a document stating that Whalen had not been the victim of any harassment. Whalen wanted a statement from Dean stating that there was nothing improper about Whalen telling the police to drop the investigation over the tape-recording and voice mail. Neither party would give. Dean fired Whalen. Whalen accused Dean of sexual harassment.

One year later, in May 1998, Whalen filed a sexual harassment suit against Dean in federal court. She alleged that Dean had begun making romantic advances toward her when they began working together on the prosecutions of James Perry and Lawrence Horn. She claimed that Dean "juggled work assignments to maximize his opportunities to travel with me on business, thereby facilitating his romantic overtures." The two began a sexual relationship, she alleged. She claimed to have copies of love poems Dean had written to her. In the fall of 1996, she claimed, she told Dean that she would no longer engage in sexual activity with him. It was after that attempt to break it off with Dean, she claimed, that she was subjected to discrimination and retaliation in the terms and conditions of her employment.

Dean was married to Diana Dean, who also worked in the State's Attorney's Office as a victim witness coordinator, and was the father of six children. He steadfastly denied Whalen's allegations, stating that they were "absolutely untrue" and that Whalen's lawsuit was "mean-spirited political defamation." A spokesperson for the fraternal order of police defended Mancuso, saying that no wiretap had taken place, and that the recording Mancuso made was with Whalen's consent. Defending Dean, Deputy State's Attorney I. Matthew Campbell, whom Whalen also sued, denied that Whalen had been the victim of any discrimination, asserting that she had been promoted consistently and given excellent job assignments by Dean.

The lawsuit came at a bad time for Dean—if such suits can ever come at a good time—because he was in the midst of his first major political campaign, seeking election to the state's attorney spot to which he had been appointed in 1996. Dean's political opponents immediately jumped on the scandal.

Meanwhile, the entire imbroglio had a collateral impact on our

Hit Man suit. Both Dean and Whalen were potential witnesses in our case, since they had been instrumental in demonstrating to two juries the importance of *Hit Man* as the blueprint for the murders of Trevor, Millie, and Janice. The sexual harassment charge was now a wild card in the case, a potential circus sideshow we didn't need.

The rift in the prosecution team of Teresa Whalen and Bob Dean became at once more unseemly and more public as Dean's election for state's attorney approached. Teresa Whalen released to the *Washington Post* the text of two love poems that Dean had sent to her. The *Post* printed the actual handwritten scrap of poetry on the front page of its Metro section. In one poem Dean wrote: "Immersed in the busy swirl of life / I pause, sometimes strain to catch a brief moment. / It brings a warm smile to my heart. / You are all that moment and all the good that it brings. . . . Your lips as they slightly turn to a smile. / When they touch mine / They speak their own language."

I felt sorry for Dean regardless of what had transpired between him and Whalen. Howard, who was Dean's friend and supporter, was less generous, not for Dean's conduct but for his literary failings. "There are those of us who can forgive infidelity," Howard said to me. "The bad poetry, however, may take this thing to a whole new level."

The next day, Independent Counsel Kenneth Starr delivered to the House of Representatives his report on the Bill Clinton/Monica Lewinsky debacle, a day on which the President issued his most heartfelt and explicit of confessions and apologies. Bob Dean followed Clinton's cue and finally admitted to his affair with Teresa Whalen. The voters were unforgiving. He lost the election.

• • •

As we hunkered down in the spring of 1998 to prepare for trial, we were forced to confront an issue that we had been conveniently able to let slide until the Supreme Court had ruled: the question of the actual identity of the author of *Hit Man*. Who was Rex Feral? We had done some investigating, through a lead given us in confidence by a newspaper reporter, and discovered the identity of the person we believed was the author. It was a woman. Her last known address was in Florida, at a trailer park. Howard, John, and I met in Howard's office in Rockville to discuss our strategy.

"So the *Hit Man* is a hit-*babe*," said John Marshall.

I was shocked at this news. Perhaps my shock was sexist. Perhaps I should have been cosmopolitan enough to imagine the profession of paid assassin as an area of equal opportunity employment. But from the text and tone of *Hit Man*, from its title, its cover drawing, its masculine voice, its machismo, I had always assumed that the actual author would be what the book itself projected, a male who had been a professional assassin and then had chosen to write about it. For some reason, perhaps sexist in itself, the revelation that the author might be a woman heightened my disgust over the whole sordid book.

Hit Man had a chapter entitled "Danger! Ego, Women, and Partners." In a long chauvinist passage, the chapter talks about how the wise hit man will keep women in their proper place in his life:

> Fortunately for the world, a woman usually makes only one
> man her target, and the nesting instinct quickly takes her off
> the street and ties her down to the little world of babies,
> laundry and housework she creates and protects for her own.
> Unfortunately, even a hit man cannot deny that what women
> have to offer is a basic necessity.

In a rambling diatribe, the chapter admonishes hit men to keep their mouths and trousers zipped around women, noting that "Women are highly emotional, rarely rational creatures," and asking, "Is ten minutes of pleasure worth your life at the hands (or tongue) of an irate spouse?"

We now had reason to believe that these words were written by a woman, not a man. She might, of course, actually have believed the sexist pig sentiments contained in the book, but my instinct was otherwise. I guessed that she had simply thrown in the bigoted bromides about women to add spice to the book, giving it more the flavor she was out to achieve, as a true narrative account of the exploits and experiences of a real hit man. If I was right, however, this was a troubling development, a setback for our side, because the next natural question was, what else in the book was simply made up. We had always treated *Hit Man* as a detailed how-to manual written by an actual assassin. That preconceived notion was now tainted with suspicion. Was our female author a real assassin herself, or had she also made that part up? Were her many "proven methods" really proven?

On one level, none of this really mattered. It wasn't whether the real Rex Feral was a real hit man, or a man at all, that counted. What counted was that the reader was convinced by the book that the instructions it contained were genuine and ought to be followed. Indeed, in some ways the fact that the author was a woman made both the author's intent and Paladin's intent all the more nefarious, for it betrayed a subjective desire to manipulate the reader, and indeed to manipulate the reader in a manner deliberately calculated to give the book greater verisimilitude.

Yet I felt queasy, troubled by the gut intuition that this startling piece of information would do our case no genuine good. Howard agreed. "The problem we've got," Howard said, was that a hit woman is just not as sinister as a hit man."

"Might depend on whether she's a real hit woman or not," I said.

"No way to know until we talk to her," said John.

"But do we really want to?" Howard asked.

We had previously sent a discovery request to Paladin Press asking that it identify the author of *Hit Man*. Kelley and Levine refused, claiming that such information was "privileged" under the First Amendment and Maryland's "shield law," a Maryland statute enacted to protect journalists from having to reveal the names of confidential sources. What Kelley and Levine didn't know was that we already knew the identity of their author—or least thought we did. We thought the claim of privilege was a weak one. "How can Paladin claim that its own author is a confidential source," I said. "Imagine the *Washington Post* gets sued for libel, for a story that doesn't run under any specific reporter's byline. When the plaintiff wants to know who wrote the story, the *Post* says, 'Sorry, that's privileged, the name of the reporter is confidential.' It wouldn't even pass the laugh test. Authors and reporters write books and stories. The people they gather information from are the sources."

"So you're saying we should be able to go in front of Judge Williams and demand that they reveal Rex's real name?"

"Maybe," I said, backtracking. "I don't think the author is a confidential source. I think on that argument they would lose. But on the other hand, I can see that they might have a First Amendment right to try to protect the author's identity. There are a few Supreme Court cases, actually, that talk about the right to publish anonymously. Nom de plums are part of the literary tradition. A tradition that is alive and thriving—take 'Anonymous,' the author of *Primary Colors*, whom we now know is Joe Klein. Now, Random House published *Primary Colors* and agreed to keep Klein's name secret. The book, however, draws a libel suit. A schoolteacher claims that an incident described in the book in which the presidential candidate sleeps with a schoolteacher during a campaign stop is actually about her. When she sues Random House, she wants to know who 'Anonymous' is. But Random House says the same thing that Paladin has said: We won't tell you, and we believe we have a First Amendment right not to tell you. It seems to me that the best solution here is for the court to insist that the publisher turn over the name of the author, but to do so under the rubric of a protective order, requiring that the plaintiffs keep the name to themselves. So we would be permitted to use Rex's real name to investigate our case, but not free to release her name to the world."

"But what happens at trial?" John asked.

"Hell if I know," I said. "She testifies with a paper bag over her head. We cross that bridge later."

"Okay, so we could force them to tell us her name," says Howard. "Or at least we think we could. The problem is, they're gonna fight like hell over this issue and turn it into a sideshow that delays the case for months, maybe longer, while we haggle over this issue. Why do we bother with this fight? Since we know her name anyway?"

"We *think* we do," John corrected.

"What do we really want out of her?" I asked. "A confession that she's a real murderer, who knew and intended that her book would be used to kill people? We'll never get that. Maybe she'll try to finger Paladin. Maybe she'll say that she wrote a book intended to be a farce, or a joke, and Paladin turned it into a real murder manual. That would be sweet. But what are the odds? What I figure is that she'll be scared witless. She'll join ranks with Paladin. She'll say as little as possible. We won't gain a thing."

"I don't think we want her in this case," said Howard. "I think we're better off letting the jury just imagine who the real Rex Feral is. They're gonna imagine somebody a lot more menacing and debauched than the real 'Hit Babe' is likely to be."

"But then why wouldn't *they* call her as a defense witness," I said, thinking out loud, and then answering my own question, "Because they *can't*, can they? Because they promised her anonymity. So they're between a rock and hard place."

"What about the fact that we technically have a lawsuit currently pending against her?" asked John. When we had originally filed our suit against Paladin Press in federal court in Maryland, we had filed an identical suit against the unknown "Rex Feral" in Maryland state court in Montgomery County. This suit had been dormant because we did not know the identity of Rex Feral, and had not been able to serve Rex with a summons and complaint, thus formally activating the suit. On the assumption that the name we had was accurate, we could hire an investigator to track down her present address, and then serve her, starting the suit.

"We just let that suit whither and die," said Howard. "If we don't even want her as a witness, don't want to depose her or interview her, then why bother to sue her? Plus, it's highly doubtful we could get jurisdiction over her here in Maryland. Paladin deliberately sold books here. But all the hit babe ever did was write a book and send it to the publisher in Colorado. So why do we want to spend a year arguing over whether we can actually sue her in Maryland when we don't really care about suing her anyhow?"

"But you know, I would like to have a better idea than we currently do on how *Hit Man* was put together," I said. "We need to launch more discovery on that point. Let's ask Paladin for all contracts, all memos, all manuscripts, edits, notes, galleys, page proofs, *everything*, every piece of paper in existence, connected to the writing and publishing of this book. I'd like to see, for example, how some of the most heinous passages in the book came into existence. Did hit babe write them in their current form? Or did some editor at Paladin jazz them up a little? Where did the photos and diagrams and charts come from?"

John was taking notes. By the end of the day we'd compiled a new set of discovery demands. Meanwhile, we decided to let the hit babe remain undercover.

•   •   •

The discovery documents from Paladin Press arrived shortly before the scheduled deposition of Peder Lund. The original query letter to Paladin from the author was included, along with portions of the author's original manuscript, the response of the Paladin editor, Virginia Thomas, and a copy of the book contract that was ultimately consummated between Paladin and the author. Also included were copies of the version of the manuscript used for the final editing pass, before the book was printed. The documents proved revealing—far more revealing than Paladin ever intended. In all of the correspondence and contract documents, the name of the author had been blackened out in the copies Tom Kelley and Steve Zansberg furnished us, so as to maintain Paladin's claim that the author's identity was confidential and privileged.

The story the documents told made Paladin look terrible. The original submission by the author had been a proposal to write a *fictional* account of a hit man's life. It was Paladin that wrote back, suggesting instead that the account be made into nonfiction, in an instructional how-to format. The author pliantly complied, wanting to land the book contract. That contract, however, contained a curious addendum. Paladin and the author agreed, in an insertion typed in different typeface from the main body of the contract and inserted at its very end, that Paladin would indemnify the author in the event of any liability suits filed as a result of material contained in the book. The addendum specifically stated that this included "any litigations or censures that may arise out of the sale, *use or misuse* of the contents of the contracted book" (emphasis added). The hit babe had obviously been worried that someone might follow the instructions in *Hit Man* to kill somebody, and that she might be sued because of it. This showed that Paladin knew, before the book had ever been published, that this was a serious risk—serious enough to be explicitly dealt with in the author's contract.

The greatest revelation of all, however, came in the manuscript itself. In the middle of the manuscript was a page in which the author's name had *not* been deleted. The name matched the name we had previously discovered. Had the lawyers for Paladin intentionally let the hit babe's name slip into the documents they provided us, or was this simply an act of negligence and oversight on the part of whoever had prepared the materials for us? Howard thought it might have been an intentional leak. My take was that it was simply a monumental blunder. Because Paladin was still taking the legal position that the author's name was confidential, we decided not to try to capitalize on this "leak," whether intentional or inadvertent, and avoid giving the name to the press or anyone outside the litigation. We would, however, confront Peder Lund with the telltale page.

28

A Marvelous Night for a Moonwalk

In the early stages of the lawsuit, the relations between the opposing teams of lawyers had been generally civilized. John and I got along easily with everyone. Howard and Kelley were ever leery and mildly testy with one another. Howard's relationship with Lee Levine, on the other hand, was genial and at times downright chummy. But as the discovery process heated up and the deposition of Peder Lund approached, reserves of patience dwindled, and relations deteriorated from civil to sardonic to caustic.

Much of the rancor was precipitated by Paladin's assertions that material we requested was confidential and privileged, but the enmity spilled into such normally routine matters such as the scheduling of depositions and requests for extensions of time to deliver documents. In a letter from Howard to Kelley and Levine on March 17, the frustration spewed like lava from a volcano: "I must offer an apology for my tone with you yesterday afternoon," Howard began. "It was uncalled for. I should have simply told you to go fuck yourself and insisted that all future communications be in writing. Alas, we all have our imperfections." Howard complained of "Tom's habit of faxing things he promised on a particular day, at the end of the day Denver time," and accused Kelley and Levine of being disingenuous in claims that they needed their client's approval to approve our requests for extensions of time, noting that we had always granted all of Paladin's requests for extensions without hesitation. The letter ended with Howard chiding that "people who serve up chick shit should not expect to be served chicken salad."

• • •

I hooked up with Howard and John at Dulles Airport for the flight to Denver. When we got to the ticket counter, I couldn't find my plane ticket. I had the receipt and boarding pass but not the ticket. Frantically, I went rummaging through my suitbag, as Howard and John looked on, amused. This was yet more proof that I was an academic after all, an absent-minded professor. "What are all the suits and ties for?" asked John, as I pillaged my bag.

"Whaddya mean? They're for the deposition." Howard and John had blank faces. "You mean you guys aren't wearing suits?"

"Nope," said Howard. "Peder's going to be the one on the camera. Not me."

"We don't dress up for this deposition," John said. "We're wearing jeans. Our 'fuck you' clothes. You did bring jeans, didn't you?"

"You mean you assholes hold a fashion meeting and nobody bothers to inform me?" I said incredulously. "Yeah, I got jeans. But if you'd told me, I wouldn't have had to lug these suits." I couldn't find my ticket, so I had to buy new one. This was tricky business, because I was financially destitute at the time, hemorrhaging money from paycheck to paycheck; my credit cards were all charged perilously close to their limits, and I was overdue and under suspension from American Express. I'd held back one credit card in reserve, to pay for a rental car in Denver and the hotel in Boulder. I wasn't sure I'd have enough to buy a new ticket and still pay for the car and hotel. I could ask Howard or John for help, but felt embarrassed to ask. By laying prostrate before the ticket agent I at least avoided the penalty fee.

On the plane we reviewed the latest salvos in the fax wars. Howard and John were smoldering over the game playing they thought Kelley and Levine were engaged in. "They've shown their true stripes," John fumed. "They portray this image of the gentlemen litigators, who want to be civil and not get down and dirty with Howard and me in the trenches, but they're the one's who pull the Mickey Mouse stunts."

I was vicariously indignant. "The only good thing," John deadpanned, "is that Howard and Lee have finally broken up."

I started to laugh, uncontrollably, to the point of tears. The infection spread, and pretty soon Howard and John were laughing just as hard. Even the lady in the seat next to us started chuckling, though she didn't know us from Adam.

"So the love affair is finally over," I said, still giggling. "Well, it was never going to work out anyway, Howard. All your friends could see it."

It had been my job to arrange for the rental car in Denver. I forgot that I'd charged it to my suspended American Express card, and when we got to the Hertz #1 Club Gold sign at the rental lot, my name had a big asterisk next to it, saying "please go to ticket counter." Howard and John looked on with a mix of surprise and embarrassment as the agent rather loudly announced that there was "a problem" with my card. Secretly wincing, I gingerly passed her the MasterCard that I hoped still had a little juice left on it. It cleared, and we were off. Snow began to fall as we wound our way up the foothills of the Colorado front range toward Boulder. We checked into the Boulderado Hotel, an old western saloon-style hotel decorated like a bordello. We watched the NCAA basketball tournament and had beers and sandwiches that night in the bar. "You nervous, Howard?"

"Not nervous. Just anxious to get it on."

John nodded. "We all are. This is what it's all about."

The deposition was in a small office in downtown Boulder, only a couple of blocks from our hotel. When we arrived the first surprise was that the room was set up with two videotape cameras. The camera crew explained that Tom Kelley wanted Howard on tape, too.

"They're afraid you're going to pull some wild-man stunt," I said. "So they want it documented. See, you shoulda packed your suit after all."

Peder Lund arrived with Tom Kelley and Steve Zansberg. Lund wore a blue suit, with a gray-and-red-paisley tie and a large cream-yellow kerchief in the breast pocket. He was wearing dark glasses, which he removed as the deposition commenced. I thought he looked uncomfortable in the witness chair, his eyes darting nervously back and forth from Howard, to John, to me, to Kelley, to Zansberg, to the camera lens. I suspect it was nothing more than normal nervousness, but I knew the camera would be unforgiving. It was the Richard Nixon principle. When the deposition was replayed on videotape, the effect of the darting eyes would be magnified, framed, and placed in greater relief by the smallness of the television screen, the physical tick enlarging the sinister to the point of caricature, like the beads of sweat on Nixon's upper lip.

After a number of preliminary skirmishes, Howard popped the first big question: "Sir, do you sell publications that contain detailed information that explains how to perpetrate criminal acts?"

"Yes," Lund replied flatly.

"And these publications are often written in a how-to format, would that be correct?"

"Sometimes."

Howard explored Lund's background, including his military career, including his training as an army Ranger and assignments in Vietnam in the Mekong Delta and Central Highlands. He asked if Lund had been involved in the CIA's Operation Phoenix, a covert operation to destroy the Viet Cong infrastructure.

"Yes," Lund replied.

Howard probed for details about Lund's association with the CIA and Operation Phoenix. Lund backtracked, claiming he had not been involved in Operation Phoenix or CIA activities in Vietnam. Dumbfounded, Howard pointed out that only moments before Lund had said he *had* been part of those efforts. Lund simply claimed that he had "corrected himself."

For seven hours, all morning and all afternoon, the deposition continued. During breaks Howard, John, and I would huddle and discuss tactics. Lund was well-prepared for the deposition, and had clearly been coached by Kelley not to say more than he needed to, and not to make any concessions. Even so, Howard was able to systematically force Lund to admit to the content of Paladin's books and to its marketing strategies. Howard asked how Paladin selected its authors, and whether they sought authors with expertise on the subjects they were writing about. Lund admitted that Paladin did look for such experts.

"Okay," said Howard. "Now, is that because, when you publish a book like *Bazooka, How to Build Your Own*, you expect that some of the people will in fact use it and want accurate information?"

"It's possible," Lund replied, adding that some people might purchase such a book to build a bazooka, and some might purchase it out of mere curiosity.

"And would the same reasoning apply to *Breath of the Dragon: Homebuilt Flamethrowers?*" Howard asked.

Tom Kelley objected to the form of the question, and several minutes of haggling ensued. Howard finally asked Lund to read the description of the *Flamethrowers* book. Lund complied: " 'Do you have anything in your arsenal that would hold off tanks or a small army of heavily armed, hostile people?' " he read. " 'What you need is your own dragon, and Ragnar is going to show you how to build one. Flamethrowers are legal, easy to build and operate, and use a fuel that is cheap and powerful—napalm (Ragnar's recipe is included, of course). Using easy-to-follow instructions and illustrations, this nontechnical manual teaches you how to design and build a customized flamethrower with common components—many of which you can pick up used at little or no cost. Plans for both backpack and vehicle-mounted flamethrowers are included. Give yourself the edge you need over most urban combat weapons. For academic study only.' "

Book after book, Howard led Lund through the Paladin catalog, forcing Lund to relate the content and apparent purpose of the publication, describing books on bombs, poisons, disposing of bodies, silencers, grenades, rocket launchers, plastic explosives, napalm, and arson. Lund admitted that he sometimes, "tongue in cheek," called many of Paladin's titles "burn and blow books."

Howard asked about a title called *Deadly Brew: Advanced Improvised Explosives*, by Seymour Lecker, a book that explained how to make the explosive C-4. "As far as you know," Howard asked, "was that one of the books that you were made aware was found in the possession of Tim McVeigh after he was arrested for blowing up the federal building in Oklahoma City?"

"I believe it was," Lund stated.

Howard asked about *The Anarchist Arsenal, Improvised Incendiary and Explosive Techniques.* Lund read the book's description into the record, including the claim that " 'Many of the innovative devices and techniques in this book have never been seen in print. You'll find detailed instructions, diagrams, and formulas on construction and installation of advanced and improvised explosives, including Semtex, C-4, land mines, FAEs, syringe fuses, car bombs, contact explosives, and many more. And you'll get an inside look at the deadly world of terrorism and counterterrorism, including actual glimpses of the IRA, PLO, SAS, Mossad and ETA in action. For information purposes only.' "

Howard pressed Lund on why Paladin sold books on how to make disposable silencers. Why, he asked, would people want a silencer to be *disposable?*

"I can't speculate, Mr. Siegel," Lund replied.

Howard asked if Lund had ever owned a silencer. He conceded that he had. "Well, what did you use it for?" Howard questioned.

"So I wouldn't annoy the neighbors when I shot," Lund replied.

Then Howard asked whether silencers were used as an instrumentality of murder.

"It's possible," Lund admitted.

"And do you have any idea why you would want to make that silencer easily disposable?"

"I would assume so that you can make another one to use," Lund explained.

Howard was incredulous. "As a hobby activity?" he demanded.

"Perhaps."

"Okay. Also, did it ever occur to you that the most likely reason for wanting to dispose of a silencer is so that, after you commit a murder, the police won't find it? Did that ever occur to you?"

"No, that didn't occur to me, Mr. Siegel."

This was a ridiculous answer, and a foolish one. When a jury heard this response, Lund's credibility would forever be impugned. No self-serving denials or evasions would ever again wash.

Howard was relentless. He examined Lund on a book that explained how to make "baby bottle bombs." Were such bombs used to blow up babies? Howard grilled.

"Possibly" was all Lund would say.

Howard asked about a book depicting something called "a hydrochloric acid goody." Reading from the book, Howard said, in a mockingly carefree voice, " 'Say you're sitting in a booth in a gay bar. You have a brown paper bag at your feet by the wall. In the bag is a gallon wine bottle. Now, being a great practical joker, you have poured about a pint of the hydrochloric acid into the bottle and nearly filled it with gasoline. The acid is on the bottom as it is heavier than the gasoline. When you've finished your beer, you drop a few chunks of aluminum cut from a pipe into the bottle and cap it tightly. Then you swish out, so you won't be noticed. Soon, the gas will burst the bottle and the gasoline will be everywhere. And if many of the dear things are smoking there will be burning faggots galore. Burning faggots, get it? Oh well.' "

Howard asked Lund if he was aware that passage was in the book. "I can't comment on something that's taken out of context," Lund insisted.

Lund had once claimed, in a press interview, that Paladin did not publish books on poisons. Howard hammered Lund on this claim, forcing him to read from Paladin books that belied the claim, describing poisons from potassium cyanide, malathion, parathion, chlordane, lindane to nicotine sulfate. " 'One of the glories of nicotine sulfate,' " Lund read, " 'is that it is absorbed by the skin and is fatal within a few minutes. Death by nicotine sulfate can only be detected by a blood test which is seldom given. A fine way to use nicotine sulfate is to carry it in a soft drink cup and act like you accidently spilled it on the victim. If he doesn't wash it off in a matter of seconds he will be dead in a matter of minutes.' "

Another passage described ways of testing poisons, including alley cats, or if a human subject is desired, winos in the street. " 'The best subject is a wino,' " Lund read. " 'In every city there are hundreds of winos sleeping out in nests in vacant lots, abandoned houses, under bridges.' " The book went on to explain how best to slip the test poison into a bottle of sweet wine.

The most petulant moments in the deposition came when Howard reviewed the documents Paladin had furnished during discovery regarding the history of *Hit Man* itself. Howard asked Lund whether he still maintained that the identity of the author, "Rex Feral," was a privileged secret. Lund said yes. Producing the manuscript page with the author's real name, Howard showed it to Lund, and asked him why Paladin had turned over to us a document with the name on it?

Lund was stunned, and Tom Kelley flabbergasted. He demanded that Howard give him the page. Howard handed it across the table to Kelley. Kelley refused to give it back. The deposition was halted, as Kelley churlishly accused Howard of unethical behavior. It was obviously a mistake that the name had been turned over to us, Kelley insisted, and the ethically appropriate thing for us to have done would have been to return the document to Paladin immediately. We kept our cool. If Paladin continued to insist that the author's name was confidential, we stated calmly, we would respect that claim. We would not reveal the author's name unless and until Judge Williams ruled that it was permissible to do so. But it was Paladin that had furnished us with the document. If it was a mistake, it was Paladin's mistake, and we were entitled to ask Lund about it.

The deposition moved forward. Howard focused on the contract with the author of *Hit Man*, quoting the language that had been added to the bottom of the contract: " 'Addendum: Publisher agrees to accept full financial and legal responsibility for any litigations or censures that may arise out of the sale, use or misuse of the contents of the contracted book. Furthermore, Publisher will, to the best of his ability, protect the true identity of the author.' "

Howard examined Lund about the circumstances that gave rise to the insertion of this language in the contract. Lund's answers were opaque, claiming he couldn't recall the details. Howard then extracted a jolting concession:

"Is it your testimony here today that, as far as you know, this is the only contract that Paladin Press has ever entered into with an author that has that addendum?"

"I believe so," Lund answered.

Howard also used the deposition to probe Lund's moral sensibilities. He asked whether Paladin would sell its books on killing to children.

"Possibly," Lund said.

"Why?"

"Because it's pure information," Lund answered.

Howard asked Lund, "Does it matter to you for what purpose your books are being ordered when you sell them?"

"No."

"Do you care?"

"No."

Later Howard asked, "If Muammar Qaddafi wrote you and said, 'I want the latest on Semtex,' you'd just mail it right off?"

"I think I'd ask him for *his* latest on Semtex," Lund jibed.

"But would you sell him *your* latest on Semtex?" Howard pressed.

"Yes."

It was as good an answer as we could ever hope to get. Howard quickly wrapped up the deposition. Snow was again falling as we walked back to the Boulderado.

• • •

Decompressing after the battle, we spent the evening after Lund's deposition drinking beer and shooting pool in the hotel bar. A bulletin came over the television screen. Arkansas federal judge Susan Weber Wright had dismissed Paula Jones's sexual harassment suit against Bill Clinton. Howard dropped his jaw. For the last two weeks he'd been all over cable-talk-land predicting that Clinton would surely lose the motion, and lambasting Clinton's lawyer for even trying it. I whooped in ecstasy, screaming *Yes!* at Clinton's upset victory, and moon-walking backward across the barroom floor, twirling my pool cue. John was as jubilant as I was, laughing as he poked at Howard with his cue. We weren't celebrating Clinton's victory, but Howard-the-Pundit's humiliating defeat. The pain in Howard's face turned from grimace to grin as I danced past the pool table.

Another beer later he confided, "We've been trying this case almost two years now. And today was the biggest surprise of the whole adventure."

"Something that Peder Lund said?" I asked.

"No. Seeing you moon-walk like Michael frigging Jackson."

• • •

On our third day in Boulder we took the deposition of Virginia Thomas, who had been editorial director at Paladin at the time the *Hit Man* manuscript was acquired, edited, and published. Thomas was a spunky, attractive, blue-eyed blond. John conducted the examination. Thomas explained that she no longer worked at Paladin. She left in 1984, the year after *Hit Man* was published, she explained, to become a freelance journalist and writer. Her most successful book was *The Beer Lovers Log Book*. Thomas was at once amiable and amnesic. She claimed that she could recall virtually nothing from her tenure at Paladin, and certainly nothing concerning *Hit Man*. When John showed her the documents Paladin had provided us, she professed an inability to remember any details concerning them.

Half an hour into the deposition, I scribbled a note to Howard.

"She's scared to death," I wrote. Howard nodded in agreement and winked. John asked her if she'd discussed this case and her deposition testimony with anyone prior to the deposition. After a long pause, Thomas said she'd discussed it with her lawyer.

John asked her who her lawyer was. She looked at Tom Kelley, who sat mute. After a few moments she asked if she could take a break. We agreed. She and Tom Kelley went into another room to confer. When they returned and the deposition continued, John again asked her again who her lawyer was.

"Mr. Kelley," she replied.

"When did you retain Mr. Kelley?" John asked.

Kelley objected, instructing Thomas not to answer on the ground that the information was covered by the attorney-client privilege. We didn't push the issue. It was obvious Thomas had retained Kelley only moments before. John tried again to extract information from Thomas, but no matter what he asked, her memory seemed to fail her. Growing frustrated, John grew increasingly sarcastic as he posed his questions. At one point Kelley intervened, objecting that John was failing to show respect for the witness. John ignored him. Meanwhile, Howard and I were beginning to find the whole farce funny. We began discretely passing notes to one another, like a couple of adolescent schoolboys, taking perverse delight in our colleague's slow burn.

John tried to question Thomas on the nature of the *Hit Man* book. He asked her what she remembered about the book.

"I would call it entertainment," said Thomas lamely.

"Would it attract people who wanted to become hit men?" John asked.

"No."

"Why not?"

Thomas refused to explain her answer, saying that it was just her opinion. The whole exercise was worthless. Thomas was terrified and obviously was not going to deviate from her avowed lack of recall. We ended the deposition.

It was only noon as we walked back to the hotel. The temperature had risen twenty degrees since breakfast, melting the morning snow. In the bright sunshine the snow-streaked mountains rimming Boulder were luminous against the dazzling blue sky.

"How far you figure it is to Rocky Mountain National Park from here?" asked John.

"I dunno. Hour, probably." As if speaking from one mind, the three of us said in unison, "Let's go."

I drove the winding highway north of Boulder to Estes Park and then on to Rocky Mountain National Park. Elk, deer, and bighorn sheep gazed indifferently at our car as we pushed up above ten thousand feet. The spring thaw was still a month away, and the park trails were heavily snowpacked, but in the warm sun we were able to hike in shirtsleeves. We took the Bear Lake Trail, a path that wound its way up the mountains past three mountain lakes, ending at a frozen pool surrounded by steep canyon walls. We were alone in a pristine land, miles from civilization, light-years from the world of lawyers and litigation. The three of us lay quiet for half an hour, our faces basking in the sun, our minds and souls adrift in private contemplation. I thought of Erin and Corey, missing them terribly, wishing they were in the mountains with me, sliding on the frozen lake, playing in the snow. And then the sun was gone, obscured beyond thick gray clouds that came unannounced from the west, rolling ominously across above the tree line. In an instant the wind picked up, and flurries of snow began to fall. A sudden spring blizzard was forming. We had an hour's hike in front of us to descend back to where we'd left the car. We scampered down the trail, half walking and half sliding on butts and backs. On the drive back to Boulder our private reveries dissolved into animated debate over the next stage of the litigation. Our strategy was fairly simple. We'd taken Lund's deposition and were elated at what we'd seen. No jury could possibly find Lund or his answers to our questions attractive. His squirming evasions would never play. Kelley and Levine had to know that.

"So what are the chances these guys might settle this case?" I asked. "I mean, hell, Lund's got to realize they're in danger of losing the whole ranch, doesn't he?"

"That's the rational reaction," said John. "But people don't necessarily act rationally in a situation like this. I think Lund's probably in denial. He probably still believes he can weasel out of this thing somehow. If it settles, it will only happen at the last possible minute, when he feels the gun pressed against his temple."

29

Sunset Boulevard

The issue of the confidentiality of Paladin's records and documents continued to be a sore point. Paladin wanted to protect the identity of its authors, the identity of its readers, and to avoid public disclosure of various other documents in its possession that it had been forced to produce to us as part of discovery. We, on the other hand, had every reason to want the press and the public to have full access to all the information produced for the trial. We had no secrets, and had no interest in helping Paladin keep its. Indeed, we thought that the more the public knew about Paladin, the more it would understand why we were suing the publisher, and what the lawsuit was about. At the same time, we didn't want to do anything to bias the jury in the case, or interfere with the fairness of the upcoming trial. In our view, Judge Luttig's opinion for the Fourth Circuit had put us in the catbird seat, and it made no sense to overreach or do anything that might screw the case up by giving Paladin grounds for complaint in a later appeal. We considered most of Paladin's assertions of confidentiality petty and capricious—grounded more in a concern that public scrutiny of its operations would be deeply embarrassing than in any plausible need to maintain genuine confidences or guard valuable trade secrets. Yet we could see at least a modicum of legitimacy to some of Paladin's

assertions. We could see why it might not want the names of its readers published in the *Washington Post*, since some of those readers
would undoubtedly be mortified if any one knew the publications
they were reading. And we could see why, if an author wrote for Paladin under a nom de plume, protecting that author's anonymity
could be justifiable.

A compromise was reached. We voluntarily agreed to a "protective
order," which would allow Paladin to label certain material confidential. Material designated confidential could be used by us to prepare our case, but we were not free to disseminate it to outsiders,
including the press. If we disagreed with Paladin's designation of any
particular exhibit or document as confidential, we would express our
objection to Paladin, and if the parties could not come to an agreement, the matter would be presented to the court for resolution.

The first major test of this process came when the printed volumes containing the deposition of Peder Lund arrived from the
court reporter. Paladin quickly designated huge chunks of the deposition—nearly 40 percent of the total deposition—as confidential.
We were infuriated. The only pages we thought appropriate for the
confidentiality label were the pages dealing with our skirmish over
the real identity of Rex Feral. We'd decided not to push Paladin on
that issue, and did not contest its desire to keep the author's name
out of the public record. But in our view Paladin had gone way
beyond that, selectively censoring large portions of Lund's testimony
that, while undoubtedly making Lund and Paladin look bad, could
not possibly be characterized as confidential. And so the confidentiality war was on. A showdown before the court was set. Paladin,
defender of the First Amendment, would be arguing against permit-
ting the media to view the full facts of this lawsuit. And the dream
team, First Amendment enemy number one, would be arguing for
open and full disclosure.

To Paladin's embarrassment, it began to appear as if many news
organizations, including organizations that had joined in supporting
Paladin as amici in the Fourth Circuit, would now oppose Paladin in

court, joining us to open up the records to public and press scrutiny. Mike Wallace and "60 Minutes" had previously done a sympathetic story about our suit against Paladin, and was now considering a follow-up "60 Minutes" segment on the hypocrisy of Paladin trying to prevent media access to Lund's deposition. A reporter for the *Washington Post* was doing a lengthy story pursuing the same angle.

To add to the irony, it was at exactly this time that I was approached by the *New York Times* about the possibility of writing an amicus curiae on behalf of a number of news organizations in a case involving press access to sealed court records. The case involved a North Carolina journalist named Kirsten Mitchell, Raleigh bureau chief for the *Wilmington Morning Star*, a newspaper owned by the New York Times Company. Mitchell inspected a settlement agreement handed to her by a federal district court clerk. The agreement confirmed information previously obtained by the *Morning Star* from independent sources, verifying that the Conoco Oil Company had settled an environmental tort suit brought by 178 trailer park residents for the sum of $36 million. The settlement agreement was contained in an envelope that was part of a stack of court records handed to Mitchell by the court clerk, in response to a request by Mitchell to the clerk asking for the court records filed subsequent to the settlement of the suit. In the process of handing Mitchell the material, the clerk extracted some documents, explaining that Mitchell could not have access to them because they were sealed. Among the materials handed to Mitchell was the envelope containing the settlement agreement. The front of the envelope contained a legend indicating that it was filed under seal and was to be opened only by the court. Mitchell testified, however, that since on her pile of materials the back of the envelope was faceup, she did not see this warning until after she had read the settlement agreement. The envelope had previously been opened, and red printing on the envelope flap, visible on the back side, which she did see, said "Opened." The initial order sealing the settlement agreement was entered without the hearing processes and substantive judicial findings required to seal a court document. Neither Kirsten Mitchell nor the *Morning Star* were parties in the underlying litigation, or bound by the terms of the sealing order.

The *Morning Star* published a story containing details of the settlement agreement, including the settlement amount. In that story the newspaper attributed its information concerning the settlement amount to unnamed confidential sources, and also stated that the amount had been confirmed through examination of official court documents given to a reporter by a court official. Applying Media Guidelines promulgated by the Department of Justice in 1980 to protect freedom of the press, Attorney General Janet Reno declined to pursue contempt prosecutions against the *Morning Star* and its reporters. Notwithstanding the attorney general's refusal to prosecute—and indeed, before the attorney general had even completed analysis of the matter—the district court appointed its own special prosecutor. The district court fined Mitchell $1,000 for criminal contempt, and held Mitchell and the *Morning Star* jointly liable for $500,000, plus costs and attorneys' fees, for civil contempt.

The case was on appeal to the Fourth Circuit, where the distinguished First Amendment attorney Floyd Abrams was joining with Mark Prak of Raleigh, also one of the top First Amendment attorneys in the country, to defend Mitchell and the New York Times Company. I agreed to write an amicus brief in support of Mitchell and the *Times*, representing a consortium of news outlets and press organizations, including the *Raleigh News & Observer*, owned by the McClatchy Company; the *Charlotte Observer*, owned by Knight-Ridder; the *Baltimore Sun*, owned by Times-Mirror; the *Richmond Times-Dispatch*, owned by Media General; the McGraw-Hill Companies; the *Washington Post*; the Gannett Company; Dow Jones & Company, publishers of the *Wall Street Journal*; the Associated Press; the North Carolina Press Association; and the Reporters Committee for Freedom of the Press. Many of my clients in the Kirsten Mitchell case were entities that had filed briefs as amici against us in the *Hit Man* litigation. Moreover, many of the legal and policy arguments that I advanced in favor of Kirsten Mitchell and her newspaper were identical to the arguments we were now making against Paladin. The courts are owned by the people, and the business of the courts, including civil trials, is public business, in which the public and the media, as the eyes and ears of the public, have a presumptive right, under the First Amendment, to full and open access to all court proceedings, exhibits, documents, or records. Litigants should be permitted to keep such materials confidential only for compelling reasons. Courts should halt the promiscuous use of protective orders, and reverse the trend of civil cases being tried largely in secret.

Borrowing from the same legal and policy arguments I had made in the Kirsten Mitchell case, we hammered away at Paladin, arguing strenuously that there was simply no legal justification for its sweeping claims of confidentiality regarding Lund's deposition.

At the last moment, Paladin backed down. We had played a game of litigation chicken, and this time it was Kelley and Levine who bailed. With huffs and puffs of righteous indignation, and piqued claims that this was all yet another example of the publicity-crazed Howard Siegel seeking to poison all prospective jurors, Paladin relented, and allowed Lund's deposition to be released, save the few offending pages that revealed the name of the hit babe.

•   •   •

I traveled to Los Angeles for three depositions, Shiri Bogan, Lawrence Horn's girlfriend; Elaine Tyler, his sister; and Corey Tyler, his nephew. The plan was to take advantage of the trip to spend time with Roger Reitzel, and I called him while waiting for my baggage to arrive at LAX airport. He was now working as a writer for Disney's "Honey, I Shrunk the Kids" show, and I planned to drive to the production company's offices to pick him up for lunch. I asked him for the address and directions.

"It's 6255 Sunset Boulevard."

"Yeah, sure," I said, "now give me your address."

He didn't get the joke. "That is my address: 6255 Sunset Boulevard."

"You're kiddin' me, right?"

"What?"

"Didn't that used to be the headquarters of Motown Records?"

"Yeah, maybe. I think I once heard that. Barry Gordy still works on my floor."

"Roger, you're not going to believe this, but the building you're now working in is where Lawrence Horn worked. It's where he wired the money to James Perry, the money that helped clinch the case against both of them."

An hour later I picked Roger up. The coincidence was already L.A. urban legend. "So get this," he told me, as he walked me to his office. Not only is this the building that Lawrence Horn once worked in, but he worked on *this floor*, right down the hall from my current office." Roger took me down the corridor and pointed to a closed door. "And that's where Barry Gordy still works."

It was a cosmic coincidence. Of all the office buildings in all of Los Angeles, Lawrence Horn, the murderer at the center of the biggest case of my life, just happened to have worked in the same building on the same floor on the same hall as my best friend.

The actual Los Angeles depositions were uneventful. I was the only member of the plaintiffs' legal team present, and Tom Kelley was the only lawyer for Paladin. Kelley and I went to lunch together during a break between depositions. The lunch was cordial. We talked about our mutual grilling before Judge Luttig. Tom let on that he wondered if Judge Luttig really should have recused himself from our case, disqualifying himself from sitting because of the murder of Luttig's father. He could never make a formal motion asking Luttig to recuse, because it would almost certainly be denied, and would only further alienate the judge, if that were possible. I didn't comment, saying nothing more than that I certainly agreed that Judge Luttig had been especially intense in the argument, an intensity that came through in his opinion. We also talked about how acrid and malevolent the litigation had become. Kelley blamed Howard. I laughed it off. "Howard's a good man," I said, "he just doesn't have enough to keep himself occupied."

Kelley laughed. "I know. I wish Howard would get another case, so he wouldn't stay up all night dreaming up ways to piss us off."

Maybe Kelley just needed to verbalize that sentiment, or maybe it was the fact that he and I had conducted the Los Angeles depositions without a trace of personal squabble or acrimony. Whatever the reason, the relationships among the lawyers took a more positive tone after Los Angeles. Kelley and Howard started talking to one another again, and a modicum of civility was restored.

•   •   •

As I thought more about Tom's suggestion that Judge Luttig should have recused himself from our case, I came to the conclusion that Tom was wrong. This wasn't the first time lawyers had challenged the propriety of Luttig sitting on cases involving murder. Indeed, Judge Luttig himself had written an opinion specifically addressing the issue. In a criminal habeas corpus case entitled *Strickler v. Pruett*, Luttig had responded to a motion by the criminal defendants to have him disqualify himself on the grounds that there were "unavoidable parallels" between the murder of his father and the murder of a woman named Leanne Whitlock, for which the criminal defendants were charged. Judge Luttig responded by stating that "the circumstances surrounding my dad's murder are so different from those surrounding the murder of Leanne Whitlock that, in my judgment, no one, except those who believe I should not sit in any murder case because my dad was the victim of a murder, could, on this ground, reasonably question my ability to sit impartially on the panel deciding this case." This was a fair enough point, but Judge Luttig went beyond that, exploring the same jurisprudential territory that the legal realists such as Oliver Wendell Holmes, Karl Llewellyn, Joseph Hutcheson, and Jerome Frank had explored earlier in the century.

"Because of the time that has elapsed since my dad's murder; the dissimilarity of the circumstances surrounding my dad's and Leanne Whitlock's murders; and the lack of any overlap in the legal issues presented in the appeals of the two cases, I do not believe that it can reasonably be maintained either that I cannot impartially sit in judgment of this appeal or that my impartiality can fairly be questioned," Judge Luttig wrote.

He then got to the nub of the matter. The purpose of the procedure that requires judges to disqualify themselves is not, he argued, to expunge from the bench judges who have been touched by life's experiences in ways that will, undoubtedly, bear upon their reaction to the cases before them. If this were so, an African-American judge who has experienced racism, or a female judge who has experienced sexism, would be disqualified from sitting in discrimination cases. "Nor, any more than recusal from discrimination cases should be required by judges who themselves, or whose families, have been subjected to invidious racial or sexual discrimination, do I believe that my recusal is required from this and all other murder cases for the reason alone that my dad was the victim of a murder," he wrote. The purpose of disqualification "is not to require recusal from the courts of all who have experienced the fullness of life—good and bad; and certainly its purpose is not to enable forum shopping by parties to litigation," he explained. "Rather, its purpose is only to ensure that the matters before the courts are decided by a judiciary that is impartial both in fact and in appearance. I do not believe that this indisputably important purpose is, in any way, compromised or disserved by my participation in this case. As I have earlier stated in open court, capital defendants are entitled to fair and impartial consideration of their claims by me when I am randomly selected to serve on the panel hearing their cases. Neither before nor after my dad's murder have they received less."

I thought Judge Luttig had the better of the argument here. Of course, Tom Kelley, stung by his loss, was entitled to think otherwise. And in fairness, perhaps I, buoyed by our victory, was also biased. But that, I guess, was the insight of the realists. Judges, lawyers, and litigants are part of a human system. We can't escape our emotions, and are not required to. What we are required to do is struggle to keep them under perspective and control. I believed Judge Luttig when he said he did that. And of course, on the merits of our case, I also thought he was right.

• • •

As trial preparations continued, two new lawyers emerged on Paladin's defense team, Stuart Pierson and Frank Kennedy. Howard met them before I did, and gave me his reactions.

"Pierson is very sharp," he said. "And relatively unflappable. Looks like a prototype for a WASP wine and cheese tasting. Suspenders and horn-rim glasses. A regular 'Prince of Prep.' He's got a pretty good sense of humor, and I can't seem to bait him."

Howard seemed to respect that in Pierson, though I suspected it drove Howard crazy. "What's Frank Kennedy like?" I asked.

"Medium build. Ruddy Irish complexion. Reddish blond hair. I lost all respect for him when he showed up for the first deposition wearing Sansabelt pants. Could have been double knit but I can't swear to it. Journeyman defense guy. Very competent in a matter-of-fact way. Thorough to a fault. Kind of guy that will beat you by actually reading all the junk that I usually throw into a pile and ignore. Would have made a terrific IRS auditor. Doubt he was in line when they handed out the creativity genes. In serious need of a personality transplant. My guess would be that he collects old Lionel trains."

When Frank Kennedy took the depositions of the Saunders family, he described the witnesses to the Saunders's lawyer Tom Heeney as "Saunders moaners and groaners." The description came after a witness described the horrible moment when Michael and Colin Saunders first learned from Detective Ed Tarney that Janice was dead. "Remind me to kick Kennedy in the balls," Howard said to me after hearing Heeney's report. I promised I would.

One of the issues we'd always wanted to try to nail down was whether there were other instances in the past in which *Hit Man* or other similar Paladin books had been used to commit violent crimes. In the discovery documents turned over to us, it appeared that law enforcement officials made inquiries to Paladin on a regular basis, asking whether a suspect had purchased instructional materials from the publisher. We had found a variety of news clippings going back decades, in which Paladin books were mentioned in crime stories, including an interview of Peder Lund on ABC's "20/20" program in which Lund was confronted with the fact that his books were used for criminal activity, and Lund, cold and nihilistic, answered that how his books were used was not his concern. When Howard had appeared on "Larry King Live," an anonymous caller from California related that he had served on a jury in a multiple-murder case in which Paladin books had been used by the murderer. And of course we knew that a Paladin book had apparently helped instruct Timothy McVeigh in the Oklahoma City bombing. But we had yet to come up with a lead on the direct use of *Hit Man* itself in a murder such as ours.

The break came in April 1998 when Phil Coglin, an FBI agent from Washington, D.C., called me in Williamsburg. He had seen in the *Washington Post* a story by Joan Biskupic on the case that included quotes from me, and he tracked down my phone number. In 1990, he told me, he had been involved in bank robbery and murder prosecutions in which the perpetrators used *Hit Man* and many other Paladin Press books to commit crimes, including murder.

"Can you give me the details?" I asked.

"Yes. Let me refer to my notes." In the methodical detail of a trained agent, Coglin told me his story. The targets of his investigation were a person named Donald Stivison and a person named William Ashley. As part of his investigation he executed a search warrant affidavit in the Eastern District of Ohio, before U.S. magistrate

Mark Abel, for a search of the premises of William Ashley at 14020 Mohler Road in Hocking County, Ohio. The search produced a copy of *Hit Man* and some thirty-eight similar how-to crime publications, apparently most of them published or distributed by Paladin. The list would be available on the return of his warrant, which is a public record.

Further investigation caused police to believe that Stivison and Ashley had been involved in the murder of a person named Richard Timmons, Jr. Stivison decided to cooperate in Ashley's prosecution in exchange for leniency. The murder prosecutions were actually handled by the Hocking County Sheriff's and Prosecutor's Office, a small town about an hour south of Columbus, Ohio. The Columbus Police Department assisted the Hocking office, which is very small, with technical expertise in the investigation. Stivison apparently testified that *Hit Man* was followed "verbatim" to kill Timmons and dispose of his body. Stivison also apparently testified that other Paladin books were relied upon for training in their various crimes. Coglin stated to me that *Hit Man* and other books found in Ashley's possession were used to train them to commit the crimes, and that they would not have had the knowledge or expertise to commit the crimes without the books. Ashley was sentenced to thirty-three years in federal prison. Stivison was sentenced to six or seven years and was probably now free or about to be released.

Coglin gave me the phone number for the Bureau of Prison's locator service. He said they would tell us the location of any federal prisoner. He thought Stivison would cooperate with us and talk to us if we wanted him to. Coglin expressed a willingness to cooperate with further information should we need it and asked that I keep him informed of how our case progressed.

Excited, we immediately followed up, calling the prosecutor's office in tiny Hocking, Ohio. The red carpet was rolled out for us. Yes, the prosecutor confirmed, *Hit Man* had been instrumental in the murders. In fact, halfway through the process of disposing of Timmons's body, Stivison and Ashley went back to their residence to retrieve their copy of *Hit Man*, to be sure they were following the instructions correctly. He invited us to come to Hocking to interview the witnesses. He would even put us up in his house as his guest. It was time somebody did something about Paladin. He wanted to help.

• • •

I'd resigned from William and Mary to accept a position in an endowed professorship, the George Allen Chair, at the University of Richmond School of Law. As I was packing boxes for the move, I began to realize how much Paladin had bombarded us with briefs, memoranda, and motions. I had a lot of boxes marked *Rice v. Paladin Press.*

By the end of August most of the trial preparation was completed, and the outlines of Paladin's defense strategy began to emerge. They were going to retry the murder cases. Juries had convicted James Perry and Lawrence Horn of murder, deciding that the proof established their guilt beyond a reasonable doubt. Now, Paladin, with apparently limitless resources, was spending enormous sums of money hiring experts to painstakingly reexamine every piece of the case.

Howard thought it was a ridiculous tactic. "They can't figure out what the hell they're supposed to do to defend themselves," Howard said, "so they're trying a murder case. So what? Do they really think they're gonna convince a jury that James Perry and Lawrence Horn didn't do this? Do they really think they're gonna convince a jury that the *Hit Man* manual didn't help? I mean, they're doing a great job as lawyers here. It's outstanding preparation. But what good do they think it's gonna do them?"

John was more circumspect. "But let's face it," he said. "It's a bad thing to say, but the truth is, money can buy you justice. Look at the O. J. Simpson case. What Paladin is doing is basically the same thing Simpson did in his criminal trial. If you spend enough money, if you pay enough investigators, enough experts, if you go through *any* police investigation, *any* prosecution and conviction, you're going to find mistakes, you're going to find loopholes, you're going to find weaknesses in the links in the chains. That's what they're doing. I'm not as cocky as Howard. But of course I'm *never* as cocky as Howard. There's no guaranteeing the outcome here."

With its seemingly inexhaustible resources, Paladin's defense team hired a cadre of experts to assist in its defense. All experts in the case were required under the Federal Rules of Civil Procedure to file written reports summarizing their expected testimony and make those reports available to the other side. We received the reports from Paladin in the last week of August, just before the September 1 deadline imposed by the court's schedule, and by September 2 had reached a decision that none of Paladin's experts were worth deposing.

Among the experts hired by Paladin was Dr. Richard Seltzer, a political science professor from Howard University in Washington. Seltzer used a market research firm to conduct a telephone survey of 238 *Hit Man* readers, obtained from a list of 314 *Hit Man* readers furnished to Seltzer by Paladin. According to Seltzer's survey, readers were more likely to be male, college educated, to have served in the military, and to have professional-management or protective service occupations. Most people, he claimed, purchased *Hit Man* because they thought it would be entertaining. Others purchased it because they thought it would be useful for writing projects, would help them protect themselves, assist them in law enforcement, or simply out of curiosity. The purchasers tended to have a high regard for Paladin publications.

Howard and I laughed out loud as we read the Seltzer report. "Funny, ain't it, that people called out of the blue about why they bought *Hit Man* don't suddenly blurt out, 'I bought it because I needed it to plan a murder,' " I said.

"Yeah," Howard cackled. "And I'm sure there's no methodological flaws in a survey of 238 *Hit Man* buyers that just happen to have come from a pool of 314 buyers furnished by Paladin, aren't you?"

I'd actually gone through the verbatim survey responses furnished by the Seltzer report. Even under the sanitized and self-serving methodology of the survey, the results were more ominous than Seltzer's conclusions seemed to reveal. One respondent actually did admit a nefarious purpose, saying that "I wanted to kill someone but didn't." Another said, "I was going through a divorce, I was just feeling crazy." Many other responses were highly ambiguous, and could easily have been masking some malevolent design.

A second Paladin expert was Raymond Toombs, a career corrections officer from Michigan. Toombs described, at length, the prisons at which James Perry had been incarcerated, and the prison culture at those institutions. There were many gangs in the prisons, he pointed out, including the Brotherhood of Islam, a gang that Perry and Thomas Turner were both in. According to Toombs, many of the criminal techniques outlined in *Hit Man* and used to commit the murders of Millie, Trevor, and Janice were techniques Perry could easily have picked up from other prisoners and from his prison gang.

The material in Toombs's report was in turn incorporated into the report of another Paladin expert, Gregg McCrary. McCrary, we'd been told by Steve Zansberg, would be a formidable witness for Paladin. A former FBI agent, McCrary had analyzed the entire crime, and concluded that *Hit Man* did not provide encouragement or significant assistance to Perry. McCrary's thesis was that it was Lawrence Horn who was the driving force behind the crimes, and Horn would have contracted for the death of Millie and Trevor whether he had ever met James Perry or not. Perry, moreover, had picked up enough knowledge of criminal techniques from prior criminal activity and stints in prison to have carried out the murders even if he'd never read *Hit Man*.

•   •   •

We gained access to the police photographs from the murder scene. They were horrendous. One photograph, showing the wounds to

Millie's eye, was too gruesome to even look at for more than a fleeting second. The photos deeply depressed Howard and John, who had known Millie and Trevor—particularly John, who had been her friend. As John drove home that night, he began to think about Peder Lund. Throughout the suit, Howard had always been able to demonize Lund. To Howard, Lund was a Nazi, and his "washing of the hands" excuse was no better than the "I was just following orders" defense at Nuremberg. But John had never quite demonized Lund. He didn't especially like the guy, but didn't hate him, didn't see him as a monster.

The pictures changed that. "I began to think," John said to me, "about the photographs, and how ordinary, decent people would react when confronted with them. If I was Peder Lund, or if you were Peder Lund, the owner of Paladin Press, and saw what this book *Hit Man* had done, what would you or I do? We'd pull it from the shelves. We'd say, 'My God, look what I've done!' Even if Lund had never thought about it before—which I don't believe—but even if he is telling the truth, and the thought never occurred to him that his book would cause people to die, once he sees what has actually happened, wouldn't the right thing be to pull the book from the shelves. Wouldn't any decent person say, 'I don't want any part of this.' But what does Lund do? He flouts the book. He has more copies printed. He sells another ten thousand! Instead of acting toward the families with decency or compassion, instead of just taking the book out of circulation, he rubs their noses in it! I mean it's one thing for the producers of a movie like *Natural Born Killers*, who have millions and millions of dollars invested, and who have produced a genuine artistic work, to say, 'We're sorry that people have imitated events in the movie, but we're not going to pull it.' But Lund doesn't make much out of *Hit Man*. For a lousy few extra thousand bucks of profit, he rubs their noses in it!"

30

Deliberate Intent

The Supreme Court announced its decision. The Court denied Paladin's petition, leaving undisturbed Judge Luttig's opinion. It was a monumental victory. The Court's action drew widespread media coverage, making the nightly news broadcasts of the major networks and the front page of the *Washington Post*. We still had the jury trial ahead of us, but my job was largely done.

In a class session with students at the University of Richmond, I was invited to reflect on our appellate victory. We had established an important principle, I suggested. A publisher who provides detailed information on techniques of violent crime with the deliberate intent that some readers will use the information to murder and maim will not find refuge in the First Amendment. The students were divided, some enthusiastically approving, some openly hostile, and many simply skeptical.

One student mentioned that in previous discussions that I had stated the First Amendment protected the right to burn the American flag as a symbol of protest, and questioned whether my position in the *Hit Man* suit was hypocritical and inconsistent.

"It seems to me," I replied, "that there is an important difference between burning the flag and assisting in murder. People may be offended by flag-burning, but it doesn't cause anybody to die."

Another student, Kathy, followed up, running me through a cross-examination. "But will the average person see all the nuances that you see?" she asked. "Aren't you worried that other courts, in other cases, will take this principle you have ordained and use it as a license to censor and suppress speech? People are going to hear about this opinion, and applaud you, and then attempt to use it as the launching pad for all kinds of mischief. What about the *Natural Born Killers* episode, for example?"

She was referring to a new decision fresh off the mint entitled *Byers v. Edmonson*, in which a Louisiana appellate court held that the victims of a convenience store shooting could sue the producers of the film *Natural Born Killers*, including Warner Brothers and Oliver Stone, on the grounds that the perpetrators of the shooting had gone on a crime and shooting spree after seeing the movie. The suit alleged that the producers of *Natural Born Killers* knew and intended that the film would inspire persons to engage in such crime and violence. The film's producers sought to have the case thrown out of court on First Amendment grounds, citing the many "copycat" cases in which television and film producers had successfully defeated such suits. The appellate court, however, held that the suit could go forward, because the plaintiffs had alleged that the producers knew and intended that the conduct depicted in the movie would be emulated. The Louisiana court relied on the holding in our *Hit Man* case as authority for its holding, quoting extensively from Judge Luttig's opinion.

"You make a good point, Kathy," I conceded. "The *Natural Born Killers* case was a defeat for the First Amendment, and thus a victory for Paladin, enabling it to crow 'I told you so.' This was precisely what Paladin and its numerous amici in our suit had warned against. We'd claimed they were all Chicken Littles shouting that the sky was falling. But now they can assert that the sky is indeed beginning to fall."

"Well, then," Kathy challenged, "how can you justify what you did in the *Hit Man* case? You *have* damaged the First Amendment."

I took a deep breath. "I think the *Natural Born Killers* case is frivolous," I said. "The producers of *Natural Born Killers* deserve to win, and I'm sure they eventually will win. But the defendants in the suit took the wrong procedural step. They tried to get the case dismissed on the pleadings, which means they were stuck with the allegations that they knew and intended that the movie would be emulated. If they'd instead moved for summary judgment, on the grounds that there was absolutely no credible proof of any such intent, I'm sure they would have won. The difference between their movie and our murder manual is that it is utterly implausible that Oliver Stone or Warner Brothers actually intended to encourage or assist crime. But that's exactly what we believe Paladin and Lund knew they were doing and intended to do."

"But there you go," said Kathy. "You have to engage in this intricate explanation to talk your way out of my question. Even if you're right, I am worried others won't follow your fine distinctions."

Another student, Chad asked, "What difference, in the end, will your triumph make? It seems to me that Paladin could weasel around your victory in future cases by just putting a new cover on books like *Hit Man*, labeling them as nonfiction novels or fantasies."

Again, I conceded the point. It was possible Judge Luttig's ruling might in the future be easily evaded by Paladin or other publishers through such cosmetic devices as dressing up a how-to book as a work of fiction. Some thought *The Turner Diaries* by William Pierce, a right-wing militia novel that described in detail how to engage in the type of bombing that took place at the federal building in Oklahoma City, was a prime example. "I agree with you, Chad," I admitted. "But that doesn't mean that what we did was not significant. Paladin, in publishing *Hit Man*, made no effort at disguise. Paladin, we claimed, wanted to market the book *Hit Man* as the genuine article, for that was much of the book's perverse appeal. A would-be hit man would rather go into business with the counsel and training of a genuine technical manual, not a novel or movie in which the hit man is never sure what is real and what is fake, what can or cannot be trusted. It may very well be that our lawsuit was one of a kind. There might never again be such a confluence of facts: an explicit how-to murder manual, a hit man who gets caught committing murders and is discovered to have followed the instructions in the manual, a publisher who stipulates to knowledge and intent in publishing it. But those were the stipulated facts upon which our case was based, and I am proud of the principle that our victory established."

Yet certitude is not the test of certainty, as Oliver Wendell Holmes once warned, and for all my show of cocksure confidence, I left the class still mulling over the questions the students had raised. What, in the final analysis, did our case mean? What had we really accomplished?

A jury would ultimately have to decide if Peder Lund and Paladin Press in fact acted with the kind of deliberate intent that we had alleged. A jury would also have to decide whether Paladin's conduct warranted an award of damages to the families of the victims, and if so, in what amount. It was possible that at the eleventh hour Paladin or its insurance company would buckle under the piling strain of impending doom and come to the negotiation table with serious offers of settlement.

For me, as a lawyer representing clients, these were critical issues. Howard, John, Tom Heeney, and I were all unflaggingly loyal to the families, devoted to their interests, and determined to achieve for them the financial recompense they deserved.

But I was not just a lawyer in this case, and the families were not just clients. Money was never the motivation for bringing the suit. Money was not what drove the families, or Howard, or John, or Tom, or me. It was principle. Sometimes money is money, and sometimes it is just a way of keeping score. We hoped a jury would someday award the survivors damages. But what we had always wanted, more than all else, was vindication.

Of course, it can be said that plaintiffs and plaintiffs' lawyers will always say that. "Oh, it's not the money, it's the principle of the thing." The very phrase has the tin-horn ring of cheap cliché.

Yet in a very genuine sense, for all of us on the plaintiffs' side, when the U.S. Court of Appeals ruled unanimously in Judge Luttig's sixty-five-page decision that Paladin's publication of *Hit Man* was not absolutely protected by the First Amendment, and when the Supreme Court of the United States refused to review and set aside that judgment, our souls found peace.

Murder had cast the lives of the survivors into a void. It was a void that Judge Luttig, whose own life had been marred by a brutal slaying, well understood. The survivors had embarked on a quest to somehow fill that void, to replace it with redemption, to instill light and good in a place that had known only blackness and evil. It was a quest for some nourishing and replenishing meaning, for the restoration of order and law and decency in lives scarred by the chaos and confusion and death. It was a quest forged in the pursuit of justice against a monstrous man who contracted for the death of his own kin, an unscrupulous two-bit thug who was willing to kill for a mangy fee, and a nihilistic publisher who deliberately set loose in the marketplace a manual that would train killers in the techniques of execution and gleefully steel them to murderous fortitude.

The survivors were on a quest to satiate a thirst that money could not quench, for money can no more calm the spirit than it can raise the dead. Only right principle can remedy wrong principle. In our victory, in our establishment of the landmark principle that what Paladin and Peder Lund did was wrong, and not above the law or outside the law but subject to the law, and answerable to society, the empty void was filled. Millie's sisters Gloria and Elaine and her daughter Tiffani believed that our victory on appeal was the ultimate memorial to the memory of Millie, Trevor, and Janice.

Here is the core of the matter: Does the publisher of a book that preaches the rectitude of contract murder, and teaches, in meticulous detail, its bloodthirsty techniques, deserve immunity from liability when the book is used to kill innocent people? Do not forget what *Hit Man* says on its opening page:

> It is my opinion that the professional hit man fills a need in society and is, at times, the only alternative for "personal"

justice. Moreover, if my advice and the proven methods in this book are followed, certainly no one will ever know.

This passage is morally abominable. It is a pariah, an outcast, to be resisted and rebuked in a decent society grounded in the rule of law. The antiseptic euphemism "personal justice" cannot mask the brutal reality of what is being proffered here—cold-blooded murder. America does not tolerate the personal justice of the lynch mob in white sheets. America does not tolerate the personal justice of the militia minuteman who bombs a federal building, massacring men, women, and children, as an expression of political protest against the perceived tyrannies of modern government and its abridgments of the putative rights of natural men. America does not tolerate the personal justice of the vigilante who bombs churches, clinics, or gay bars, or the terrorist who explodes a packed airliner, plummeting hundreds to screaming death. America does not tolerate the personal justice of the estranged husband who knifes his wife in the night, or the avaricious con man who kills for the insurance money. The "personal justice" of *Hit Man* mocks the genuine ideal of justice. It is the antithesis of justice. Society exists to replace the personal justice of the jungle with the community justice of trials, juries, and judges. In the social contract, deliberate murder is outlawed, replaced with deliberative due process. The "personal justice" that *Hit Man* preaches is nothing less than personal murder.

Personal, that is, to the Lawrence Horns of the world, who make the decision to hire someone to kill. But impersonal to the man who is hired. This is the second driving message of *Hit Man*. Here is a book that opens with the premise that it is perfectly acceptable for Lawrence Horn to step outside the social compact that binds us all and become a god and a law unto himself. And here is a book that cajoles the James Perrys of the world to embrace the schemes of the Lawrence Horns without the encumbrances of remorseful second thought. For after touting society's need for the hit man, the book in the next breath absolves the assassin of all worry and guilt:

Some people would argue that in taking the life of another after premeditation, you act as God—judging and issuing a death sentence. But it is the employer, the man who pays for the service, whatever his reason might be, who acts as judge. The hit man is merely the executioner, an enforcer who carries out the sentence.

Yet for all its repugnance, if this were all that *Hit Man* did, if the worst that could be said of it was that it preached the moral propriety of private execution and advanced the abstract proposition that hit men were members of an honorable profession, I would not maintain that the book deserved legal censure. I would condemn the book, I would rail against it with all my fiber and fury, but I would not support its punishment in law. For I believe in the social compact, and I believe that the American social compact embraces a wonderful and emancipating and robust conception of freedom of speech, a conception so bold and liberty-loving that even expression espousing revolution, violence, and murder must be tolerated, as long as those views are advanced as mere abstract teaching. Judge Luttig expressed the point eloquently when he noted the paradox of American freedom. In this country we have embraced the remarkable faith that our law includes the right to advocate lawlessness. As Judge Luttig wrote: "Without freedom to criticize that which constrains, there is no freedom at all."

So if all that *Hit Man* did was preach, all that I would do is preach back. But *Hit Man* also teaches. The book not only preaches and teaches, it exhorts, cajoles, encourages, steels, incites. And in that combination, in that evil alchemy of nihilistic philosophy, calculating instruction, and black exhortation, *Hit Man* forfeited the protections of the U.S. Constitution. Freedom of speech is not freedom to kill. *Hit Man* causes murder. Perhaps not in a direct, literal, and immediate sense. The mere touching of the book, the mere fondling of its malignant pages, will not result in instant death. But its blend of incitement, justification, and training in the dark arts of murder does result in the real slaughter of real innocents. To be sure, every reader who buys *Hit Man* doesn't use it to plot and kill. Of course not. But some do. Peder Lund and Paladin Press knew that some do. And they didn't care.

Throughout our lawsuit, Paladin had incessantly argued in the highest tones of indignation that the First Amendment protects it. My response was to put to Paladin the fundamental question: Why? Under what vision of a free society, what theory of the meaning of freedom of speech, did Paladin believe it was free to do what it did without being held responsible for the death and destruction caused by its actions? As our free speech tradition has evolved, jurists and scholars have identified several transcending purposes served by freedom of expression. One is the idea of the open marketplace, the rationale that humankind's search for truth is best advanced by a free trade in ideas—in the words of Justice Oliver Wendell Holmes, that "the best test of truth is the power of the thought to get itself accepted in the competition of the market." A second great purpose is the vindication of human dignity. Freedom of speech is not valuable solely for its role in the pursuit of truth, but also as an end in itself, an end inextricably intertwined with individual creativity and fulfillment. In the words of Justice Thurgood Marshall, "The First Amendment serves not only the needs of the polity but also those of the human spirit—a spirit that demands self-expression." And finally, there is a special relationship between freedom of speech and the processes of democratic self-governance. As Justice Louis Brandeis wrote, "[F]reedom to think as you will and to speak as you think are means indispensable to the discovery and spread of political truth."

If these are the wonderful and grandiloquent purposes that undergird the First Amendment, how does the murder manual *Hit Man* stack up when measured against them? The marketplace of ideas will not be impoverished by imposing liability on those who traffic in such murderous contraband. *Hit Man* can stake no plausible claim to the nourishment of the human spirit. The training and incitement of killers does not advance the rule of law or contribute to the deliberative processes of democracy.

• • •

One month before the jury trial was to begin, the nation was stunned when two students at Columbine High School in Littleton, Colorado, used guns and homemade bombs to commit a massacre that left fifteen people dead and twenty-three wounded. Paladin's lawyers filed a motion to postpone the Hit Man case, arguing that the national obsession with the Littleton killings would make it impossible for Paladin to receive a fair trial.

Howard and John were steeped in last-minute preparations, and so it fell on me to respond to Paladin's motion to postpone. We appeared before Judge Alexander Williams on May 19, four days before the trial was to start. I hit back hard. The people of Littleton were doing their best to get on with their lives and heal, I argued, and so were the people of the nation. Yet the business of the country had to go on, including the business of the court. Judge Williams denied Paladin's motion. The very next day, the argument proved lamentably prescient, as headlines announced another school shooting, this time with six students wounded, in Conyers, Georgia.

The pressure on Paladin and its insurance company was building. An intense burst of settlement negotiations suddenly began. Howard and John handled the negotiations brilliantly. On Friday, May 21, the last business day before the trial was to commence, the case was settled. Paladin's insurance company agreed to a multimillion dollar compensation payment to the families. Paladin also agreed to make yearly contributions to two charities of the plaintiff's choice. "I wanted one for the people of Littleton," Howard said to me, "and the other for Oklahoma City." Most important, Paladin agreed to take the book *Hit Man* from the market. Paladin would sell it no more.

We had achieved total victory. I was at once numb and humbled. Nothing we had done could bring back anyone's life, not Trevor's, not Millie's, not Janice's, not any of those killed across the country by assassins and terrorists. But if their lives cannot be retrieved, in their deaths there is now perhaps at least a measure of redemption and meaning. The law will never be the same. We have struck a blow against the culture of violence. Freedom to speak is not freedom to kill.

Index